Time and Reality
in American
Philosophy

TIME AND REALITY
in
American
Philosophy

Bertrand P. Helm

The University of Massachusetts Press

Amherst, 1985

Library of Congress Cataloging-in-Publication Data

Helm, Bertrand P., 1929–
Time and reality in American philosophy.

Includes index.
1. Philosophy, American—20th century. 2. Time—
History—20th century. I. Title.
B944.T54H45   1985   115'.0973   85-8583
ISBN 0-87023-493-5 (alk. paper)

Acknowledgment is made for permission granted to quote from the following books under copyright:

John Dewey: The Early Works, 1882–1898, ed. Jo Ann Boydston (Carbondale: Southern Illinois University Press); vol. 1 © 1969, vol. 2 © 1967, by Southern Illinois University Press. Reprinted by permission of the publisher.

John Dewey and Arthur Bentley, *Knowing and the Known* (Boston: Beacon Press, 1949), reprinted with the permission of the Center for Dewey Studies, Southern Illinois University at Carbondale.

John Dewey, *Experience and Nature* (1958 edition), © 1925, 1929 by the Open Court Publishing Company. Reprinted by permission of Open Court Publishing Company.

Alfred North Whitehead's Early Philosophy of Space and Time, by Janet A. Fitzgerald, © 1979 by University Press of America, Inc. Reprinted by permission of the publishers.

The Aims of Education, by Alfred N. Whitehead, © 1929 by Macmillan Publishing Company, renewed 1957 by Evelyn Whitehead. *Science and the Modern World*, by Alfred N. Whitehead, © 1925 by Macmillan Publishing Company, renewed 1953 by Evelyn Whitehead. Reprinted by permission of Macmillan Publishing Company and Cambridge University Press.

C O N T E N T S

A C K N O W L E D G M E N T S

Earlier versions of the chapters on Charles S. Peirce, William James, and George Santayana have appeared in various journals. I gratefully acknowledge permission given by the editor of *The Monist* to use my study of Peirce, "The Nature and Modes of Time," which appeared in 1980 in a double issue of *The Monist*, "The Relevance of Charles Peirce." For permission to use "William James on the Nature of Time," from *Tulane Studies in Philosophy* 24 (1975), I thank the editor. Also, I wish to thank the editor of the *Southern Journal of Philosophy* for permission to use my essay, "Santayana: The Temporal Compulsion," which appeared in 1972 as part of that journal's Special Issue on Santayana.

I am indebted to Barbara Massello, formerly of Southwest Missouri State University, for her help in obtaining articles and books needed for these studies, and to Mildred Wilcox for typing the manuscript. I am indebted to the Southwest Missouri State University Foundation for a grant to help with the preparation of the manuscript for publication. I wish to thank Carol Schoen, my copy editor at The University of Massachusetts Press, for the steady pressure she exerted on the entire manuscript, drawing clarity out of vagueness many times over. Any difficulties of style that remain are my own.

A special note of thanks is expressed for the support given me by members of my family, especially my wife, during the preparation of this book.

Time and Reality
in American
Philosophy

AMERICAN intellectual history plainly shows that there is neither a continuing persistence of received ideas nor an unfailing loyalty to a single cluster of themes. Not only does American thought display a gradual expansion of the fundamental beliefs laid down during the colonial period, but it also reveals some radical discontinuities in its basic philosophical assumptions. These were due to variations in the national patterns of social life, to the incorporation of philosophical novelties imported from abroad, and to developments in the natural sciences which seemed to shake the very foundations of the more traditional habitations of the mind.

Relatively mild changes in American thought were registered in such movements as New England Transcendentalism, which was more of a literary enterprise for responding to the initial influx of German idealism, and in the Scottish common-sense realism, which was more of a curricular philosophy for bridging the gap between Christian apologetics and the molding of sturdy characters. But more dramatic variations in thought patterns accumulated across the middle decades of the nineteenth century until they were set loose with unexpected power in the last decades of that century. The impact of these departures from the past was only heightened by their almost simultaneous occurrence in several different areas of experience.

I. SOME BACKGROUND THEMES

The existing complex of ideas and institutions challenged by new forces in the 1870s and 1880s included the following staple elements:

1. The idea of a settled causal order in the world of nature, ruling out real novelty and emphasizing hidden, beneficent repetitions
2. The notion of a transcendent deity who oversees and mostly regularizes the natural order, except for occasional miraculous intrusions
3. The conviction of a formal center of conscious autonomy within each person which allows one to steer through the inexorable workings of this natural order toward a divine destiny
4. The assumption of a fixed space-time matrix within which interactions between nature, man, and God took place as natural, social, and religious events
5. The acceptance of a rational theory of natural law which provided justification for redressing social wrongs and personal injuries according to formally exact processes
6. The adherence to a stable system of higher education which exposited these themes in an authoritative curriculum that emphasized changelessness in nature, man, God, space, and time, and in the law
7. The Enlightenment belief in a sure progress in history, as reworked to allow for economic progress through industrial technologies.

These seven pillars of traditional wisdom supported the intellectual and spiritual edifice of American thought during the middle decades of the nineteenth century. It was their fate to crumble almost simultaneously before a complex of powerful new forces. To speak of the turmoil of the 1890s is to refer, at least in part, to the buckling of an entire interlocking system of belief. Assaults upon two or three of these staple elements would have required major realignments. But if most or all are concurrently challenged, then social theorists and philosophers are set the task not only of reconstructing a system of supports, but also of discerning new compass points for aligning that system, for the traditional orientation markers were all but obliterated in the rapid flow of events and ideas.

The decade of the 1890s is crucial in American intellectual history, for it is both an ending and a beginning. Henry Steele Commager designated the decade as "the Watershed of the Nineties."[1] Most of the aforementioned supports had crumbled by then. Chief among the casualties was the supernaturalist belief. Merle Curti believes that the blow struck against this part of the traditional complex of belief was "the most striking event in the intellectual history in the last third of the nineteenth century."[2] This event, moreover, represented both an intellectual and an institu-

tional change. Challenges—both to the hold of Scottish realism upon the curricula of colleges and also to the traditional mission of the institutions of higher education—were implied in the rejection of supernaturalism. Perry Miller speaks of the displacing and disappearance of Scottish realism as "one of the most radical revolutions in the history of the American mind."[3] The revolution in the late decades of the nineteenth century was hastened along by basic institutional changes, especially at Harvard. There, a spirit of change and experimentation was introduced by Charles William Eliot after he became the president of Harvard in 1869. The title of his pivotal *Atlantic Monthly* article of that same year, "The New Education: Its Organization," became a reform slogan.[4] Science, both pure and applied, and living European languages were key features of his reform initiatives. George Santayana's trenchant appraisal of the Harvard reforms must stand for all time as the archetypical academic response to dispersive tendencies in the curricula of modern American universities.[5] In any case, Eliot's reorganization was central to displacing another traditional pillar of American thought, and to erecting more inventive structures in its place. It is no accident that most of the philosophers who comprise the golden age of American philosophy were associated with Eliot's Harvard, or that philosophy as an autonomous discipline freed from sectarian restraints received a powerful impetus at that university.

The demise of the supernaturalist emphasis was due neither to mere institutional changes nor to the increasing prestige of some scientific theories, including the Darwinian version of biological evolution. Indeed, it is quite doubtful that any scientific world view by itself can obviate a powerful and vital body of religious doctrine. Rather, the external assault on the supernaturalist dispensation was paralleled, if not fortified, by internal theological criticism of the reigning system of religious belief. The new biblical criticism, one of the most significant imports of nineteenth-century German scholarship, coupled with the deepening interest in comparative religion, made paralyzing inroads into the traditional Judaeo-Christian *Weltanschauung*. It was due to an internal realignment of basic theological doctrine, in harness with an external criticism set out by Darwinian naturalism, that the supernaturalist standards were undone. The displacement of American theology toward more of a social gospel was the most obvious result of the decline and fall of Scottish realism. The entire process was calculated to introduce much more of a temporalist idiom into American intellectual history.

Another tradition superannuated in the last decades of the nineteenth century was the conviction that there is a formal center of consciousness—a stable self or soul which is the ground of personal identity across

time—which provides victory over time, and which has an eternal destiny. This conviction was unable to survive the Darwinian criticism from without and the psychological criticism from within. With the publication of Darwin's *The Descent of Man* (1871), along with the independent but confirming work in experimental psychology imported from the German universities—especially in the physiological psychology of William James from the late 1860s on—man's psyche was naturalized as a denizen of this world. The famous paper by William James, "Does 'Consciousness' Exist?", had almost posed a rhetorical question by the time it was published in 1904. James argued that it existed not as a formal entity or self-conscious substance, but as a function or series of functions across time. Such a view threw new emphasis upon the nonrational, noncognitive sides of the psyche, upon feeling and emotion, and upon appetition and aversion. If there is no transcendent ego with a supernatural destiny, then the essential interests of humans are to be realized, if at all, in some indefinite future in this world. The past and present can no longer be springboards into the heavens, but can provide propulsion into the future.

Oliver Wendell Holmes, Jr., recapitulated this line of thought in mounting an offensive against another bastion of traditional wisdom in American thought: the law. If other philosophers, in expressing the mood of the times, attacked the sway of formal necessity in some of the natural sciences, Holmes assailed necessity and form as the controlling features of the dominant legal philosophy. Holmes was one of the young lions in the Metaphysical Club of Charles Sanders Peirce in the early 1870s, and he was to apply some of its initiatives in revolutionizing American jurisprudence. Indeed, his prediction theory of law may have extended outside of jurisprudence proper to provide the germ from which grew some of the most distinctive features of the philosophy of pragmatism as it was elaborated by Peirce, James, and John Dewey.

According to Max Fisch, pragmatism may have arisen as "a generalization of the prediction theory of law."[6] A somewhat different explanation of the close relation between Holmes and the pragmatists is presented by Morton White, who perceives not only an intellectual tie between them but also a more deep-lying cultural tie.[7] The social and cultural changes find expression alternatively in both the legal philosophy and the more technical philosophy proper. The changes represent what White speaks of as a "revolt against formalism." Dewey and Holmes "emphasize that the life of science, economics and law was not logic but experience in some streaming social sense."[8]

On naturalistic grounds, Holmes uprooted the earlier underpinnings of the law. According to Stow Persons, Holmes "found in the universe no

evidence of purpose or of moral order. As a lawyer, he rejected the belief of Marshall, of Story, and of Kent that human law derived its authority ultimately from the law of nature and of God.'"⁹ Holmes looked elsewhere for backing and justification of the law, and found it in the evolution of man and societies. His legal realism reflects this passage from a scholarly concern with the law's past toward a scientific interest in the law as giving adaptive guidance for the present and the future. Learning smacks too much of an antiquarian concern with the past, whereas science and good legislation treat the present and the future.¹⁰ Thus, Holmes's predictive theory of the law: law is a prediction of what judges will do and what courts will decide. Such a view amounts to dismantling the more traditional American jurisprudence and its associated mythic features. The spirit of temporalism—evident in a concern for a past as energized to enhance the quality of present and future life—is reinforced through Holmes's naturalistic jurisprudence.

The temporalizing and naturalizing of the law, taken together with the temporalizing and naturalizing of religion as an adaptive set of beliefs, was critically important in American intellectual history because of the symbolic and mythic values associated with law and religion. Law, especially the higher constitutional law as grounded in rational principles, and religion, especially the theology concerned with a providential human destiny, were two supports that helped unify and direct the diverse, tumultuous American experience since the closing decades of the eighteenth century. As these mythic elements crumbled, the American mind seemed flung into a precarious, risk-laden future, one with no sure rational structure or providential denouement.

Americans, it seemed to Commager, had almost invented time.¹¹ They were not so much concerned with timing or punctuality as they were with vistas opening into a brighter future that beckoned with new promises. The pioneer experience, along with its unreflective extension into industrial technology, conspired to emphasize changing scenes and novel products for requiting human needs. It was only subsequent to the unregulated spurt of industrial expansion that some kinds of change appeared to weaken possibilities for other lines of social development. In *The Response to Industrialism: 1885–1914*, Samuel P. Hays also treats the 1890s as a watershed decade, as had Commager. In his chapter, "The Shock of Change," Hays treats the "Turmoil of the Nineties" as a critical experience, and notes that "a series of events in the 1890s sharpened and intensified reactions to industrialism and heightened the shock of rapid change."¹² Change had almost become the industrial law of the land, a law that was too much a law of the jungle, one that was supported and justified

by Social Darwinism. The stream of machines had become too much like new wine in old wineskins. Machines had too greatly shattered the calm of the lingering pastoral mind-set.[13] With the critical reaction to uncontrolled growth and change, yet another of the main pillars of traditional wisdom was toppled. Amid the shambles of the naive doctrine of progress rewritten as industrial progress, it became clear to social scientists and philosophers that later events do not always bring more shining promises. In this way, too, was attention turned to the fundamental temporal processes, and to the interrelations between present, past, and future.

Attention fell upon the temporal stream of events when physicalistic schemes of explanation were supplanted by evolutionary schemes which had allowed for the appearance of novelties and accidental sports, and uprooted the traditional causal conceptions. With the eclipse of supernaturalism and its transfixing concepts about eternity, attention fell upon the temporal stream of events. With the dissolution of the self as a self-conscious substance—so that consciousness became construed as a shifting balance of adaptations to natural occurrences—attention fell upon the temporal stream of events. With the fundamental change in scientific and mathematical conceptions of space and time—whereby space is treated as a function of a force field and time is treated as a unidirectional continuum spearing into the future[14]—attention fell upon the temporal stream of events. With the dislodging of the law from the dead hand of the past, and the law's regrouping in terms of present modes of social life that lead into an expansive future, attention fell upon the temporal stream of events. As a result of the revolution in higher education and in attitudes toward industrial technology—so that these fundamental institutions become experimental and risk-laden bearers of both social good and social turmoil—attention fell upon the temporal stream of events.

The undoing of the supports for much of the traditional wisdom of the American mind seemed to radicalize that mind and throw it off balance into a risky future. No more striking evaluation of the entire process can be found than in the observations of the sympathetic foreign observer, Jacques Maritain. In his *Reflections on America*, Maritain, a French neo-Thomist philosopher, said of America that "this country is entirely turned toward the future, not the past. An appeal of this kind, a suction so to speak, exercised by the future upon the whole nation to such a degree and with such power, is in my opinion something new in human history, and is no doubt an element in the greatness of America."[15] Beyond the poetic utterance of Archibald MacLeish that "America is promises," Maritain treats America as a pilgrimage into the future. For in his chapter "The American Pilgrimage," Maritain adds that this may reflect a "Christian

sense of the impermanence of earthly things. . . . In this sense of becoming and impermanence one may discern a feeling of evangelical origin which has been projected into temporal activity."[16]

Although Maritain's description of the phenomenon of America does seem peculiarly apt, perhaps his religious interpretation of the phenomenon should be paralleled by something closer at hand. Charles Sanders Peirce made the intriguing observation that time is a domain that allows for exemptions or reprieves from the law of contradiction. The law of contradiction is the view that an object or phenomenon cannot both have and not have the same trait or characteristic at the same time and in the same respect. But a phenomenon such as the life of a nation can resolve some of its apparent contradictions by displacing the traits or characteristics to different positions in the present and future.

It has been amply observed that the American experience is shot through with contradictions. Typical is Max Lerner's view that "every generalization about American thought can be offset by a countergeneralization."[17] We are both egoistic and not egoistic, religious and not religious, compassionate and predatory. The list goes on. But from this point of view, contradictions in the American character provide the propulsive power that casts us into the future.

A somewhat different approach to the conflicting traits in the American experience can be found in Michael Kammen's study, *People of Paradox* (1972). His general approach to the American character is to read it in terms of polarities, not contradictories. The concept of biformity is his frame of reference. He believes that biformity is a universal trait of colonial cultures. "What finally matters," he judges, "is the particular configuration of tensions within a national setting, as well as the behavioral, intellectual, and emotional consequences of that configuration."[18] Our civilization is contrapuntal. Now whether we deploy otherwise contradictory characteristics across time so as to lower the levels of conflict, or whether we hold contraries together in a tense, contrapuntal balance within a temporal configuration, still the American national experience conspired, in the closing decades of the nineteenth century, to throw the temporal features of experience into prominence. This, then, is the intellectual and spiritual milieu of our most typical, nationally prominent philosophers. Although such a judgment can hardly apply to Alfred North Whitehead, who came to the United States in 1924, his career in philosophy does reveal analogous circumstances, as we shall see. Still, the golden age of American philosophy raised with special urgency foundational questions about the nature of time and its relation to reality. Peirce, James, Royce, Santayana, Dewey, and Whitehead are of a single voice in asserting the

centrality of the theme of time, but they answer the questions in an idiom peculiar to the philosophical perspective each occupies.

2. PHILOSOPHERS IN THE FOREGROUND

More than any other American philosophers who were active during the late nineteenth and early twentieth centuries, Peirce, James, Royce, Santayana, Dewey, and Whitehead channeled the course of subsequent American philosophy. The roster could be prefaced with an older contemporary of Peirce and James in order to include Chauncey Wright steadily voicing a new dispensation. The list could best conclude with some attention to Dewey's contemporary and colleague, George Herbert Mead. Mead is at the crosscurrents of temporalist emphases in American philosophy. At Harvard he was a student of both Royce and James. As a colleague of Dewey at the University of Chicago, he both influenced and was influenced by Dewey's temporalistic naturalism and instrumentalism and, to a greater degree than Dewey, was alert to the significance of Whitehead's process philosophy. Inasmuch as both Whitehead and Dewey thought highly of Mead, it is fitting to offer an overview of Mead's philosophy of the present in our epilogue.

Chauncey Wright (1830–75) was an independent spirit who evidenced a style of philosophy free of any sectarian mold. Living in Boston, and at home in scientific and professional groups around Harvard, he occasionally lectured there at the invitaton of Charles Eliot.[19] But he pursued the philosophy of science and metaphysics with a dispassionate expertise that won him an expanding reputation and considerable influence in both the United States and England. Early on, Wright was a critic of philosophy as pursued under any kind of sectarian or metaphysical restraints. He "devoted a good part of his metaphysical writing to negative criticism of the Scottish realists."[20] In the judgment of Edward H. Madden, perhaps the leading expositor of the views of the man he called "the Socrates of Bow Street," Wright was the dialectician who began to force philosophy along new paths. "Wright is a pivotal figure in American philosophy—with him began the 'golden age' of Peirce, James, Dewey, Royce and Santayana."[21] He was arguably the central figure in the Metaphysical Club, an informal group that grew out of an idea suggested in a letter from William James to Wendell Holmes in 1868.[22] Wright did more than his share of analyzing into strands and regrouping into more deft patterns the ideas of Peirce, James, Holmes, Nicolas St. John Green, and John Warner. Like Holmes, the latter two members of the discussion group were lawyers. Perhaps the predictive theory of the law, as well as the very pragmatic axiom itself,

assumed a certain obviousness and luster in later decades because of Wright's ability to give all of the Metaphysical Club's efforts a more polished appearance.

Of special importance for our purposes was Wright's relationship with Francis Ellingwood Abbot (1836–1903), who propounded a doctrine of the objectivity of relations in the real world. Abbot was an occasional participant in the discussions of the Metaphysical Club.[23] His early work on the philosophy of space and time attracted the attention of both Wright and Peirce, and drew spirited responses from them. Abbot's first published work was a long paper appearing in the *North American Review* entitled "The Philosophy of Space and Time" (1864). This article is not only the most obvious point of departure for an independent metaphysical treatment of space and time in American philosophy, but it also bears on the reception of Kant's critical realism in American thought. Abbot's paper opens with this claim: "In the higher metaphysics no ideas are more worthy of critical examination than the ideas of Space and Time, or yield richer rewards to a careful and patient analysis. Ramifying in all directions, they connect themselves with almost every important philosophical inquiry."[24] Abbot proceeds to discuss "the essential difference between Space and Extension" and, *mutatis mutandis*, the difference between time and protension.

But Abbot never wins his way clear to an independent treatment of time because he tends to model time after space. He spatializes time, almost entirely ignoring the cardinal relation of earlier-and-later as a unique characteristic of temporal change. "For the sake of brevity," he asserts, "we shall confine ourselves in this undertaking to Space alone, since the general characteristics of the two ideas of Space and Time are identical."[25] Both Wright and Peirce criticized Abbot's views, and none of the other classical American philosophers analyzed time solely according to spatial models.[26] Wright does lead into the golden age of American philosophy, although he did not achieve, perhaps because of his early and untimely death, the same philosophical stature enjoyed by the others who define that period. His work in the philosophy of science, especially his distinctions between the biological and physical sciences; his expert analyses and assessments of the theories associated with biological evolution (some of which Darwin valued so highly that he had them distributed in England); his philosophy of mind that was scaled to an empirical and evolutionary approach; his criticisms of many of the pale abstractions of Scottish realism; and his knowledge and criticism of the philosophy of space and time as elaborated by Francis Abbot: these themes all found their register in the work of the leading American philosophers during his own lifetime and

during the decades immediately following. His work helped establish the agenda and identify the unfinished business for a distinctively American philosophy. Charles Peirce, Wendell Holmes, and William James set out views about the interest-oriented nature of the human psyche, and about the nature of time and reality that are, in part at least, extensions of their early contacts with Wright in the Metaphysical Club. In Holmes's words, they "twisted the tail" of the cosmos in those early discussions. Peirce and James, not content with such limited sightings and contacts, also decided to cage the animal, to encompass the cosmos within the trammels of elaborate philosophical constructions.

Charles Sanders Peirce (1839–1914) was the most intense, most idiosyncratic, of the major American philosophers. A son of the accomplished Harvard mathematician, Benjamin Peirce, his own training at Harvard was in the natural sciences as well as in mathematics. With the exception of some of his articles for *Popular Science Monthly*, he wrote both philosophy and science in a technical and exacting vein. His work was severe and precise, framed according to the strictest lines of logical analysis and division. Some of it seems to break open only after a second or third reading. James K. Feibleman's *An Introduction to the Philosophy of Charles S. Peirce* (1946) is still the most accessible route into the system that is implied but never fully stated in the work of Peirce himself.

Like Chauncey Wright, Peirce was in the ambit of Harvard and partook of its intellectual life, but he never enjoyed a permanent appointment there. Occasionally lecturing but not as a regular academic, he often seemed to use an almost private vocabulary to elucidate his main distinctions in logic and in metaphysics. Still, more than any of the other major American philosophers, he retained some of the indistinct religious suppositions and metaphysical perspectives that typified the Scottish realism that he, Wright, and James hastened into abrupt retirement. What is plain enough is that he reworked those suppositions and perspectives in the light of evolutionary theory. Our chapter on Peirce opens with his creationist-evolutionist account of natural laws and their growing complexity across time. As opposed to Wright, Peirce held that evolution does account for the present laws of nature.[27] Given his quasi-theistic account of the origin of all that is, such that a primal act of will or power lies behind all of nature's laws, Peirce refused to accept the absolute sway of causality, for those laws cannot be rationally necessary if they arise from something like an absolute will. Wright, however, had accepted universal causality.[28] But for Peirce there is openness, plurality, and chance in the universe due to its ultimately arbitrary origin. In these respects, he influenced the thought of James.[29] Peirce's account of the nature and modes of time close-

ly adheres to these foundational matters, and his labored prose seems to capture some of the obscurity surrounding such issues.

It is increasingly being recognized that Peirce's philosophy is salient to further developments in twentieth-century thought. That there is no definitive chronological edition of the body of his writings is now being corrected.[30] Stages in the development of his philosophy can be more exactly defined as those textual questions are more fully answered. Accordingly, our chapter on Peirce's philosophy was framed in a more nondevelopmental, systematic manner than any of the other chapters. Although the result gives us less of the man and of the progress of the man's thought, perhaps limiting the discussion to a smaller number of interrelated themes can help clarify the idea we noted in Francis Abbot's philosophy of time: for metaphysics, no ideas are more worthy of critical examination than the ideas of space and time. As we shall see, Peirce argued for a clear distinction between the near and the remote future. The impetus for uttering that distinction, we may hazard, lay embedded in that general restlessness of the American mind that led Commager to comment that Americans invented time. The distant future seems too much wooed by the merely possible or the fervently eschatological. Max Lerner might almost echo Peirce's distinction about the two senses of the future when he says, "American thought has moved from the Utopian and the millennialist to a focusing on the calculable future."[31] The immediate future is that hazardous realm for testing and experimentation that prediction helps evoke. For the pragmatist or instrumentalist, experiment helps create or provoke a determinate kind of future just as much as the future acts as a lure for experiment. Such transactions between the ideas of prediction, experiment, chance, and the future make up the very stuff of the Peirce-James-Dewey axis in American thought, showing all the while that the cultural milieu of a pioneering and industrialist society is helping energize the development of thought.

Accounted by Bertrand Russell as "the recognized leader of American philosophy,"[32] William James (1842–1910) gained during his lifetime an international reputation as a philosopher of process, development, and the stream of consciousness. From our angle of approach, his thought discloses several major "actors" whose interrelations give us the world as we experience it. He sets forth five key factors that comprise reality: time, space, consciousness, qualia, and, as a shadowy surrogate or afterimage of God, the More. These five turn out to be equally real, but not of equal value. For all his emphasis upon time and the streaming processes of reality, James, like Abbot, judges that space is the most valuable of all continua—although, unlike Abbot, for James time is an independent continuum not to

be construed according to the ground plan of space. We may well wonder whether James ever escaped from the world of necessity and inevitability which had so severely vexed him. If we pull nature out of the traditional trio of which reality was comprised—nature, man, and God—it appears that James has attacked nature by main force, analyzing it into its constituent elements of some neutral stuff (properties or qualia), the space in which those qualia are dispersed, and the "time-buds" within which the qualia interplay with each other. If anything at all is left over as an integrative element from the original unity of qualia, space, and time, then perhaps it is given in James's pure experience as a monistic nature *redivivus*. James may never have achieved a unified philosophy, and attending closely to his views of time and the way time relates to the other constituents of reality only reinforces the overall pluralistic effect of his findings.

Some intellectual historians think that James's pluralistic philosophy is too much of a projection of the many-sided dispersive character of the American experience. Perhaps Lewis Mumford stands in the forefront of the revolt against pragmatism when he writes of "the Pragmatic Acquiescence."[33] The argument is that the culture of the middle and later decades of the nineteenth century could no longer flourish; the living energies receded from the dispensation that Mark Twain satirized (with his coauthor, Charles D. Warner) in *The Gilded Age* (1873). Mumford continues that William James simply preserved the separated parts and exalted them into a philosophy, giving us "a blessed anesthetic." James "gave this attitude of compromise and acquiescence a name: he called it pragmatism; and the name stands not merely for his own philosophy, but for something in which that philosophy was deeply if unconsciously entangled, the spirit of a whole age."[34] He has reported, Mumford, concluded, "the hash of everyday experience." Mumford's characterization, we may note, also extended to the thought of John Dewey. According to Mumford, the main difference between the two pragmatists is that we recover pioneer America in the thought of James, and industrialist America in the work of Dewey.

A more carefully wrought analysis of the pluralistic, dispersive aspects of pragmatism is given in the influential study by Arthur O. Lovejoy, "The Thirteen Pragmatisms" (1908). Where Mumford gives an external analysis of James's pluralism and temporalism, Lovejoy gives an internal analysis of some of the most important pragmatic doctrines. He argues that some of those key themes "are not only distinct but logically independent."[35] Pragmatism, then, seems to disintegrate into its species, and it means quite different things depending on whether it is taken as a theory of meaning, of truth, of validity, or as an ontological theory. Lovejoy concludes that these various theories are incompatible with each other. Although the

overall effect of his analysis is more damaging than Mumford's external approach, he is also more sympathetic to the movement as a whole, holding that his study is presented as something of a prolegomenon to a future pragmatism.[36]

A more recent, sympathetic treatment of James's thought, one that finds a central vision unifying the various strands in his philosophy, is set out in an essay by Richard Bernstein. Indeed, as opposed to those who hold that James never achieved a mature, integrated statement of his philosophy, Bernstein argues that *A Pluralistic Universe* gives precisely such a statement. The various lectures comprising James's book are neither random nor desultory. Rather, Bernstein holds, "they are beautifully orchestrated—themes are introduced, developed, and tied together into an integral and synoptic whole."[37] This appraisal of James's thought, one that stresses the continued relevance of its themes in countering the formalism and intellectualism in present-day thought, is reinforced and powerfully augmented in the recent study by Jacques Barzun, *A Stroll with William James* (1983). Barzun has simply raised to a new level the question of how best to assess the work of James in the sweep of American intellectual history. Perhaps he, the historian of ideas and movements, and James, the philosopher who described his work as "my *flux*-philosophy," have enjoyed an uncommon meeting of minds, at least from the one side, in this "stroll." It is due to both minds having a sense of history. James "is the historian among philosophers. In everything he wrote—letters, books, lectures, jottings—his habit is to introduce his theme by sketching what has led to its present state, in his mind or in the world. In developing his ideas, he cites cases, illustrates with historical events and persons, reports recent views and public facts; and he often finds in a philosophic position of the past a prop for his new one."[38] But through it all, there is a vision animating the whole, a vision that was projected from the magnanimous personage who seemed to be without guilt and without guile. "The conspicuous fact about James is that he harbored no sense of wrong," Barzun believes.[39] Thus, James seems to have recapitulated in his own life a dominant trait of the American character: it is guileless and guiltless. As against Mumford, it becomes quite clear from Barzun's pages that James gives us no anesthetic hash of the multifarious American experience, but has thrust American character open from within to disclose at its center something like an artesian will or a mysterious innocence. In any case, our own chapter on James concludes that he presents us all over again with a mystery at the crux of things.

Josiah Royce (1855–1916) presents some of the strongest evidence of the living influence of William James and Charles Peirce. James was responsi-

ble for bringing Royce to Harvard, and was his senior in the philosophy faculty. Where James has five coequal elements of reality, Royce has but one. That one, his Absolute, is a living, creative will. James's pluralistic realism and naturalism helped call forth from Royce an absolute kind of pragmatism unified around the idea of a will that articulates itself into a system of true individuals. Each individual has its own specious time, but all are integrated within the self-representative Absolute whose time plan is the perpetual or the eternal.

Aside from James's influence, and perhaps more powerfully, the diversity and vigor of the American experience—especially as it was found in California—are registered in Royce's version of voluntaristic idealism. The very tumult and randomness of the early social life of that state, where Royce was brought up and where he taught before joining the Harvard faculty, helped pose the problem of how to integrate within a single system of loyalties the competing if not contradictory acts of frontier lawlessness. There is some analogy between the philosophical program Josiah Royce framed for himself, with its unifying and purifying ground plan for the reform of the intellect and moral experience, and the unifying legislative plans for the reform of a disintegrating nation so single-mindedly pursued by the early Israelite royal figure for whom Royce was named, King Josiah. Certainly American religious circles, once the attenuated religiometaphysical philosophy of Scottish realism had been dethroned from its ideological control of much of American higher education, were looking for a new champion. They believed they had found him in Josiah Royce and could easily enough discern an absolute center in the modified version of German idealism that Royce assembled into a vaulting architecture of reason aimed at the eternal.

Much of Royce's discussion of nature and time and its subsumption under the perpetual and the eternal seems to parallel Augustinian and Franciscan views about the restless journey of the finite soul back to its eternal and saving ground. Royce's later work was fortified by James's realistic and naturalistic analyses of the life of the psyche at the lower levels, and honed to logical excellence through the studies in the newer symbolic logic to which Peirce pushed him. This same work, framed around a deepened awareness of the reality of relations, must stand as one of the very best examples of how philosophies imported into the American experience undergo realignments which emphasize the concepts of the individual, the will, the inwardness of personal life, and the logic of the shared social mind. That Royce could consistently position these features toward each other without any loss of the integrative power of his system (centered around his idea of the logos that he called "System Sigma") is indirectly

but powerfully shown by the quality of the rebuttal he elicited from both George Santayana and John Dewey. The sometimes not so genteel exchanges between the three philosophers did much to raise the standard of autonomous intellectual inquiry in American thought to the levels it enjoyed in later decades.

But systems of idealistic philosophy have not fared well in twentieth-century American philosophy. They have not captured the center because they do not sufficiently reflect the distinctive idiom of American experience. Still, Royce's deep sympathy for symbolic logic and the logic of relations, his almost consuming interest in the conceptual schemes of the natural and mathematical sciences, his concern with the problem of integrating personal and social ethics, and his relating these to earlier developments in the history of philosophy (he held the chair in the history of philosophy at Harvard), all helped set the benchmark for academic philosophy in American higher education. In this respect, he did for American philosophy what T. H. Green did for English philosophy: they elevated the sights of informed, university-trained minds whose goals were social goals.

A self-confessed stranger in a foreign land, George Santayana (1863–1952) both is and is not an American philosopher. With the possible exception of Whitehead, his philosophical sources run more deeply and widely than any other classical American thinker. His is more of a Graeco-Roman presence, more indeed of a Latin presence, than any of the others. John Smith does not include him in his critically important study, *The Spirit of American Philosophy* (1963). By way of contrast, H. B. VanWesep excludes Royce but does treat Santayana in his *Seven Sages* (1960), another key treatment of persons and themes in American thought. Perhaps because of Santayana's immersion in the larger stream of perennial Western philosophy and, contrariwise, because of his embedded presence in Harvard's intellectual life at the turn of the century, we can discern in his work the most fruitful kinds of interaction between imported philosophical motifs and the more typical temporalism, naturalism, and voluntarism of "the American spirit."

There is a strategic reason, beyond desiring a more complete treatment of the philosophers who comprise the golden age, for assigning Santayana a place in these studies of time and its relation to reality, for Santayana's temporalism finds its deepest root in the pre-Socratic philosophers and the Hellenic colonial experience, especially that of Heraclitus at Ephesus. Following the view of Jacques Maritain mentioned earlier, what we might otherwise consider a unique, time-energizing complex of experiences in American national life at the close of the nineteenth century may be—if we adopt the longer view to which Santayana's work invites us—a recur-

rent feature in the development of the intellectual life of different civilizations at widely separate places. Perhaps, the argument would go, comparative studies in the intellectual history of diverse civilizations will show that common features of temporalism, naturalism, and voluntarism arise out of a special dialectic between the earlier colonial experience and a maturing civilization that has caught its stride, is confirming a common set of deep-lying categories, and is poised for a fully flowering cultural life. That is, Santayana's special perspectives call up questions about the philosophy of history which only Whitehead was to raise with equal intensity.

Such a viewpoint would require that we probe more deeply behind the genetic explanation (by Lewis Mumford) and the critical dissolution (by Arthur Lovejoy) of American pragmatism. Does perhaps the spirit of American philosophy, taken primarily in the sense of the spirit of pragmatism, instrumentalism, and radical empiricism, reflect the skeptical animus of the philosophe and the sophist and then a gathering, constructive response to it? From this point of view, Peirce, Santayana, Royce and Whitehead were looking for the grounds of constancy in a world of process and hazard in ways that James and Dewey were not. But whether arguing for a relativistic and evolutionary approach, or against it in not allowing those emphases to have the final word, questions about the nature and modes of time are pressed to the forefront on the agenda of American thought.

John Dewey (1859–1952) had a career more complexly related to the vicissitudes of American intellectual history and American national life than any of the other leading American philosophers. He played a key role in measuring the more traditional philosophical schemes and finding them lacking. Committed strongly to some features of those schemes in his earlier, idealistic period, he found that none was scaled to the new tasks that arose as the ground of the nation's experience shifted. Under the influence of the organic, life-oriented philosophies of Leibniz and James, and convinced by the naturalism and experimentalism of Peirce, James, and, to a degree, G. H. Mead, Dewey rejected the content of most of his earlier views and set out to develop a nonidealistic, evolutionary account of mind and nature.

Perhaps the most typical of his books, in the sense of its challenging the perennial Western mode of philosophy, was *Reconstruction in Philosophy* (1920). In it he established a dialogue with the classical Hellenic world view as channeled through the Judaeo-Christian tradition. He found classical philosophy and some of its rationalist and empiricist offshoots in modern times to be intellectually sterile, scientifically lisping, and socially and morally demeaning. Under the Baconian banner of social engineering, he

argued away the static English empiricism in favor of a wide-ranging experimentalism, and raised the standard of applying a revised scientific procedure to man's moral and social problems. The book is an early and brilliant example of what is now called the "sociology of knowledge," and one of its most effective devices is the regular displacement of hierarchical schemes of explanation in favor of temporally organized, functional schemes of explanation. *Reconstruction in Philosophy* is comprised of a series of lectures Dewey gave in Japan immediately after the First World War. Perhaps specially stimulated by a non-Western intellectual milieu, the lectures call for the displacement of existing props for man's view of himself and nature by means of a redesigned set. *Reconstruction* is neither Dewey's best book nor his theoretically most satisfying, but it is the most compelling overview of all of his themes as orchestrated for a single purpose: to call for a radical change in the direction of Western philosophy.

But therein lies a most interesting problem. To the degree that its main lines of argument are successful in discounting the cogency of the Greek basis of Western philosophy, those same lines of argument can be used to discount the reconstructed philosophy he plans to erect in its stead. For he views the mainstays of the classical philosophy—with its theory of changeless forms, its theory of a changeless Good as legislating over nature and over human moral experience, and its dualistic contrast of the ideal and the real—as simply a register at the intellectual level of the traditional hierarchy of Greek social life and the separation between the economic classes in that society. But if Dewey is ever to arrive, by extension, at what Karl Mannheim (in *Ideology and Utopia*) called both a general and total conception of the ideological grounds of all explanation, then Dewey must also allow that the impetus of his thought reflects and does not transcend the American experience and all of its interacting complexities and shifting scenes of conflicting groups. His reconstruction, then, would be a deconstruction of philosophical schemes into temporary instruments for adapting to a hazardous and evolving future. But indeed, what I have called a problem is no problem at all for Dewey, for our tentative adaptations to a changing world of experience, one flung forward in time, and one which allows for real but limited realizations of value, is for him the simple truth of the matter.

Optimistic to the end of his life about almost everything but time (as we shall see), socially and politically active in all manner of national and international causes, Dewey became an exemplar in his own lifetime of the democratic man who was aristocratic in the etymological sense of the term: releasing the best that is in us from the trammels of tradition in order to self-consciously bring into being for our own time and place the strong-

est values we can gain and enjoy. He seems to be what Gabriel Marcel called *homo viator,* a man-on-the-way. Dewey's is a journey from nature, through nature, and back into nature. The whole of it is calculated, in each of its several phases, to highlight the experience of time and the relationship of time to the rest of reality.

One other leading philosopher who was deeply interested in the notions of process and event rounds out the golden age of American thought. Initially another voice from abroad, he gave to American philosophy a deeper infusion of scientific experience than allowed by Dewey's rapprochement with English philosophy in the second decade of the twentieth century. Alfred North Whitehead (1861–1947) came to American shores in 1924 to accept an appointment in philosophy at Harvard. Unlike Dewey, who was not himself a natural scientist, Whitehead was throughout the whole of his academic career in England a mathematical physicist and mathematician. Like Dewey, however, he was immensely invested in education at several levels, and carried a heavy load of educational administration during his active years in England.

With James and Dewey, Whitehead affirms the primacy of experience. But unlike either of those American figures, he was to find, certainly in his later work in philosophy proper, traces of eternality and intimations of immortality within that experience. Reminiscent of Santayana's realm of essences and of Peirce's domain of Firsts, there is in Whitehead's realism a domain of ideas or forms (called by him "eternal objects") which must be consulted in order to give an adequate account of the vistas that open out within experience itself. Time and events cannot be adequately explained, he thought, without the punctuation provided by these more timeless ingredients. The eternal objects are graded into experience and give to it some of its marks as an interrelated whole. The forms or eternal objects, it turns out, are related to the developing consequences of God's own nature, a processual nature of burgeoning value which gives to events or actual occasions their existence and their power of being known.

Whitehead's philosophy of process and events, and of the relationships of time, process, and events to eternal objects and other factors of reality, is dealt with at greater length across two chapters (as opposed to the single chapters devoted to the work of each of the others), simply because of the much greater role these notions play in the whole of his philosophical production. Whitehead gives us two very distinctive philosophies of events and time. Although there is passage from the first of them to the second, there is no real sense in which we could anticipate or predict his second, more metaphysical account of events, emergence, and creativity by simply attending to the first, more physicalistic account and then attempting to

determine what sort of metaphysics is implied in it. But we should mention at least one methodological postulate that controls the development of both accounts alike: experience is to be explained in terms that come from experience itself. Although this postulate is broadly consistent with the fundamental convictions of our other American philosophers, Whitehead carries out its implications with a resoluteness of attention that is unique in his case.

This is not to suggest, however, that Whitehead somehow synthesizes the main temporalist themes of the other leading American philosophers in his work, say, from 1925 on, commencing with *Science and the Modern World*. There simply is no way to tie together all of these other vigorous projects of thought in his metaphysics. The development of philosophy, and perhaps especially the development of American philosophy, cannot be so simplistic and jejune as all that. Besides, professional opinion is still divided as to whether Whitehead has managed, without contradiction or real contrariety, to bring together the several perspectives of his own thought under the vice-regency of his Categoreal Scheme in *Process and Reality*. More to the point, is there process and temporality in God's own nature? Is there temporality and value in eternity? Although it is hoped that our analysis of some of Whitehead's views helps clarify some of the terms involved in such questions, any judgment as to whether Whitehead was ultimately able to answer them must be approached through the work of Charles Hartshorne and Robert Whittemore. But there is an antecedent question, the textual question, that must be answered, having to do with the order in which the main parts of Whitehead's metaphysical writings are to be treated. In this area, the studies of Lewis Ford are beginning to provide a kind of guidance unavailable until very recently. Whereas Professor Ford's approach in *The Emergence of Whitehead's Metaphysics* (1984) is still to be evaluated for its overall effect, he has clearly thrown light on some controversial passages by arranging them in a more correct order. A close reading of those passages is pivotal in judging the consistency and adequacy of Whitehead's philosophy.

Peirce and the Prevalence
of Time

A TOPIC that regularly appears in
even the most casual inventory of philosophical problems is the problem
of time. Time is such a pervasive, resilient feature of experience that it cannot be ignored. But time is also vague enough that almost any analysis or
tracking procedure we use to enhance and purify its signals, in order that
we might better understand it, seems to override or baffle those signals. We
begin to study the phenomenon of temporality and find that our attention
is displaced from our subject to our ways of probing into it. Hence, one of
the paradoxes about time: time seems to mirror our investigative method
back to us, with only the method more deeply clarified. Such a paradox is
caught up in some of Kant's beliefs about time as a pure form of intuition.
Even though it is the most general form of experience, it cannot be grasped
apart from particular experiences. "Time," he says, "is nothing but the
form of the internal sense, that is, of our intuition of ourselves and of our
internal state."[1] To assert that time is a form of self-awareness is to assert
that a study of time will reflect our categorial apparatus back to us empty
of all content that is nonself. We simply have come to see part of the structure of our own minds.

Charles Sanders Peirce frequently dealt with the problem of time in
a way befitting its vague, pervasive character: by conducting many sorties
into the topic but never a single, strategic campaign. His longest passages
are short when compared with the extensive discussions of time by many
other scientists and philosophers. Much of the diversity in his handling of
temporal questions is related to the fact that he is treating specialized problems in empirical sciences, in mathematics, or in philosophy at a level

where it is altogether natural to allude to time.[2] In the aggregate, his writings reveal a wealth of material on the different problems of temporality. With few exceptions, his different pronouncements fit together effectively if we qualify them by their actual context. Moreover, his doctrines about time are not peripheral—mere incidents to his scientific investigations and philosophy—but clearly go to essentials. For insofar as his thought is synechistic, it is also temporalistic.

Time, Peirce argues, is a paradigm for all other continua whose main features are foreshadowed by the structure, the modes, and the laws of time. Inasmuch as time is the best version of continuity, and in that continuity is "the form of forms" in Peirce's philosophy,[3] it follows that his philosophy of time is at the center of his system, determining lines of development in his metaphysics, his pragmaticism, and his account of the logic of the sciences. Nevertheless, no matter how regal time may be in his philosophy, it is not imperial. Other factors do limit time's superintending functions.

I. THE ORIGIN OF TIME

Some of the most conspicuous features of the universe are found in its continuous sequences, and in the ways these sequences and changing scenes modify each other. Some augment, some diminish. But whatever the lines of action, we still summarize the wealth of such evidences of changing worldscapes by saying that reality is temporal and that time is a dominant feature of all of the guises in which the world appears. But Peirce did not think that the world was always this way. He believed that temporality is a character that has arisen in the course of things. Some traits of reality were present before time was present. Time is episodic in, but not constitutive of, a wider reality.

There are four major alternatives regarding the origin of time: (1) time was created, (2) time has evolved, (3) time was both created and has evolved, and (4) time was neither created nor evolved, but always was. Peirce did not think that this last alternative, the most Hellenic of them, was a serious option. It would make the universe eternal and recurrent.[4] It would, moreover, rule out novelty and chance. Peirce rejected the doctrine of the eternality of time while affirming the third of the above alternatives.[5] If time were eternal, if there never was when time was not, it would then be coeternal with God, and would thus limit or constrain Him. "It is a degraded conception to conceive God as subject to Time, which is rather one of His creatures" (4.67).[6] Making God subject to or limited by time would constrain God by the necessary relations that hold for the forms of continuity that characterize time.

For Peirce, then, time is in some sense due to the action of a creative ground. Although the same thought appears in Royce's work, there the idea of ground seems more implicative than creative, more of the nature of a ground-consequent relation. But for Peirce, time has an arbitrary beginning, and one must look directly at the features of temporality in order to understand them. Time is rooted in a creative power that is divine (6.505–6). God created it and is still creating it. But Peirce also thought that time evolved or developed.[7] In its most primitive sense, time is a kind of cadence, perhaps a sequencing of otherwise amorphous processes. As part of a universe which gradually arose, time itself has a beginning. There must have been "a state of things before time was organized" (6.214). Qualities of such a state would be akin to Peirce's Firsts. There were circumstances and complexes such that time was not but other things were: such is the assumption Peirce is entertaining.[8] Under these conditions— the mythopoeic account continues—there was vagueness, and then there was sheer potentiality. Out of this primal zone of fecundity, both time and the universe arose (6.193). Just as feeling takes on habit in becoming character, so too potentiality takes on time in becoming existence. Time and space would make up the good manners of the universe, but then so too would essences or forms be aspects of the well-ordered behavior of the existing world. Even the Platonic forms once were not, but have come to be in some kind of evolutionary process (6.194).[9] Like time, they are modes of the manifestation of a primary potentiality.

Peirce's story of origins goes about like this: In the beginning was an arche that was a zone of power, but it was not yet a stage of orderedness. Flashes of potentiality illumined the primal condition but had not yet ordered it into a world. As the original zone took on organization, the swarm of disparate potentialities became the universe, and temporal and spatial forms are the raiment the universe sparingly dons. Time and space are the garb for all that exists. "Existence is a stage of evolution" (6.195). But existence is neither the first nor the last word about things. It is a species of reality, one which assumes the modes of space and time. Peirce's metaphysics is only tactically, not essentially, synechistic. Where the spatiotemporal forms of continuity are epiphenomenal, a metaphysics stressing continuity (synechism) will have only a penultimate validity.

For Peirce, time is the constancy and the intent of God's creative activity as it is manifested in the existing universe. Time is created but not caused, for cause presupposes a temporal order in which relations of consequence and antecedence are seated.[10] Peirce thought that there was a clear connection between the argument from design and the belief that the material universe had an arbitrary beginning (6.419). A meaningful argument

from design requires that time and space had a beginning, and that matter began with them. In such a finite, material universe, there can be real patterns of reactions.

It is the spate of real reactions in a noneternal material universe that sets real time off from mathematical time. Mathematical time is governed by the principle of noncontradiction, whereas the principle of existential reaction is typical of processes in real time. Mathematical time, Peirce held, is mere possibleness (6.326). As such, it has no arbitrary beginning, but is equally consistent with any beginning. It is time without limits, an endless, abstract, eternal kind of time. As Peirce would have it, a flaw in Hellenic cosmology is that Greek philosophers too often patterned natural or real time after mathematical time. They hypostatized mathematical time and, working with such a misleading model, could come to the conclusion that the cosmos is eternal.

To fix our attention upon the features of novelty and uniqueness in experience, Peirce uses the notions of First, Second, and Third as his most universal categories. Firsts are precisely these qualitylike elements of novelty and uniqueness, features that are simply there. Seconds are the more reactive features whose unique elements oppose each other, and one or the other, beyond simply being, is also said to exist. Thirds are elements of mediation and connectedness, elements like time and space and states of the universe. It appears that, for Peirce, time has evolved after its creation and partly as a result of continuing creation. Peirce can have it both ways without serious difficulty if he treats God in traditional terms. And he does. He believed that creation is not adventitious, a one-time-only act, but is an essential attribute of God. "Creative Activity is an inseparable attribute of God" (6.506). As creator, He is Absolute First, and as terminus, He is Absolute Second (1.362). Peirce adds here that "every state of the universe at a measurable point of time is the third." Judgments about the level of complexity to which existing reality has evolved are, thus, also comments on the stage God's career has reached in passing from His Primal to His Consequential nature. In Peirce, elements of absolute idealism are plainly present in these passages, that are at once both theogonic and cosmogonic. In a similar vein, Alfred North Whitehead located developmental features of this cosmos within God's nature. For both Peirce and Whitehead, God is a principle of creation and limitation.

2. THE NATURE OF TIME: THE PRIME CONTINUUM

Although it is a dominant feature of experience, time is not a dominating feature. It is continually present, but hardly noticed, for we lack the neces-

sary experiential contrasts (1.134). We do not have a nontemporal form of awareness. Although our awareness of time is mind-dependent, the fact of time is not. Peirce believed that time is a continuum that welds the world into a greater unity. Objectively outside of us, it also appears in human experience, binding us to the world. Time is important for our knowledge of the continua of the material world, especially as exhibited in physics (6.387). Indeed, time is the most excellent kind of continuum (6.86); it provides paradigms for all other types of continua.

Peirce believed that continuity is "the leading conception of science" and that it plays a part in all the laws of physics and psychics (1.62). If we hold that time is the paradigm for continuity, and that kinds of continuity provide us the leading conceptions of the various sciences, we can conclude that the temporal continuum gives the sciences the leading ideas for organizing their different subject matters.[11] In addition, the temporal continuum will receive special attention in those philosophies based in the natural sciences. Peirce believed that continuity had been stressed for 300 years by scientists, mathematicians, and by some philosophers like Hegel (1.41), and he threw in his lot with this group. He found the entire topic of continuity "entrancing" (1.171).[12] All things are awash in continua.

Peirce could conceive of his work as a synthesis of the various movements in modern science insofar as they treated continuity under the twin forms of time and space. He assigned the label 'synechism' to the doctrine that all that exists is continuous (1.172).[13] The work of Aristotle, Kant, and Hegel on continuity was important to Peirce's own work, for continuity is a fundamental idea in philosophy, and synechism is the doctrine that says as much (6.103). Emphasizing continuity over chance, Peirce called his system synechism, and not tychism (6.202), for tychism emphasizes Firstness, whereas synechism stresses Thirdness.[14] Indeed, continuity is Thirdness almost to perfection (1.337).

Time is so preeminently an archetype for continua that Peirce asserted "we envisage every other continuum" according to its devices (6.86). To support this contention, he defines two others—the mathematical and the spatial—in terms of the time continuum (6.164). The definitions are set up as analogies, and the implication is clear: the grammar of temporality provides the structure for all other continua which hold in the realm of actual reactions. Time gives the reactions in the spatial continuum their unique, nongeneral marks and initial constraints, those of exact location and full concreteness (6.82). Indirectly, in that they embody the conditions of possibility, time and space are together inherent in the continuity of nature (4.172).[15] But they are not the sole grounds for continuity in nature. Other grounds for the community of things are found in the conditions

of generality, as in the ways properties are shared by different natural complexes.[16]

Time may be the most excellent kind of continuum, but it is not perfectly continuous (1.412). Time is also a zone where forceful reactions occur, reactions that dislocate or interrupt to a degree the temporal continuum. Thus, time seems to be continual rather than continuous, sometimes more intermittent than unremitting. The suggestion is that Peirce was pursuing some of the implications of regarding time in nonspatial terms, for we do not speak of continual lines or continual surfaces, whereas continual or intermittent time is an acceptable locution directly grounded in experience.[17] But how could there be a discontinuous continuity? Peirce's views on time seem to require such a condition. We can imagine a continual continuity if we reject images of time as a flowing stream or as the "time-line" used in the classroom, in favor of other images. A mile relay race run by four quarter-milers, with some overlapping of the laps and with the all-important baton being handed on from the finished event of the first lap to the dawning event of the second lap, would be an example of a continual continuity.[18] A rope is an example of a continual continuity. It is a perissad with superfluous, uneven, or successive elements that make of it a twisted abundance. In some ways, time is like that for Peirce. A coil of rope fifty feet long has no fifty-foot fibers in it, but is composed of endless overlappings, side-wise interweavings, and braidings. The fibers are like the "topical singularities" that interrupt or divide a continuum at a lower level of generality (4.642). Thus, a rope or a relay race are suitable images of a discontinuous continuum, continual as regards its partial singularities but continuous as a complex interacting whole.

Let us call that trait of time in virtue of which it is a discontinuous continuum its Peirce-continuity, and hereafter, its P-continuity. Stated formally, P-continuity is simply "a discontinuous series with additional possibilities" (1.170). Peirce chose this phrasing to emphasize the most obvious features of real continuity. It has to do with the way one aspect of mind is continuous with another aspect, or the way something that is to a degree past is nevertheless part of the present. Josiah Royce and G. H. Mead also show that the past operates within the present. Relating the definition of P-continuity to the rope metaphor, we would say that the individual fibers make up the discontinuous series, and the overlappings and braidings would be part of the additional possibilities. Elsewhere, Peirce held that the parts of a continuum which interrupt its perfect continuity arise out of the act of defining (6.168). In our image, the hemp fibers are what the rope resolves into through high definition.

Time, then, is a kind of order where different phases of things overlap

and feed into each other without ceasing. It is the way entailment is graded into processes and reaction. "Our hypothesis therefore amounts to this, that time is the form under which logic presents itself to objective intuition" (6.87). This hypothesis is reminiscent of Plato's doctrine that time is the moving image of eternity. For both Peirce and Plato, the temporal scene is a kind of transparency through which forms and relations are projected, leaving behind shadowy replicas that help order and grade existence. Peirce held both that time is our best example of continuity, and continuity is Thirdness almost to perfection. We must now draw together the other features of continuity that determine time's nature and that, therefore, condition all processes in time.

In addition to the formal property of the continuum that we have called its P-continuity, Peirce held that continuity had defining features which he called Kanticity and Aristotelicity. The Kanticity of a continuum is its endless divisibility or infinite intermediation (4.121; 6.166). This means that between any two points in a continuous series there are more points.[19] This Kant-continuity or K-continuity means that every part of a true continuum has parts of the same kind (6.168). Between any putative isolates set off against each other, there are new isolates which modulate the relation between the initial features, and these new constituents are like the original parts.

The third essential feature of time as the prime continuum is Aristotelicity. The Aristotle-continuity or A-continuity is the property that any two points of a continuum have a common limit (4.122; 6.164). If we take all of the existing points in a continuous series, at any intensified degree of K-continuity that we choose, the last member of one part of the series is also the first member of the next part. Taken strictly, A-continuity would signify that the continuous series is never fully disconnected. A continuous series retains connexity in some sense. Every point can be taken as the limit to an endless series (6.166). As applied to time, this would mean that every part or element of a temporal continuum can be related to every other part.

K-continuity stresses the sense in which time seems to be composed of intervals or durations. A-continuity stresses the sense in which the temporal continuum is composed of instants or moments. If in addition every part of a continuum is composed just of parts like itself, then there is no true novelty in time but only a combinatory novelty. It was to insure the feature of real beginnings that Peirce apparently worked with the idea of a discontinuous continuum.[20] This additional property of the temporal continuum suggests the way that the continuum is open to additional properties, qualities, and reactions, to Firsts and to Seconds. P-continuity

is needed to make sense of the additional possibilities from outside a given continuum.[21] Thus, P-continuity would mean that real time is multipli- or n-tracked, even though still unidirectional. Time has branches and confluences, and would be n-tracked in those ways.[22] There are always, P-continuity would remind us, two or more braided continua in the existing world of reactions.

3. THE REALITY OF TIME

Time is some sort of objective order independent of any perceiving subject. This is the view Peirce wanted to maintain against Kant. Cusanus, Bruno, and Leibniz all held that space and time are our creations, and Newton's doctrines about the objectivity and absoluteness of space and time notwithstanding, Kant had followed them.[23] But according to Peirce, time is not ideal; it is real (5.458; 6.96). It is the way conditions of objective possibility are displayed in the existing universe. The laws of continuity must be geared down in order to become entrained in the world as we know it. Real time is time that is present (6.387; 6.506). The logical laws of being, including the laws of the continuum, take on increasing specificity in becoming first the metaphysical laws of reality and then the physical laws of reality.[24] In discussing this transition from timeless being to temporal reality, Peirce uses the categories of actuality, nascence, and possibility, three categories that are, respectively, versions of Firstness, Secondness, and Thirdness.[25] Historical influences from Aristotle as regards the emphasis upon actuality, and from Duns Scotus as regards the idea of haecceity, influence this part of Peirce's theory of time.

For Peirce, to exist is to endure in time or to stand out in time as an actual event. Anything that does not exist for a time does not exist at all (3.93n). Thus, a necessary mark of existence is being in time. Another mark of existence is being general. There is no such thing as a sheer particular, for being requires endurance through change, with relations holding between the earlier and later stages of change. In order to speak of the same thing inhering through these changing stages, there must be an underlying relational identity of which the different stages are special cases. Thus, Peirce can conclude, only general beings exist. There are qualitative possibilities, such as characteristics or properties, that have a kind of being as Firsts. But they would not have the change and reactivity associated with being in time, and Peirce does not speak of them as existing. Existence is a stage of evolution where time has arisen and force is exerted (6.195). It is the zone where reactions occur and actualities come to be. It is the realm of *faits accomplis*.

The mode of actuality is the mode of being where time really acts upon us (5.459), in about the same way that existing objects act upon us: it influences us as an existent in its own right. Still, time is not merely an existent, for inasmuch as all existing things and states are general in some sense, so is time. Time is a form or law (6.96). In addition to being a power and a general law, time is also a nascency where form and power blend as contracted possibilities or actual events. The actuality of an event consists in its happening there and then (1.24). It becomes partially arrested in time and space through entering into objective relations with other existents. Actuality is something brute, like a sheriff's hand upon one's shoulder, as Peirce was accustomed to saying. The leading edge of the actual is the nascent state of the present. It is where happenings here and now become impervious to additional influences, and become part of the sum of *faits accomplis*.[26] The here and now fades insensibly by degrees into the there and then. The leading edge of the actual, the *hic et nunc* of things, is an aggressive stubbornness, and this obstinacy of things is their *haecceitas* (1.405). Qualitative possibilities are braided together in this nascent state of the actual, and their reactions are limited by what has already become a *fait accompli*. The *hic et nunc* is where the actual and the possible overlap. The resultant reaction is brute, blind force (7.532).[27] Possibilities are really welded together. These welds, which are reactions that involve qualitative elements like Firsts, have all the here and nowness of events which might be called pretemporal or prototemporal (6.200). Peirce had to allow for such quasi-temporal happenings in order to underwrite his belief that the entire Platonic set of abstract possibilities, both forms and relations, did in fact evolve.

4. THE MODES OF TIME: PAST, PRESENT, AND FUTURE

Peirce uses the traditional categories of modality—possibility, actuality, and necessity—to draw distinctions between the three modes of time: present, past, and future. To study this side of Peirce's philosophy is to realize that the modal categories and the modes of time are not to be paired off with each other in any obvious way.[28] One of the most interesting sides of Peirce's contribution to the philosophy of time arises from his examination of the relations between logical and temporal modality.

Time is related to objective modality, Peirce believed, as species is related to genus. Time is "a particular variety of objective modality" (5.459); the obvious modes of time are past, present, and future. Peirce called these features "general determinations of time" (5.458), determinations that in some respects arise out of the categories of logical modality.

The past is what is actual; the mode of the past is the mode of actuality (5.459). The future is full of new determinations, as guided by law, but it is also full of potentialities, replete with what might become fact, but also might not. Accordingly, the modes of the future are those of necessity and possibility (5.461). The three modal categories of actuality, possibility, and necessity are assigned as features to the past and to the future. What, then, is the mode of the present?

In some places Peirce proceeds as if all three modal categories characterize the present. Elsewhere it appears that none of them applies to the present, that the present is nonexistent and thus cannot be modally designated. In the former case, all three categories could apply to the present if the present is where the past and the future overlap and is jointly composed of them. This position is sometimes underwritten by Peirce; the present is half past and half to come (6.126). Following this view, the present would be the zone where the actual, the necessary, and the possible mingle.

Peirce's more customary doctrine, however, is that the present, taken as the present instant, simply has no independent existence. It is at best something like a point instant. We cannot seize the immediate present (3.343). Indeed, the present seems to be nontemporal. Flatly stated, we would say that the present contains no time (1.38); it is outside of time, cut off from the actual and the possible. Taken as a kind of instant, the present is simply a *quale*-consciousness, utterly severed from the past and the future (6.231). It is where the future flows into the past, and where the past mirrors the destiny of the future to the future. But at this juncture of past and future, there is nothing present. There is, to put it bluntly, no present (1.493). There may be the mere possibility of a conceptual cut across an idealized kind of continuum that mathematics can describe, but there is nothing at the present in the durational sense.[29]

The reason there is no present is that the flow of time keeps all of time's content in a constant process of relocation. There is no present because the fact or actuality that is to be present to us is already past (2.84). One result of this radical effervescence of the present is the interruption of the laws of the conservation of mass and energy. The past is broken off from the future, and there is independence of the actual instant (6.87). The past does not enslave the future, and the present is a boundary beyond which the power of the past cannot reach (7.536). There is no sheriff's hand in the future, and the claims of the past have no direct agency in the future. Peirce is deeply committed to this break in time's passage. The present represents to him a boundary situation in which chance is real and novelty can arise.

Such a break in time's passage, almost by definition, defies determination and analysis. The present, Peirce holds, is inscrutable (5.458). It is

a zone where strange powers are found. It is occult (2.85). Itself lacking duration, it nevertheless accumulates and endures to become the substance of the past. The present has the peculiar property of being atemporal in the sense of having no time in it, yet it accumulates in wholes of time (7.675). It is a sheer surd, a presence without determinations or modalities. It is a haecceity (1.405). It seems to be something only in relation to the other two, the future and the past. With them, it forms a conventional triad, for time is triadic (6.330–31). Apart from them, the present is nothing at all.[30]

The following diagrams represent Peirce's stance on the modes of time and their relations:

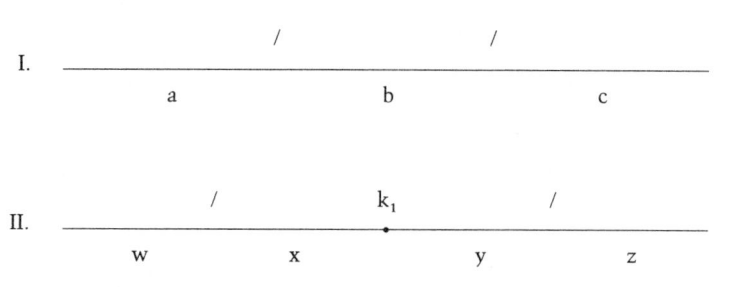

Case I illustrates a more traditional time line, one which symbolizes that the present has duration. Segment a would stand for the past, segment b for the present, and segment c for the future. But Case I will not do for Peirce, for he denies that the present, as represented here by segment b, is a locus for anything at all. At best, the present b is where the past a and the future c overlap or blend. But Case I seems to deny to the intuition any sense of a and c overlapping at all. Peirce's view requires that something happen to b so that it becomes a power zone, yet without extent. Under the double pressure of efficient causation (the force of the past) and final causation (the necessitation of general laws governing the future), the present implodes and becomes occult, effervescent, and titanic.

A better representation of Peirce's view is shown in Case II. There, segments w and x represent the remote and the near past, respectively, and segments y and z stand for the near and the remote future, respectively.[31] Segments x and y, the near past and the near future, respectively, are what we call the present.[32] Xy would have entangling alliances with the efficacy of the past and the potentiality of the future; xy is a region of conflicting powers, where the residual malleability from the future suffers contraction so as to be compossible with ineluctable past fact.

Peirce explicitly distinguishes between the near and the remote future. The indefinite, more remote future is that part of the future that the modal

category of possibility applies to, or segment z in the diagram. The indefinite future is truly general and cannot be fully realized (2.148). But that part of the future that the modal category of necessity applies to is the near future, or segment y. This immediate future, according to Peirce, is inevitable (7.536). In this zone, general laws governing possible relations are really becoming operative. This close-up, real future is predetermined (7.666). Given Peirce's application of the modalities of possibility and necessity to the future, and his division of the future into the indefinitely general and the inevitably determined, it is clear that the future is both open (as regards its more distant, general possibilities) and closed (as regards its constraining laws).

The past is also divided into two parts by Peirce, though not as clearly as the future is divided. The mode of the past is the mode of actuality. He then makes a distinction about actuality that in effect gives the two-fold division. Part of the past is nascent. Our segment x in Case II represents this part of the past. But part of the past is dead, the part symbolized by segment w. The nascent state of the actual he did call the present (5.462), but Peirce also said there is no present because what is present is already past (2.84). The nascent state of the actual is still alive in some sense, with power and force working there, but the dead, finished state of the past, that region of actuality no longer open to any kind of modification, is the realm of *faits accomplis*. We tend to say that the present is what now is; it is the existential mode of time. But Peirce pushes this sense of time into the close past. For him, the past is the existential mode of time (5.458).

The present, we have seen, does not exist for Peirce except as it is revealed through the interplay of past and future. It is an epiphenomenon of their permutations. They, moreover, do not exist apart from each other. There is no time future by itself, nor a time past just by itself. The past/future distinction, he says, is a polar distinction (1.330; 5.450; 5.458), which means that we have a temporal field made up of waxing and waning events whose durations overlap or interweave. P-continuity is especially characteristic of this temporal field. Any event in the field can be taken as having both antecedents and consequences. If we consider its antecedents, we have an event as the crest or high tide of other conditions. In relation to the other conditions, the event is their end or telos, the high tide of their range of influence. Finally, although there is no knife-edge present, there are knife-edge distinctions we can make in the present. Such a knife-edge instant, k_1 in the second diagram, is the result of an act of abstraction: Any number of such distinctions—k_2, k_3, ... k_n—can be drawn in addition to k_1, and all of the marks of A-continuity and K-continuity apply to these rather precise point instants. As we shall see in the following section, these

instants can be graded into our understanding of this existing world of forceful interactions, but the instants are not to be confused with the durations in which the world's work is done.

Final causes work from the future (6.66).[33] They help determine what can be. This is the sense in which we say that the future weeds out the past (7.667). But though an event is *in futuro* with respect to some things, it also has the stance *in praeterito* with respect to others. It trails off into other events and helps determine what they are. It forces them, in the sense of being an irresistible restraint upon what else is compossible in them. So taken, the past is an efficient cause working upon the future, in part forcing the future to be a determinate sort of something. Psychologically, for example, the past acts on the future as memory (1.325). To say that past and future stand in a polar relation is to say that they are concurrent in every event. Trying to think of the future by itself is no help whatever, certainly not if we picture that future as a length of time (5.330). Every event has both past and future aspects, and thus must be understood under the double rubric of final and efficient causes. As half past and half to come, the present, or what we take as present, must always be understood in a polar sense.

As half to come, the future is a potentiality. Potential being is being *in futuro* (1.218). It is what may come to be in the relations between things. The future acts teleologically upon the past, in terms of Thirds (1.325), but it is the more remote future that so acts, that part of the future whose modal character is possibility. Indeed, the future is a world of ideas (6.192); it is the realm of generality that has not yet become fixed in relation to some existing past. As unfixed, the future is undifferentiated (6.191); it is nonego (7.536). But when the future becomes ours and takes on concreteness, it is then already part of the past. The analogy Peirce uses seems to be this: the nonego is to the ego as the future is to the past.

5. THE CONSTITUENTS OF TIME

The constituent parts of time for Peirce are instants, intervals, events, and stream. The first three are ways to indicate different aspects of the diversity of time, whereas the idea of the stream of time as a forward flowing of the world's contents suggests that there is a continuous unity underlying the diversity. Instants are most akin to Firsts in the sense that what we take as Firsts are features of experience exhibited in instants. In a similar phenomenological vein, intervals are most like Seconds, and events are most akin to Thirds. Then, as if to emphasize that instants, intervals, and events are given together in any existing complex, Peirce uses the idea of

time's flow. In this analysis lies the significance of Peirce's belief that although time is real, it is not an absolute. Time is simply a characteristic of the present stage of the universe. This doctrine controls some of the lines of his discussion concerning the constituent parts of time.

a. Instants. An instant is something "in stance." It has a relatively fixed posture in comparison with its context. An instant is where a change of quality is judged to occur or some new quality seems to appear. If a person is walking slowly, sees a friend, and then speeds up, the instant is where we make a cut, saying that the increased speed replaced the slower speed. There is movement underlying the specified instant, and a change of quality signifies the ending of one condition and the beginning of another.

Time, Peirce holds, is made up of instants (1.317). Time is in stance where the element of Firstness predominates, where we are conscious of a new quality. Consciousness, in an instant of time, is *quale*-consciousness (6.231), a feature of the now that differs from what falls before and after it. The very idea of time is the idea of a continuous series of such instants (7.416), each of which can be correlated with the series of conscious states. Indeed, the idea of feeling is sometimes defined by Peirce as that sort of consciousness that can be included within an instant of time (1.377). The time series and the series of psychological states are closely enough related that, for him, time parallels the life of the psyche. In addition, Peirce thought that time as a series of instants could reflect actual time and space (6.182), that there is no evidence that the series of instants does not have such real and objective reference. His argument here reflects Kant's view that time has a schematizing function. For if the time series parallels the life of the psyche or ego, and if that same time series can reflect the spatio-temporal structures of the world, then the time series does superintend the relations between ego and world.

The independent instants in the continuous series represent nontemporal intrusions where an exchange of quality has occurred between two temporal phases, each of which has its own duration through a time of relative stasis. This moment of relative stability has both a forward-looking and a backward-looking side, with the two divided by, but also meeting in, some distinct quality appearing there. Instants have two sides, and each instant is a polarity (1.380; 1.389), identifiable by its antecedents and consequences.[34] Indeed, instants are microcosms of the polarity of time and the past/future modalities.

The instants are independent, but not really discrete (4.641). If they were discrete, for example, we could have no memory of things. In some respects, instants have duration; they must carry over into each other with accumulations of qualities passed on to the later states. However brief they

may be, instants are not instantaneous (5.284). They are less like geometrical points than they are like perceptions of qualities here and now.[35] Instants are where Firsts are revealed. So the temporal continuum is discontinuous with respect to the appearance of a new quality, but it has continuity with respect to the way this new quality impinges on, relates to, and causes changes in other qualities. The temporal continuum is discontinuous as regards Firsts, but it is continuous as regards Seconds and Thirds.

A final observation about instants is that Peirce did not think of absolute instants in the sense that all other instants fall before or after them (6.318). All instants do not admit of being placed in simple order in a single continuum.[36] Thus, time is not centered, not all of a single strand. Rather, there must be time strands, overlapping and crisscrossing like fibers in a weave or strands in a rope. Time once arose, but all of it may not have arisen at once. This leaves open the possibility that new time orders may come into being as extensions or modifications of special kinds of processes.

b. *Intervals*. If we suggest that there are two time thoughts and not just one, then we say that a new or different feature has appeared which sets time thoughts distinctively apart and prevents them from being the iteration of the same thought. Peirce says that two thoughts are separated by an interval of time (5.288). An interval has parts, but an instant has sides or aspects. A finite interval is composed of an innumerable series of feelings which, as parts of consciousness, also occupy parts of the duration of consciousness (6.137). What is present during an entire interval is also present during each of its parts (7.352). It seems clear that although time is made up of instants, intervals, and events, an interval of time having duration is not made up of instants. An interval is like a unit of time's work where efficacy and reaction are busily incubating appearances of new properties. Such appearances amount to the breaking off of durations such that we say something has happened. An instant is analogous to a time-point, but durations are more analogous to surfaces, each portion of which is also a surface. We might say that durations are made of moments but not instants, where moments would be different size units of duration. Moments have duration because moments overlap (6.111). Elsewhere, Peirce also tells us that moments take time.[37] A moment for him seems to be the shortest duration an interval can occupy and still be said to take time, i.e., to fall between instants and be measurable by clocks.

c. *Events*.[38] According to Peirce, the event is the third basic element of which time is composed. Here, we are referring to real events, ones which take place in time or have dates in time (1.492), not those quasi-logical events of a nontemporal nature during which there is development in the

Platonic realm of universals and potentialities. Antecedence and consequence in that realm are not like before and after in real time. An event can only take place in real time (7.535). When an event in the physical world overlaps and reacts with the consciousness of minds, additional events take place, which are called experiences. Every new experience is an event occupying time.

Every real event has a front and a back. Unlike the two sides of the instant, which are divided by the appearance of a quality, the two phases of an event stand in contradiction. All events involve the juncture of contradictory inherences in subjects existentially the same (1.493). This means that events, considered as wholes, are not internally consistent. If something happens as a real event, logical opposition is a significant part of the happening.[39] A real event is an existential junction of incompossible facts (1.494). Just as space allows us to have (indeed, is defined as) an ordering of two subjects with a single predicate—the order of coexistence—so too does time allow us to have (indeed, is defined as) one subject with two opposing predicates, which gives us the temporal order of sequence.

Peirce lists several necessary conditions for events (1.493). First, an event contains a contradiction, i.e., it is typified by both a and non-a. Second, the contradictory phases of the event must each actually be embodied in existence. Third, there must be a juncture of the contradictory characters into a single existential subject. And finally, one of the contradictory phases is earlier than the other; if they occurred at a single instant, that instant would be the crossover point where we would begin to have a spatial, not a temporal, deployment of existence.

d. Flow. The question surely arises as to how the three elements of which time is composed are related to each other. Peirce's key metaphors for this interrelation of parts are those of the flow of time and of time as a welding medium, one where real continua are found. One characteristic of time as a whole that is often an early casualty of the spirit of analysis is the flow of time. Peirce's treatment is balanced in that, despite his close analysis of time's parts and modes, he also deals rather often with the flow of time. The idea of the flow of time is his device for synthesizing the results of earlier acts of analysis. Another synthesizing idea is that of time's welding together its different contents. "Flow" and "weld" are ways of emphasizing Thirds.

The purest sort of temporal action, Peirce holds, is the temporal flow itself (7.490). Events, instants, and durations are blended together. Time flows through contradictory states (6.325), and conflicting predicates are the way stations that mark its passage. To connect such stations to the front and back of events is to weld the contrasting conditions into a unity,

or to have a confluence of different streams. Time, Peirce says, is a current or a river (1.273; 6.325). At any rate, real time is a river. But he thought that the river analogy was too limited. In particular, it would not do when dealing with mathematical time, for mathematical time does not flow through contradictory states (6.325). But when talking about real time, the idea of its flow helps suggest that time is transitive. Indeed, the flow of time is the same as time's transitivity (6.128–29). The flow, moreover, is in one direction. Real time cannot reverse itself.

Mathematical time goes forward or backward with equal facility. It is not marked by forcible encounters or real reactions. But it is otherwise for time taken as objective sequence and passage. This time is one way (6.127). This unidirectionality of objective time is a law of mind that Peirce believes time follows.[40] If we then impute time to the universe, so that the marks of irreversibility are thought of as lodged there, we are also imputing to the universe a quasi ego (7.536). And he does so impute. There is, Peirce says, no *saltus* in nature (7.413). It is as if everything happens within a spiritual universe, where time would be the form of intuition that sets all happenings in different sequential orders. The denial of any real disconnections between things, the assertion that there are no leaps or gaps, is to say that the universe is a temporal plenum. Leibnizian and Schellingian influences are revealed in such occasional remarks by Peirce. His use of the German transcendental philosophy seems obvious when he asserts that the idea of time belongs to genuine synthesis (1.384). But this tilt to his philosophy of time seems oriented to past positions that the sciences were steadily vacating.

4. CONCLUSION

Peirce's philosophy of time is a carefully qualified temporalism, one which allows us to see several emphases of his metaphysics transposed into the idiom of the temporal categories. He held, for example, that time is the prime exemplar for all forms of continuity. Inasmuch as he preferred to name his philosophy "synechism" (from the Greek word for "continuity"; also see n. 14), he in effect identified his philosophy as a form of temporalism. But as he examined the idea of continuity, it evidently became clear that some pluralistic characteristics were to be registered within it. I have used such tortured expressions as "discontinuous continuity" or "continual continuity" to reflect his composite definition of time as a continuum with essential interruptions. There are open places in the continuity of nature, intervals of a kind where chance occurrences and variations can

struggle to expression. This element of chance in the world is caught up by Peirce in his concept "tychism" (from the Greek word for "chance"). He preferred synechism over tychism as a name for his metaphysical position; entry into his view of the world—as chance occurrences in a stream of necessity—can be gained through his philosophy of time.

But this philosophy is a qualified temporalism, because time, he thought, once was not. It came into being as a joint product of creation and evolution. That is, time is prevalent during the present stage of cosmic evolution. The concept of creation suggests activity that is nonrational in some respects. It conveys the notion of an ontological discontinuity between creative ground and created product. Thus, for Peirce, behind time as the prime continuum is a deep-seated primal discontinuity. Moreover, there are other factors of reality, such as qualities or Firsts, which seem eternal in some respects, though changeful in others. Accordingly, we have both a qualified synechism and a qualified temporalism.

Another emphasis of his thought which is reflected in his view of time concerns his reading of the 300-year record of modern science, mathematics, and philosophy. At the very threshold of the disciplines in these areas, he concluded, were key notions concerned with time. Science investigates continua, and continua are specially revealed in temporal notions. Thus, all of the sciences are specially concerned with ideas about time among their foundational concepts. This not only would serve as a reminder that we are to proceed functionally and experimentally in our investigations, with an eye open to the practical consequences of our beliefs, but also would include an invitation to be alert to the metaphysical assumptions we bring into play immediately as we examine new continuities in nature. Peirce's emphasis upon the inclusion of the temporal idiom as a part of the preamble of all sciences is suggestive of a similar idea in Whitehead's philosophy of science, for Whitehead held that to be a theorist is to be a student of temporal relations.

Inasmuch as a key to Peirce's understanding of the modes of time (past, present, and future) lies in the way the laws of logical modality (possibility, necessity, actuality) apply to sequences of states in this changing world, it is clear that the modes of time are derivative. To speak of Peirce's "futurism" or of his emphasis upon the future suggests that he grants the future a kind of independent status in which our aspirations are achieved or our beliefs are confirmed or disconfirmed. But any such independence of the future would be strictly nominal for him. It is much more informative to speak of the interplay of necessity and possibility with actuality in the various states of the world's passage. The relations of before/after and of

earlier/later are more significant for him than the relation of past/future. Even as a form of shorthand, "futurism" has been too boldly written into our expositions of Peirce's work.

Finally, we should note that Peirce distinguishes mathematical time from real time. He thus repeats a standard lesson of modern Western philosophy that the temporal processes of the natural world and the topical time of psyches and societies differ from the abstract, overly domesticated time of mathematics. Whereas time as we experience it is not delusory, it is illusory and of the nature of an appearance. Peirce and the other classical American philosophers set themselves the task of discovering the ground of time and temporality. But in his very concern for that deeper ground, we find a possible source for the most serious drawback of Peirce's account of time. His account of time and time's domain lacks categories which could make sense of those aspects of human creativity that are revealed in poetry, literature, and drama.[41] The world's great literature immerses us in those categories of experience which call us back into ourselves, where we are anxious about our choices and guilty about the apparent irrevocability of wrong choices. Time does vex the earthbound heart. No philosophy of time can be fully adequate which fails to account for the vexacious, aversive, destructive aspects of human finitude which gnaw at the time-worn mind.

James on the Plurality
of Times

$\mathbf{T}$HE puzzlement of some Western philosophers who deal with the problem of time was foreshadowed by Augustine in Book XI of his *Confessions.* It seems that we are directly acquainted with time and treat it in a comfortable and familiar way until asked about its distinguishing features. If we then seek to give a rational account of the nature of time, we find that the subject seems to unravel before our eyes into separate kinds of process or change. But we sense that analyses or descriptions of these special topics in time's domain may not really settle all of time's accounts. Fearing that its object falls outside of experience, the philosophical impulse is often to weakly reckon it "a mystery" and, threatened with bankruptcy, turn to more rewarding tasks. Such a reckoning, we shall see, may well be William James's final assessment of time.

Short of that final word, however, James resolutely discusses many of the special topics falling under the heading of the problem of time. The topics he discusses arise from his treatment of the following kinds of questions: (1) How is the time we feel related to the time we think about? (2) How are the time experiences of different persons related to the public times of societies? (3) How is human time, both personal and social, related to the temporal processes and periodicities we find in nature? (4) How are the many human and natural times related to or grounded in a single, invariant time order that some postulate for the whole of reality? And

(5) how would an invariant time order be related to other candidates for invariance, such as consciousness or space? James develops fairly effective answers to the first four of these questions, but he treats the fifth question weakly, only hinting at its solution. In effect, he leaves it a mystery.

The preceding questions can be recognized as special versions of some central problems of philosophy, problems which have simply been expressed in the domain of time. The five questions about time are special cases of, respectively, (1) the epistemological question about the connection between percepts and concepts, (2) the psychological and ethical question of the relation between the personal and social aspects of human nature, (3) the anthropological question of man's relation to the surrounding world, (4) the ontological question about the one and the many, and (5) the metaphysical question about what there is and what is really real. To see how James handles questions about the nature of time is partly to see how he approaches these more general questions. Indeed, his answers to questions about time ballast his positions as he moves into those deeper waters.

In the discussion that follows, we examine James's beliefs about time and its different guises, and then gather together some of our findings into direct answers to the five questions given above. We proceed roughly in reverse order, dealing with (4) and (5) first, and with materials bearing on (1) last. This approach admittedly emphasizes some of James's final writings, including those first published posthumously. But it also reflects his belief that the problem of the one and the many is "the most central of all philosophic problems."[1] Accordingly, we begin with time in nature and whether it is a many or a one.

I. REAL TIME. A CONTINUUM IN NATURE

In the closing decades of the nineteenth century and into the first decade of the twentieth century, time was taken as a necessary condition of reality in at least two ways. One view was that the temporal order, perhaps along with the spatial order, was a matrix or receptacle in which the entire inventory of things is seated. Another view was to consider time as a feature of the whole of reality in some or most of its parts, but not as a trait of reality as a whole. The first view is Newton's and the second is James's. Arguing against the determinism and monism implicit in the prevailing scientific idea of absolute time, James claimed that times are absolute, but time is not. There are many different processes, and they are probably not even fluent in the same river of change.[2] But even change itself cannot encompass all that is real. For James, reality is essentially but not solely temporal, even while extending itself into new creations temporally, on a

day-by-day basis.[3] There is no ultimate, all-inclusive time which includes all smaller times within itself, and against which they can be averaged and plotted. In his discussion of some aspects of James's cosmology, Bernard Brennan sets out the close connection of temporal and plural features: "James's attitudes toward the universe were profoundly reverential; but his reverence was directed toward the temporal rather than the eternal, the many rather than the few."[4] Brennan goes on to detail the preferences for the dynamic, concrete, and particular over the static, abstract, and universal that James registers in his accounts of the universe.

For James, nature has times, but no one time. An important implication of this viewpoint is that there can be no such thing as nature at an instant. The decline of one natural process to its final stage may very well parallel the ascent of another process to its zenith. The very identification of such a parallel, moreover, must be seated in yet a third process external to the other two. James simply denied that there was a single, master time flow in relation to which an invariant system of cross-references could be exhibited. Nature proceeds organically and not additively. Real time, James believed, comes in drops or buds. In this respect, his view is analogous to the epochal conception of time set out by Whitehead in his philosophy of organism—though Whitehead sees events or occasions as internally, not externally, related. Real time comes in drops and not in fixed, quantitative increments. According to James's organic naturalism, nature's elements are qualitative, rather like the "seeds" of Anaxagoras, the "seminal principles" of Augustine, or the "monads" of Leibniz. "Nature doesn't make eggs by making first half an egg, then a quarter, then an eighth, etc., and adding them together. She either makes a whole egg at once or none at all, *and so of all her other units.*"[5] According to this view, nature is not merely a system of mass-points distributed spatially and temporally in orders of coexistence and sequence. Such a conception does apply to reality, but only in the way that a map exhibits certain relations that hold within a territory. It is for James an intellectualist construction, an abstraction all too often mistaken for its referent. Idealized points of time are serviceable fictions for mapping, but "time itself comes in drops."[6] These drops, the real cells of which nature is composed, are caught up internally in waxing and waning processes. They are incommensurate with each other; they are fecund.[7] With some obvious exceptions (most of them are spatially voluminous; their "windows" are to a degree open to each other, and thus to a degree there are external relations between them), the drops share many traits with Leibniz's monads. In a more direct way, Dewey relied upon Leibniz's organismic views to show how living things are essentially caught up in temporal development. Leibniz is a common source for both men. James's temporal drops or buds also seem to possess the three princi-

pal traits of Augustine's seminal principles (unity, form, and order), but they did not arise *all at once* as did Augustine's seminal principles.

Novelty is an essential part of James's pluralism. The drops or buds through which nature extends itself are never perfect duplicates of each other. Elements or phases of different buds may be alike, but not the buds themselves, for nature does not progress by cloning, through the mere repetition of some of its members. "If the time-content of the world be not one monistic block of being, if some part, at least, of the future is added to the past without being virtually one therewith, or implicitly contained therein, then it is absent really as well as phenomenally and may be called an absolute novelty in the world's history in so far forth."[8] In the Newtonian version of absolute time, there can be a future moment or instant which follows this instant and which, without novelty, exactly repeats the content of this instant. But for James, real novelty and a real future are results of the incommensurability of time drops. All are dissimilar when compared with each other.[9] The future is never obsequious to the past. Inasmuch as no two units repeat each other in all respects, nature is not in any way redundant or sterile. With such a view of time, where the units or drops have duration, there cannot be any point to the paradoxes of Zeno or any real conflict disclosed in Kant's antinomies.[10] Such puzzles can arise only if we hypostatize our abstract space-time mappings.

For James, reality is essentially temporal, but not merely temporal. In addition to the component of time, the other real components of which nature is composed include space and psyche (instead of 'psyche', James sometimes uses 'self', 'ego', or 'consciousness'). Space, time, and self are the three archetypal *continua*, a triumvirate that governs and directs all that is. They are the grounds for all union and coherence.[11] Each of these matrices for relatedness has independent being. Neither one of them nor two of them undergo any modification due to the presence of the third.[12] The claim that these controlling factors are quite independent of each other is an essential element in James's arguments against idealistic philosophies (which in their "tender-minded" way make space and time subjective, mere forms of the intuition of an enveloping psyche or consciousness), and against materialistic and deterministic philosophies (which in their "tough-minded" way make psyche an epiphenomenon of a system of mass-points distributed in space and time). The trio of time, space, and psyche are bridges; they are mediating links.[13] They partially overcome the discontinuities between all existing qualities.

The basic elements of space, time, and matter secure James's pluralism. Insofar as they are a many, their alternative modes of combination will still leave our world a many, a multiverse. With this understanding, reality cannot be merely monistic and psychelike. In letters to Renouvier in 1880

and 1884—before *The Principles of Psychology* was completed, and prior to the famous 1886 article, "The Perception of Time"—we find James discussing this triad of reals.[14] All three are given as *continua*, and consciousness or ego is not allowed to include or supplant the other two. In the letters to Renouvier, space and time are autonomous. They exist by themselves and must be conceived through themselves. If space and time are not *in se*, he argues, we would be tempted to turn to a universal ego in order to introduce continuity into the world.

2. REAL TIME: ITS PLACE IN THE HIERARCHY OF NATURE'S CONTINUA

For James, time, space, and consciousness are equally real, but not of equal value. Space and time are more important bonds of union than consciousness. James believes that all things and qualities can partake of time and space without being completely contained within time and space. "Why may not the world be a sort of republican banquet of this sort, where all the qualities of being respect one another's personal sacredness, yet sit at the common table of space and time?"[15] The ego would meet other qualities and other egos at this banquet. The psyche would simply be another celebrant at that common table. Our minds can meet things because both mind and thing partake of time and space. "It is a gift that we can approach things at all, and, by means of the time and space which our minds and they partake, alter our actions so as to meet them."[16] The space-time matrix provides for some of the unity of the world, though the world is not in space-time as in a receptacle.

Consciousness is a different kind of unifying continuum. It provides an internal bonding, not the external kinds of bonding typical of time and space. Consciousness draws things together through time and space, and then superadds its own sort of cohesiveness. Because space and time are *in se*, they are not simply forms of intuition, *though they are partly that for consciousness*. As unifying relations, space and time do not penetrate into the terms they relate so as to violate the "personal sacredness" of things. Space and time are like those ancient gods of Greek and Roman mythology, the Termini, the beings who watch over and guard the limits of things. "Hegel in daring to insult the spotless [sophrosyne] of space and time, the bound-respecters . . . seems to me to manifest his own deformity."[17] Time and space provide the grounds for external relations. But if, as with Hegel, they are vassals of the ego as forms of its intuitions, then all things can ultimately be perceived as internally related within a single grand mind or Absolute Spirit.

Space and time are forums for union; qualities and psyche intermingle

and have liaisons there. But space and time are not substantial bonds of union, for they still work to separate things. They keep existence moving, from collapsing into iteration and ultimate self-identity. Space is the primary distancing medium for James, and is especially exhibited in conjunction with aversive experiences. Indeed, James holds that pain is incipiently spatial and makes up part of what we mean by space.[18] His image of space and time at the center of the republican banquet is a most telling image in support of the judgment that he never relapses into some kind of mentalism or panpsychism. All of the thought-families that fall under denominations of that kind require that some sort of psyche or consciousness is the host, in whose presence and by whose means all other celebrants meet. Conversely, some version of pluralistic realism is entailed by the image of a republican banquet where all things meet across space and time. Thus, space and time are more important than psyche. In addition, space is more important than time. Peirce, as we have seen, had the opposite emphasis. Space, James says, is the "paragon of unity."[19] It provides the most clear and obvious versions of relatedness because it allows a greater diversity of qualities to be harmonized through it. The ways things meet in space are more intricate than time's sequences allow, and are more stable and less vagrant than the psyche's modes of connectedness permit.[20] Space is a higher type of continuum than time because of the greater number of its objective dimensions. It has three dimensions, whereas the objective directions in time are only two, before and after.

So far, then, James's metaphysics provides for three basic reals ranked in a hierarchy of value, such that space is a higher type of relatedness than time, and both space and time are more important than consciousness. Space and time for him are not forms or concepts, but are relations that enable the psyche and its concepts to make telling connections with the qualities of things.[21] Space and time are the continua which make possible some degree of communion between the psyche and the fourth basic kind of reality that James recognizes, namely, the entire collection of qualities and facts. The members of this domain comprise the "one primal stuff or material in the world, a stuff of which everything is composed."[22] Though James calls this stuff "experience," it clearly is neither a psychical nor a physical stuff, but can become psychical or physical through the agency of the continua of consciousness and space-time. In itself, this basic stuff is neutral. The bonds of space, time, and psyche transform the congeries of neutral qualities into a congress, and provide it with its forms and its constitution.

But what will insure that the forms of connectedness provided by the three continua will be compatible with each other? They seem, for ex-

ample, to share some common nature, in that all are forms of relatedness. In virtue of what can they sometimes cooperate to build up a harmony out of the chaos of qualities? Pressed by these considerations, James is not silent, but neither is he very helpful. The notion of "the More"—utilized in his Gifford lectures, *The Varieties of Religious Experience*—is pressed into service. In the piecemeal, droplet-type world of qualities and continua, there is no absolute agency that would apportion all of them their proper roles. If some qualities organize by means of time, and other qualities organize through the devices of space, what is to keep those two networks of organization from conflicting with each other? What can relate the temporal mode of being to the spatial mode of being? At this point James leaves us with a mystery. He says that a "more" accounts for the partial blending and interconnectedness of the spatial and temporal continua: "Everything that happens to us brings its own duration and extension, and both are vaguely surrounded by a marginal 'more' that runs into the duration and extension of the next thing that comes."[23] It seems, then, that a fifth factor of being helps comprise reality along with the other four. The fifth factor, the More, has a schematizing function, and works to bring qualities, times, spaces, and egos into some kind of working harmony. Because it differs from the other four, it is some sort of apeiron like that of Anaximander: it is propertyless, spaceless, timeless, a nonconscious penumbra where some things can run over into other things. It can somehow help seat things at the table of space and time.

3. HUMAN TIME: THE CATEGORY OF TIME IN SOCIETIES

In the cosmological context, space is more important than time. Both are real, but space has greater value as a paradigm of relatedness. But in the human sphere, the comparative values of space and time are reversed. James believes that time is the most important continuum in human affairs, but Peirce had more generally taken time as the prime continuum in every forum of experience. This emphasis arises out of one of the most telling metaphors about time that can be found in James's works. He compares the moving, thick present in which we are immersed to the comparatively soft but dynamic growth rings of trees.[24] Although not making use of James's metaphor, Eisendrath precisely captures the sense of the metaphor when he judges that, in contrast to some phenomenologists and logical positivists, "the James-Whitehead philosophy comes closest to that point where real things are making themselves up out of the materials of their own existence."[25] For the growth ring of the tree is exactly where the tree makes itself up out of its own materials. This active ring

in the tree, James says, is "the dynamic belt of quivering uncertainty."[26] He claims, moreover, that both past and future are ingredients in this zone of the moving present. This growth zone is both the demarcation and the overlap between a closed, sealed past and an open, individualizing future. He reasons that "simply because the active ring, whatever its bulk, is *elementary*, I hold that the study of its conditions (be these never so 'proximate') is the highest of topics for the social philosopher."[27] A philosophy of time, a philosophy of the growing, dynamic present, must be the preamble of any adequate social philosophy.

To be sure, our ideas about space and time are basic to *any* part of philosophy because they are included among the categories. In a passage where James discusses the ultimate categories, time and space appear in the list of those basal conceptions. James thinks they can withstand any violent change of belief because the categories are our oldest truths; their claims to control experience rest upon prescriptive right. "Their influence is absolutely controlling. Loyalty to them is the first principle—in most cases it is the only principle."[28] A conception of time built upon the present as a fecund source of novelty is central to all important investigations into human affairs.

Time, then, is one of a group of common-sense categories. For James, these categories are forms which provide for a continuity of experience from one person to the next. Contrary to Kant's position, he did not treat them as necessary forms for all possible human experience, but as sufficient conditions for some human experience.[29] In response to the question about the origin of the categories, James thought they arose from a constant usage that had settled down into very dependable forms across long periods of human history. "They were developed through generalizations from experience by some men, and then were found to be serviceable by other men across many generations." This seems to be James's answer to the question about the origin of the categories. At any rate, it is clear that for him the categories arose out of experience and were not the timeless conditions of experience. "My thesis now is this, that *our fundamental ways of thinking about things are discoveries of exceedingly remote ancestors, which have been able to preserve themselves through the experience of all subsequent time.* They form one great stage in the equilibrium in the human mind's development, the stage of *common sense.*"[30] According to this view, time and the other categories are simply more seasoned techniques for structuring experience. They have survival value. Their right to dictate a grammar to experience is based upon immemorial custom. As opposed to Kant's objective and subjective deductions of the categories, but consistent with historicizing tendencies in some of the post-

Kantian German idealists, James gives an historical and social deduction of the categories.

It is because time is a synthesizing category that operates upon qualities within experience that the present includes the past. The past is included within the present because it is registered within the temporal categories that organize the present. The category of time, moreover, is given in the consciousness of the individual because it is a part of the structure of his social consciousness, a structure that solidified during the immemorial past of previous generations. According to James, time is fundamentally rooted in social process, too. Wilshire—in his study of James where the American pragmatist is positioned toward the main trends in European phenomenology—is correct in showing that James relates our notion of time to brain processes. But Wilshire makes too much of the physiological and neurological processes and not enough of James's emphases upon the equally important psychosocial processes.[31] We arrange events in the social receptacles of time, but the receptacles so framed are not a real part of time in nature. The *category* of time is an artifact that the individual uses to wedge his experiences into alignment with the experiences of others. The harmony of interests that is gained enables cooperation with others to progress more smoothly. The primitive or nascent mind has its social consciousness and its temporal organization of experience developing abreast of each other. "Young children and inferior animals" have no knowledge of time and space as "world receptacles."[32] On the other hand, most persons brought up in a social context where the ideas of space and time are appealed to frequently, so that those ideas become almost second nature to them, do accept space and time as containers in which their individual experiences and the experiences of others fit together. These imposed receptacles, however, are different from "the loose unordered time-and-space experiences of natural men. . . . The great majority of the human race never use these notions, but live in plural times and plural spaces, interpenetrant and *durcheinander*."[33]

Given James's historical deduction of the categories, it would appear that the categories would provide some of the conditions that would make possible the social contracts of a Hobbes and a Rousseau. The categories help steady experience, giving it equilibrium and continuity, thereby freeing men to attend to the future thrust of their own special forms of individuation. There is an incipient philosophy of history in James's remarks along these lines.[34] Perhaps he consciously steered away from developing his own philosophy of history because of his arguments against the idealists. They were in his judgment "tender-minded," and were the very philosophers who did most to cultivate those speculative views of history.

Perhaps his scattered thoughts about time and history would have been pulled into a more rigorous framework had he ever been able to write the systematic, substantial book in philosophy which he sorely desired.[35]

4. HUMAN TIME: TIME FOR INDIVIDUAL PERSONS

The lived time of the individual person only fitfully overlaps with the lived times of other persons. But each person to some degree is a party to the "social contract," where some of the cadences of private time are muted in favor of a more public, calibrated time. This more objective public time is not directly experienced. We memorize it and accept it as a condition for cooperating with others in molding a future that will be more consistent with our interests than the past has been. The future, for James, will ameliorate the conditions of our lives.[36] The lives to be lived in that future ought to be closer to the expectations which grow out of our private, lived times. The social, averaged time, which is an enabling condition for our joint ventures, is, however, experienced indirectly and retrospectively. Natural time is also experienced indirectly, but we come to know it prospectively and through anticipation, for the growth and forward movement of nature is also revealed as a power within the individual psyche.[37] We experience cosmological processes in our own lives as a kind of tug into an open future. It is only lived time that we experience directly, immediately, and introspectively in the present.

Time is immediately given in experience. It is directly felt as a datum. James says that it is a "genuine sensation."[38] Although it is given as a datum, it is a complex sense datum. Sensed, perceived time is always complex. To believe that there is such a thing as a simple sensation is to be working with a fiction.[39] Fibers from the past in the guise of remembered ideas are always wound into the smallest perceived units of duration. Inasmuch as the pasts of individuals differ, it would follow that the time perceptions of individuals also differ. But they do not differ completely, for the times that are felt or perceived coexist with and interpenetrate each other.[40] Our lived times are not wholly separate, or as separate as our most intimately subjective times. For example, James held that the times in dreams of different persons are separate.[41] But our lived times are not completely averaged into a public, objective time. Objective, public time arises out of lived time, but only through the mediation of conceptual time. Public time is constructed out of conceptual time, and both arise out of lived time.[42]

According to James, lived, perceptual time is continuous, although it does wax and wane. But conceptual, constructed time is discontinuous.

As we shall see further on, this emphasis is reversed in the thought of Whitehead, for whom lived, perceptual time is discontinuous and actual, whereas conceptual, constructed time is continuous and deals with the possible. For James, conceptual time arises when attention decomposes the originally given synthetic wholes of experience into various elements. Our notions of past and future arise out of these discriminating acts of attention. Further on, we examine a similar view of past and future held by G. H. Mead. Past and future have only a conceptual existence for James: both are concepts;[43] neither is directly given in experience. Admittedly, attention can set up a single point where the past touches on the future,[44] but this single point or instantaneous present is itself an abstraction. James uses several different expressions for exhibiting the idea of the present as a point in time. He speaks in different places of the "strict present" and "actual present," and "time instant," and "real minima."[45] What is common to these different usages is that they all refer to abstractions. Although they are the flesh and blood of the paradoxes and antinomies of time, they are lifeless in the real world of process and change. Their essence is that they are the hypothesized absolute crests of the processual waves that compose nature.

There can be no pointillist composition that would present us with the sweep of experience. For James, all real experience is voluminous and intense, whereas sensed time is thick and enduring. In one of his most famous images, James spoke of lived time as a saddle-back, and not a knife-edge.[46] We sit astride a specious present. Perhaps disembodied intelligences or angels can perch on time-points, but men know time in terms of durational units. We are astride a changing present, mounted on and living through its different time units. Thick, overlapping, in phase, sensed: these are the characteristics that James ascribes to the specious present. Conceived time, by way of contrast, is a pale shadow of our direct experience of the specious present. This felt, living present, with its prospective, retrospective, and introspective strands inherently entangled, is "the paragon and prototype of all conceived times."[47] As with the classical empiricists, James viewed the specious present as the percept to which we trace our concepts of time so as to authenticate them. But unlike those empiricists, James recognizes that the percept or sensation of time has relations that are real and not merely mind-dependent.

Time as empty; time as a container or receptacle; time as a pure form of intuition: these too are abstractions according to James. But there is a feature in lived time that lies at the root of these concepts. There are circumstances where the human sensorium is, relatively speaking, dormant and in a condition of latency. This condition is sometimes called the threshold

of awareness. But the fact that no *obvious* content is being presented in experience does not mean that unobvious, bare threshold conditions are not there. James speaks of this condition as "the muted play of inner rhythms."[48] For both Josiah Royce and John Dewey, the concept of rhythm plays an important role in the way they develop a philosophy of time, and James may very well have influenced them in this respect. When we then perceive something, the perception rides atop that surface of inner rhythms. When the perception crests, wanes, and then lapses, the lapsing is also experienced against that background play of physiological and neurological patterns. It is against this steady-state condition of a living equilibrium that particular budding "nows" or droplets can be seen as beginning and ending.

The contrast between relatively full time, due to the perception of external things, and relatively empty time, due to the rolling ground-swells of our latent inner environment, provides the basis for understanding James's two laws of perceived time: they are the Law of Time's Discrete Flow and the Law of Time's Discontinuous Succession.[49] According to the Law of Time's Discrete Flow, time is composed of units of duration that flow, in the sense that the waning of some experiences overlaps with the intensifying development of others. But because the crests or high tides of the successive experiences are separate, the durational units are really distinct units. This first of James's laws of time makes of our experience a one-in-many: many cresting waves of experience in one transitive flow. But why are the crests separate? Why cannot two experiential processes reach their zenith at the same moment? James's other law of perceived time handles that situation. The Law of Time's Discontinuous Succession says in effect that the changing intensities of experience have to take turns in preempting the latent sensorium if they are to register within it at all. In more modern terms, we would say that a neuron must repolarize before another impulse can proceed along it. James's second law is sound in this respect, and simply reminds us that one of the key functions of the sensory apparatus is a pacing function, whereby some sensory traffic cannot cut into or overtake other traffic. These two laws of perceived time are strikingly similar to two of the salient marks of the passage of events or occasions discussed by Whitehead as the prehensive and separative characteristics of temporal processes (see chap. 7). We can interpret James's two laws together by saying that inner, lived time must relate things by separating them. Just as a turnstile at a sporting event reduces a throng of people massed on one side of the turnstile into a more orderly file of individuals on the other side, so too the latent sensorium operates so as to pace experience, and orders its sensory traffic into a coherent inner flow. Thus,

using James's construction, the succession of mental states is a discontinuous stream. His stream of consciousness more closely resembles a series of locks in a continuous canal than a surging river at flood tide.

5. JAMES'S ANSWERS TO THE QUESTIONS ON TIME

At the beginning of our discussion of James, we cited some of the key questions that a sound philosophy of time must answer. Let us set out appropriate Jamesian answers to those questions by translating some of the preceding discussion into terms that link his leading ideas. Let us also indicate how some of the answers to these questions about time provide access to those larger problems of philosophy that stirred James but which he was never to treat systematically.

1. *How is the time we feel related to the time we think about?* The mediating idea for James in this case would be "abstraction from living experience." Given as a conclusion to a traditional syllogism, his answer to the question about time at this level would be: no felt times are thought times. This is because all thought times are abstractions from living experience, and none of the felt times is such an abstraction from experience. In short, time as felt and time as thought are related by exclusion. This doctrine that no felt or sensed time is the same time as the time that is thought or reasoned directly assails any rationalistic epistemology, which would proffer that conceived relations in the mind are congruent with the felt continuities given in the specious present. Mind-order and world-order are aspects of the same configuration of processes, we might allow, but they are different crests or high tides in that processual order.

2. *How are the times of different persons related to the public times of societies?* The connecting idea James developed here is that of the "historically grounded socializing categories." Stated as a claim based upon the grounds given in other key concepts, his answer to this question would be: no lived times of persons are public times of societies. This would be substantiated, in that no lived times of persons are historically grounded, socializing categories, whereas all public times of societies are such historically grounded categories. The pragmatic doctrine that calendar-and-clock time is a social device for furthering human ends lets the emphasis fall upon the individual in case there should be conflicts between individual and society. Presumptively, what is important in the life of each participant in society will fall at least partly outside society's moral claims on him. His own special good is still in the making. It is James's double emphasis upon the individual's responsibility and upon social pluralism that is caught up in the spirit of Barrett's remark about James that "he

speaks to us now, I believe, more forcefully than at any time since his death in 1910."[50]

3. *How are the lived times of humans related to nature's real times?* According to James, nature's real times are buds or drops, and new ones are always arising. The new temporal content makes the future of the natural world an open, noniterative future in important respects. The mediating idea that can justly be ascribed to James here is "nature's plural undetermined times." This idea would allow the transitive inclusion of some natural temporal sequences within the sequences of human temporality. Presented as an argument, James's answer at this level is that all lived human times are open to nature's future, in that all of nature's plural undetermined times are open to nature's future, and all lived human times are included in nature's plural undetermined times. From a naturalistic point of view, such an argument suggests that our forms of personal and social living are subject to constant transition because the passage of nature itself is manifest in them, too.

4. *How are the times of human subjects and of natural processes related to an absolute, cosmic time?* James's pluralistic temporalism issues, I think, in its most resolute statement here. Both his cosmological and psychological views on the nature of time meet in what we can summarize as his idea, that of "plural time-drops possessing extension." Mindful of this notion of many voluminous time droplets as a mediating concept, an answer to question 4 would be that no cosmic, absolute times are human and natural times. This belief follows from the premises that all human and natural times are composed of plural time-drops having extension, and that no cosmic, absolute times are times composed of plural time-drops having extension. Clearly, the time James is dealing with here is not the Newtonian time of the late nineteenth century. Time may itself be a one-in-many, but abstract physical time is not that one.

5. *Finally, how is time related to things like space and consciousness?* Here, the only available linkage is James's idea of the More, but every explicit appeal to the More is questionable in James's philosophy. This concept functions as a wild card and means different things in different contexts. In this sense, at least, James's philosophy of time has at its crest a mystery. We will find in our analysis of Dewey's account of time that he also sounds a note of mystery at the very heart of the topic. James may very well have influenced Dewey's judgment on the matter.

CHAPTER III

Royce, Eternity, and Time

CONTEMPORARY cinematograph-
ic technique provides us with effective devices for fastening our attention
upon what is essential in long, continuous processes. To observe the
growth of a flower or a vine by means of time-lapse photography is to have
presented to us unforgettable, flowing images of maturing life forms. The
very meaning of the idea of organic growth is exhibited with a freshness of
detail not readily captured in any other way.

Surely the organic growth manifested through the successive stages
of the philosophy and literary activity of Josiah Royce can be perceived
almost as if in motion, when we note some of his most telling themes and
follow them through to their mature stages. With the singular intensity
and clarity of sudden insight, Royce seizes upon his root conceptions and
then pursues them through a series of remarkable expansions. He feeds
them with new detail gained through his endlessly rich empirical studies,
until they achieve a fullness of spread and connectedness that seems, in
the process, to make of us less observers of developing lines of thought
than participants in a living project.

Royce's view takes root in the idea that time arises out of and is dependent upon the order and direction of the will. This voluntaristic conception is further secured and embodied by the idea that we project our intentions of the present moment forward into a future and backward into a
past. Royce's student, G. H. Mead, interpreted past and future in much the
same way. These modes of time are projects of the will, later to develop

into deftly adjusted projects of the dialectic between the will of the individual and the will of the community. Finally, the entire evolving structure impinges upon and is then caught up in a view of eternity. In the Hegelian idiom, time is *aufgehobt* into eternity, giving to eternity an endlessly variegated, actual content. Or, in the idiom of Byron, Royce could let his speculations pursue the poet's stanzas and agree in full that:

> Heaven is free
> From clouds, but of all colours seems to be,—
> Melted to one vast Iris of the West,—
> Where the day joins the past Eternity.

The time that arises from the will of the individual as it pursues its interests; the time of the communal or corporate will as it interprets different individuals and groups to each other; the time of Absolute as it draws the finite perspectives of individuals and groups into itself so as to grace them with insights that are *sub specie aeternitatis:* such is the entire moving image of Royce's philosophy of time. This view is unique among the classical American philosophers. Whitehead ascribes an integrative function to God's eternal nature, but his divine ground is much more of a creative process than is Royce's Absolute. Even as Absolute Will, the Absolute is one of interpretation, not origination.

   The context for Royce's approach to the question of time was framed in part by two emphases of late nineteenth-century thought, the same emphases that Charles Sanders Peirce had responded to in his treatment of time. One of the two was part of the world view of classical modern physics at the height of its success: that most changes in nature can be accounted for in terms of positional properties steadied into configurations at instants of time, with an interchangeability of material particles having those properties. According to this view, qualities are reducible to different combinations of quantifiable properties. The other emphasis arose in the Romantic movement in both philosophy and literature, especially reflecting its pessimistic side: that almost all change was the reappearance or return of events or circumstances that had occurred previously.[1] Nature runs through a repertoire of appearances and then starts again at the beginning. Apparent novelty is reducible to yet another return of an earlier appearance. This theory was especially striking in Nietzsche's doctrine of eternal recurrence. Common to both the physicalistic and Romantic theories was the conclusion that the significance and urgency of the present was to be explained in terms of essentially nontemporal features of reality, and thus explained away.

I. TIME AND THE WILL

In his 1880 article, "On Purpose in Thought," Royce worked against the mechanistic doctrine by emphasizing that the uniformity required in that doctrine is in fact derived from a fundamental purposive axiom.[2] In addition, he countered the doctrine of the eternal return by stressing the value-creating activity of the will. He argued that the time stream is a construct on its formal side and is thoroughly contingent with respect to its episodic content. The key to what is in effect Royce's double rebuttal lay in showing that the spatial emphasis in each is based on a surface analysis, that a deeper analysis would develop the lingering temporal nuances in each doctrine, and that time itself should be seen as arising out of prescriptive acts of the will. These prescriptive acts are anticipations of experience. The axiom of uniformity, so central to the sciences, is one of the ways we anticipate experience. According to this axiom, there is a necessary element in experience, "some kind of regularity and fixity of succession, and . . . under like conditions, like results will always follow given agencies."[3] This axiom is to be understood, moreover, in the light of the axiom of time, which holds that "*facta* cannot become *infecta*, that the past can never be undone."[4] The past moment is irrevocable. It stands, then, that when all future moments in turn become past, they too are inviolate. When they become past, they will never again be open or potential. If, Royce argues, we treat past moments as *infecta*, as corruptible or mutable and therefore subject to reconstitution, then we are no longer dealing with tides in experience that are truly set in motion by the will. "Because if we conceived time of such a nature that its moments are capable of return, we should be conceiving of it, not as time but as space."[5] For points in space can be occupied, vacated, and reoccupied.

Now this assumption that there is a time future, whose moments will become irrefragable when they become past, is not based upon any other principle. It is a regulative principle, one which at best would allow an indirect proof. In this proof, denying there is a future is asserting it, for we must assert a future condition from whose vantage point we could judge that the future has now ceased. We cannot, Royce would have it, abstract ourselves from our condition of temporality. Absolutely foundational for him is the assertion that there will be a future. With this value claim or axiom, "we attained perfect confidence."[6] This axiom lies at the base of the previously mentioned time axiom, namely, that *facta* cannot become *infecta*. This axiom that there will be a future also lies at the base of all other anticipations of experience. For when "we intend to believe in a future we do believe in a future. The purpose and its fulfillment are insepara-

bly joined."[7] From the primal act, "I will," there is derived "there will be." This internal meaning and its external embodiments in time constructs are a unity for Royce.

Royce relates the axiom of time to the resultant axiom of uniformity as the "I will" is related to the "there will be." The will undertakes its constructive activity, and the dimensions of the future and the past arise out of that activity. Where Plotinus had reasoned that time is the life of the soul, Royce appears to argue that time is the life of the will, the exterior embodiment of the internal intent of the will. The past and the future devolve from "thought working upon the data given in the present moment of consciousness."[8] Thought, following the behests of the will, arranged that data will fall into the before and after sequences found in the flow of time. Thus is laid down the foundation for the axiom of uniformity. Past and future, Royce avers, are projections away from present activity, and they proceed under certain laws that order or arrange their content.[9] Mechanism, so far as it goes in its characterization of reality, is accurate enough. But it is not ultimate; it merely maps the appearances of a deeper kind of activity. In this early article, Royce exactly prefigures the criticism of realism found in his first series of Gifford lectures, a criticism that turns on the idea that philosophical realism mistakes surface appearances for the nature of things.

The time order is clearly not real in itself when taken as a mode or projection of will and reason as they work over and through present experience. The time order rests upon the will, in senses yet to be described, and the uniformities in nature in their turn rest upon this time order. Royce explicitly reduces the axiom of uniformity to structured anticipations. He also says "that by future and by past we mean only certain notions we have, that are here and now framed by a present thought-activity dealing with the present data of feeling."[10] (For added emphasis, Royce italicized all of these words.)

Royce believes that to assert that past and future are projections or constructs of an activity of will and reason is also to deny that past and future are discerned or directly sensed in some way. "Past and future, as past and future, are never immediately given. This is a great fact of thought and of conscious life generally."[11] The present moment is immediately given and appreciated, whereas past and future are extensions of the present moment: "The present moment is the builder of both branches of the conceived time stream." As these branchings grow outward, they provide a medium for future constructive activity. A world picture is projected across these idealized modes of time. The architecture of our projected world view, in its turn, becomes the uniformity we subsequently "find" in analysis. A goal shared by this idealizing activity of will and reason is to

display a unity of origin through a diversity of developmental lines. "The end of thought in assuming the axiom of uniformity is the construction of an ideal picture of a world of experience that shall be seen as one."[12] The relations found in one part of the time stream are representative samples of the arrangements in other parts of the time stream. If nature tends to replicate itself, it is because the copies arise as amplifications of the activity of reason and will in the present moment.

In another article also published in 1880, "Tests of Right and Wrong," Royce refined some of the positions we have just noted. Common to his approach to the question of time in both papers is his locating issues of temporality in the practical field of the will and its activities. Such an approach will facilitate his later treatment of time as a problem with significant ethical dimensions. The second of these two 1880 investigations explicates more finely how different aspects of the will are associated with diverse characteristics of the present moment of experience. Indeed, the general nature of knowledge depends upon contrasts and comparisons between different moments or aspects of experience.[13] In particular, experience always displays at least three features that provide the grounds for judgments of likeness or difference, and also provide the basis of our separation of time into its modes of present, past, and future.

The first of these features is that "something is given to us as a fact of momentary experience."[14] This is the *datum*, wherein perception discloses features that seem "absolutely to be forced" upon us. All of our knowledge is based upon these irresistible givens in experience. A second feature is that the presented datum is also representational. We amplify the datum so that it is taken as significant. It points beyond itself to something else. We project an aspect of the datum so that it has another feature of the datum as its referent. This would show that experience resonates. Part of it is a recognition in memory of our responses to similar moments. Part of the present datum thus is a resounding of features of past data, of features they had when they were immediately given in a present. This acknowledgment of something real or valid that can never *not* be there is an absolute or eternal feature of the present moment.[15] This fixed aspect of the present moment Royce calls the *positum*, which arises as a projection away from the present and is the firm ground of our sense of the past.

In addition to the *datum* and the *positum*, there is a third feature that experience regularly exhibits. It is an amplifying feature whereby we project some aspects of the datum toward the possibility of future experience. This third feature is an outgrowth of our expectations. Expectancy is the ground of the future. For Royce it is the most important element of knowledge, in that it is the basis of practical action. Neither the future nor the past is immediately experienced. The future is not a datum, but a *postu-*

latum.[16] Insofar as we expect future experience, there will be future experience. We expect and we postulate, and these postulations *are* the future. If
for Royce the *datum* is the forceful, intensive aspect of the present moment of experience, the *positum* is the ostensive aspect of experience, and
the *postulatum* is the protensive aspect. All judgments concerned with
possible experience are synthesized out of what is posited and what is expected. Such synthetic judgments lead him to some basic analogies that
provide the structure for time past and time future. But the basal analogy is
that the future expected is like the past remembered, and if either is shown
to have certain additional marks, then the other has those temporal marks,
too. This basic analogical principle about time would lie behind and give
body to any belief we might have that some parts of reality mirror or replicate each other. Royce is standing here in that ancient tradition that runs
from Plotinus, Augustine, Bonaventure, and Cusanus up to Leibniz and
Lotze. Such a tradition, we shall see later, was also sounded by Whitehead
and Mead.

In Royce's treatment of this doctrine that the different parts of reality
mirror each other, it develops that the conjunction of the future and the
past gives us the realm of the possible. The possible arises from projects
that lead away from the present moment:

> Conduct is as a rule more and more complex according as the future
> experience that is expected at the moment of acting is more and
> more extended. For expectation of an extended future experience is
> commonly attended with an acknowledgement of a past experience
> proportionately extended.[17]

Past and future, Royce continued, are not only proportionate in extent, but
also proportionate in definiteness. The longer the view taken of the past,
the longer the view of the future. Acts vary in their complexity with the
sweep of time that is included. Thus, a rule that would govern our acts
would be an imperative attached to a time scale: "In thy acts treat all the
future as if it were present."[18] Cleaving to such an imperative would,
Royce believed, free us from the illusion of time perspective. This illusion
arises to the degree that we treat the data of present moments of experience
as critical and absolute.

Time illusions arise out of the partiality of the individual agent who
mostly pursues his own present interests. "My conduct is not approved if I
give myself over to the illusion of time perspective. . . . Approved action
consists in weighing all future consequences according to their conceived
value, not according to the value my passion gives them."[19] The time illusion is dispelled, however, the more consciousness moves out of its specious present into a generalized future and past, projecting through the

force of its insight other worlds as *desiderata.* "The essence of conduct is putting insight before desire, when naturally desire is before insight." But how can the finite will induce the power to project its interests into a future beyond its present limits? Royce does not raise such an issue here, but he treats the question in the context of the community in one of his last works, *The Problem of Christianity.* Still, as we extend our ideas of past and future, we convert the experience of the present moment into "symbols of a real universe." Some parts of immediate experience becomes surrogates for all other parts in the time series. This would indeed go beyond the popular idea of time.

In a conventional vein, we think of time as fitful, passing, evanescent, and destructive. But the claim of knowledge and the requirements for right action apparently demand a reassessment. Royce clearly wants us to discount the popular notion of time because of the limitations of its ethical dimensions: "The ethical finds not enough room in the philosophy of time. The world is studied, but not the active human will, without whose interference the world is wholly devoid of human significance."[20] By "philosophy of time," Royce is referring to both the popular and naturalistic conceptions of temporal passage. Neither makes enough of the human will and some of its first fruits, time and consciousness. "The Evolution Theory," he scolds, "is one-sided because of the subordinate place it gives to consciousness."[21] If we restrict ourselves to a study of how life evolves in the evolutionary process, then we will cut ourselves off from considering how life is to be conducted. We will not be able to move outside the "moment-atoms" of the present into the open vistas of an extended future and extended past.

2. TIME IN ITS RELIGIOUS ASPECT

Gathering together temporalist elements from those early papers in epistemology and ethics, Royce introduces a distinctly new dimension of his philosophy of time in *The Religious Aspect of Philosophy* (1885). This book also contains important themes that will be fully developed only in his Gifford lectures fifteen years later. Included among these themes is a deepening critique of philosophical realism that serves to prepare for the more inclusive philosophical horizons of an absolute idealism.

Although a popular metaphysics has it that the world exists in space and time, where real things are external to each other and interact through efficient causes, a more adequate philosophy which maintains contact with man's religious interests will present the world of nature *sub specie aeternitatis.* "The world . . . cannot be supposed to be either a power or a heap of powers. For powers have their being only in time, and only in rela-

tion to one another." Religious concerns require a comprehension of the issue of time that includes, but goes beyond, the more practical concerns of the will and reason. The religious consciousness needs a world that is more than an evolutionary development amidst warring powers. "So long as you look upon the world as a growth in time, as a product of natural forces, as an historical development, you can never make it certain, or even probable, that this world is not such a scene of endless warfare." The religious aspects of philosophy require an approach to the questions of historical development and evolution that goes quite beyond the realist view of time and space as containers of all of reality. The causal postulate to which the realists appeal, Royce holds, is a subordinate postulate. For him, the relation of ground to consequent is more important than the causal relation. Time, Royce argues, must be grounded in the idea of eternity, in something abiding and changeless, not in the causal sequences around us where attention and interest bring about illusory projections. He invites us to "declare time once for all present in all its moments to an universal all-inclusive thought." This declaration sets the tone for most of Royce's subsequent reflections about the relation of time to eternity.[22]

Certain other of Royce's earlier speculations about time that are repeated in this book are now embedded in the context of his views about an omniscient, total consciousness. Again he says that the past and the future are postulated, and time is said to be real. But the real processes in nature do not cause our ideas of time. Rather, nature's sequences are a counterpart of our willed time-orders. Real time that we thus read into natural processes are an external embodiment of the internal notions of time. The future is again said to be an outgrowth of expectations we associate with an experienced present.[23] But significantly, these ideas—that the past is a posit and the future an expectation, with a sense of the eternal as their proper ground—are linked for the first time with a mathematical analogy.

Royce's mathematical approach is set out to exemplify a principle of method that he seems to read off the logical law of inverse variation between the intension and the extension of concepts: As the intension of a concept increases, the extension decreases, or remains the same. In his 1882 article, "How Beliefs Are Made," Royce gives a "law of the mind" which reads as follows: "Our consciousness constantly tends to a minimum of complexity and a maximum of definiteness."[24] A more elaborate version of this principle appears in The Religious Aspect of Philosophy. It now reads:

The aim of the whole process [on conceiving an external reality] seems to be to reach as complete and united a concept of reality as is possible, a conception wherein the greatest fullness of data shall be

combined with the greatest simplicity of conception. The effort of consciousness seems to be to combine the greatest richness of content with the greatest definiteness of organization.[25]

Royce then connects this principle of the plenitude of exemplification with the idea of properties of mathematical objects that are unified under a single equation. All of time is present to a universal, infinite thought in the same way that all the properties of a curve are contained in the equation for that curve.[26] The universal, infinite thought is an eternal ground. Specific times are related to it in the same manner in which points on a curve are related to the equation for the curve.

Royce secured some of his initial views on the religious aspects of time by grounding them in the history of philosophy. His professorship at Harvard was in this field, and his lectures on modern philosophy, published as *The Spirit of Modern Philosophy* (1892), revealed how deeply the ideas of time, process, and will were channeled in Western thought. These lectures also show him struggling to resolve the opposition between different approaches to the problems of time and space.

With Spinoza, Royce held that the nature of substance or God is eternal, and thus no temporal approach can adequately sound that nature. To the spirit of Spinoza's thought, Royce hoped to be true.[27] With Kant, Royce held that time and space are not themselves experienced, but are the forms under which the world of experience appears to us. "Know what space and time are, and you will know something about the truths that condition the world's very existence." But Royce also believed that Kant should be corrected. He came to feel that his earlier doctoral work on Kant was based on a misinterpretation. His studies of Schelling and Schopenhauer helped lead Royce to a proper point of departure from Kant. Kant indeed is hero and guide to modern philosophy, but Kant had overly intellectualized perception and its pure forms, space and time.[28] Partly through Schopenhauer's emphasis upon the will as the ground of all reality, Royce was led to his most significant emendations of the Kantian philosophy.[29] If analysis can show us that time and space are pure forms of intuition that underlie all perception; and if time is the more important of the two because it is the form of *internal* perception, positions which Kant had held; then analysis is simply exhibiting what will and attention first laid down as the before-and-after and the side-by-side aspects of all experience. Thus, for Royce, time becomes the order and the form of the will, and not the form of intuition. The will in question, moreover, is not the arbitrary will of a finite self, but a far more grand Will that has as its proper expression the creation of an external nature.

The true World-Will is not a phenomenon in space and time.[30] Indeed,

the world was not created in time, although it does have temporal features. There are processes in time, but we need to transcend temporality in order to characterize them correctly. To make sense of time is somehow to achieve the perspective of an eternal thought. Such a perspective, Royce believed, was inherent in understanding that all natural events are expressions of fairly exact laws. Thus, all events are present "in one time-transcending instant to the insight of the Logos."[31] Royce used a musical analogy to suggest that such time-transcending moments are available to us here and now. Such moments are like the unity of perception achieved by the listener who experiences the whole symphony.[32] In particular, Mozart had spoken of grasping the significance of an entire musical composition by somehow standing outside of time; he "possessed all the succession of restless musical strivings in one artistic glance." In time itself there is a necessary restlessness, a striving for moments yet to come. Time, like the will, is restless and insatiable: this thought of Schopenhauer's probably led Royce to attach special significance to the musical analogies he so often used in his later work. "The truth of time must be seen by the absolute Knower, as Mozart saw his whole compositions."[33] The truth and the unity of time are Royce's marks of eternity.

The mathematical and musical analogies we have examined show that Royce seeks to understand time less by analyzing its internal structure and properties than by setting it in the proper milieu within a more inclusive whole. He sets out a view of endless or infinite time in which natural or evolutionary time is seated as one of its phases. In an expanded version of the time-triad we examined earlier comprised of *datum, positum,* and *postulatum,* he set out this threefold structure:[34]

$$\longleftarrow \rule{3cm}{0.4pt} P \mid E \mid F \rule{3cm}{0.4pt} \longrightarrow$$

In his diagram, P stands for an endless time projected into the past, where aggregations of matter were small and relations within those aggregates few. P thus refers to an epoch of relatively formless content. E stands for the finite portion of time where evolution reigns, where world processes of the present go on, where laws of nature as we know them control the details of development and the retention of structure. F stands for an endless future on the other side of present nature, where evolution as we know it is no more. Peirce had also held that evolution, and time with it, was a topical feature of the present cosmic epoch.

Now temporal processes as we know them are restricted to the E epoch of infinite time. Time in our epoch is real but only provisionally so.[35] Nature as a whole is a drama of three acts, and time's role is played out in the second act. Other, future possibilities also bound this actual temporal

world. The Absolute alone, freed from our own feverish temporal perspectives, knows all these possibilities and their relations to present actualities. Finite forms of consciousness are mainly aware of the E phase of things, but they nevertheless partake in full of the entire –P–E–F– structure. We are temporal beings, urgently so, but we are not merely temporal. "This temporal order, rigid and necessary in itself, is it not after all only one of infinitely numerous possible world orders . . . ?"[36] The Absolute, it now seemed clear to Royce, would have to be perceived as a system of all of these possible world systems, an Eternal Order whose elements are themselves replicas of that Order in the sense of mirroring its structure internally in their own more special natures.

3. THE TEMPORAL AS A MODE OF THE ETERNAL

In his Gifford lectures—given in two series in 1899 and 1900, at the University of Aberdeen, and published in the two volumes of *The World and the Individual*—Royce fully orchestrates into a single grand conception the foregoing themes about time and eternity. Three emphases in the lectures significantly expand his previous investigations into the nature of time, all the while bringing the results of those investigations into a greater unity: (1) Time is treated more positively and less as an illusion by appealing to a wider range of experience; for even the illusory is a limited appearance of reality, and the limited reality that is exhibited can be grasped by means of more careful, empirical studies. (2) This more empirical approach to time is carefully subsumed under, and then drawn into, his understanding of the nature of the eternal. Royce fortifies this emphasis with some exacting exegeses of themes about the perpetual and eternal that are set out in perennial Western philosophy. And, (3) an understanding of time *sub specie aeternitatis* is reinforced internally by making use of some mathematical and logical conceptions that were being worked out by Dedekind, Cantor, and Peirce concerning self-representative systems, the infinite, and the theory of relations. Firmly embedded in all of these emphases is Royce's conviction that time and eternity must be understood in terms of triadic structures, and that these structures replicate or mirror themselves endlessly in new and more precise forms.[37] Whitehead's view of the internal relatedness between events or actual occasions neatly parallels Royce's approach to this topic.

An examination of the nature of time appeared late in Royce's first Gifford lecture series at Aberdeen. It opens with a distinction between time as experienced and time as conceived. Past, present, and future are parts of *conceived* temporality. The past is not experienced or actual to us as past,

although the process of the present settling into the past is actual. Regarding the past, present, and future, "their sequence is the actuality of the temporal order."[38] From this point of view, the earlier-later relation—or what McTaggart was to call the B series in his influential paper, "The Unreality of Time"—is the primary actuality and is the ground of the past-present-future relation, or what McTaggart called the A series.[39] Past, present, and future are distinguished on the basis of an actual sequence, but they are not themselves separate parts of time in the actual world. It is illusory, Royce believed, to view the future as sundered from the present. The illusion comes from ignoring other features of the actual sequences as they are presented to us so as to favor our own personal center. A proper social setting for judgments about the actual sequences would, he concluded, free us from such illusions.[40]

On its positive side, illusion is after all a partial or finite manifestation of the real. These partial manifestations can be set into more extensive, coherent complexes so as to balance and offset the initial limitations of subjective viewpoints. Thus, through a social corrective, what was illusory or unreal can be understood as a limited revelation of an unlimited reality. To act so as to reveal in one's actions some fulfillment of the interests of others frees the act from mere partiality. An ethical imperative, analogous to the one Royce discussed in "Tests of Right and Wrong," should control the way we sequence our acts. Time, he holds, is "the form of ethically significant process." Our understanding of time is subject to the present time span of our consciousness. But that time span can be enlarged as the interests of others are increasingly registered in it, for our limited time span is an arbitrary matter.[41] Because the time span varies with the moral agent involved, a more capacious moral agent, one who is sensitive to a much larger social good, would have a time span almost different enough to constitute a new being. Summarizing Royce's discussion on this point, illusion varies inversely with time span: the smaller the time span that lies at the base of our acts and judgments, the greater the partiality and the illusion. The greater the time span, the less the illusion and the more the moral agent verges on enacting and judging the real nature of things. The conclusion is that a moral agent with an infinite or eternal time span at the base of its acts and judgment will always envision a full reality.

Such a conclusion leads directly to a concept that Royce first used in his initial series of Gifford lectures. It is the concept of the *totum simul*. Boethius had introduced the expression into medieval discussions, and Thomas Aquinas had regularized the *totum simul* as part of the vocabulary for treating the relations of time to eternity. In his earliest papers that touched on the question of time, Royce had held that there was an eternal

or immutable feature in the present moment. His argument in *The World and the Individual* up to this point allowed him to attach that changeless aspect of the *positum* to the idea of the *totum simul*, a sort of simultaneous whole that can be verified in conscious experience here and now. In the present moment, there is an eternal consciousness, "definable as one for which all the facts of the whole time-stream, just so far as time is a final form of consciousness, have the same type of unity that your present momentary consciousness, even now within its time-span, surveys."[42] The analogy Royce uses here is completed with the thought that for the divine mind the whole of temporal succession is present all at once in an absolute insight.[43] The whole of time—with all of its ethical significance in terms of progressively more wide-ranging social relations, which overcome the illusion associated with the individual consciousness—will be caught up in perpetuity in the *totum simul* of the Absolute.[44]

In his second series of Gifford lectures, Royce presents his most careful analysis of the relations between time and eternity.[45] The ideas that temporal illusions are nevertheless partial revelations of the real world, and that time is ultimately unified in a perpetual *totum simul*, fix the outer limits of his analysis. He asserts that the theory of time and eternity (which he gives in his third lecture) is "of central importance for all the problems of the later lectures." The problem of distinguishing time and eternity is held to be one of the most delicate and yet simplest of the main problems of philosophy. It is one of the simplest, according to Royce, because its answer is given in every moment of experience and in every justifiable claim made upon us by an ethical imperative.

The principle that time is not illusory but is a partial manifestation of being provides Royce with a justification for collecting many of the salient properties of temporality from our empirical consciousness. Indeed, our metaphysical views of time can only gain by being grounded in our more immediate temporal perceptions. These direct perceptions disclose five primary marks of time.[46] One aspect of all our moments of perception is change. All of our conscious states are signalized by process and variation. These changing moments are, in the second place, characterized by succession. There is a cadence to change, so that some given event has another hard by it in a succession of events. Out of the succession of events arises a third mark, one which sets time apart from space. Events have their successors, and the ordering of *before and after* cannot be traversed in either direction as spatial orderings allow. Time has a direction, and its direction is experienced by us as intimately related to the directional or goal-oriented nature of acts of the will. "This direction of the stream of time forms one of its most notable empirical features. It is obviously

related to that direction of the acts of the will. . . ." If the will in question is fitful and capricious, the illusory aspect of time will seem predominant. But if the will is steadied through social extension, the revelatory nature of time, where eternal aspects of being are disclosed, would come to dominate.

Yet a fourth mark of the empirical time consciousness is the unity into which the ordered succession of events falls. The earlier and later members of the succession are present in the same whole act of perception. If we take the third of these properties of temporality, a succession of events, and relate it to this fourth mark of a single event of succession, then we would say that time is a unity-in-diversity. It is, in a double sense of 'present', always a present time. A succession or order of moments is present at once in this specious present, i.e., in this time span unified with respect to its diverse *befores* and afters. The present is, for Royce, holistic and exclusionary at the same time: *afters* and *befores* are distinguished and exclusive of each other because they are presented together at once.

> This extremely simple and familiar character of our consciousness of succession, —this essentially double aspect of every experience of a present series of events, —this inevitably twofold sense in which the term *present* can be used in regard to our perception of temporal happenings, —this is a matter of the most fundamental importance for our whole conception of Time, and, as I may at once add, for our conception of Eternity.[47]

A fifth characteristic of perceptual time is a pragmatic feature. We not only sense irreversible successions as unified wholes, but we attach to such perceptions certain marks of our favor or disfavor. We are interested in how these successions bear upon our prospects for good or ill, and we gain an impression of our own will as being an event within the succession of events that can modify or augment the succession. That is, time is a perception, a feeling, and an interest. We perceive its distinct moments, we feel them unified in a whole of attention, and we are interested in our prospects in relation to it. Time, it seems, is found at every level of the psyche, and is especially clear at the level of the will. "Our temporal form of experience is thus peculiarly the form of the will as such."[48] Time as the form of the will is the form of practical activity.

The aspect of time that the realist is most apt to stress is the externality of time's moments with regard to each other. The events given in the sequences of time are taken as really separate. The aspect of time that the mystic is likely to stress is its immediate unity, where the succession of moments is given as a whole in this present moment. The separate events

are taken as blended into a single, fused whole. The aspect of time that the critical rationalist is apt to emphasize is the directedness of time toward a larger possible experience given in the future. Practical reason works to enlarge possible experience so as to discover objective grounds for all valid relations, whether actual or not. Thus, all of the historical conceptions of being that Royce explicates in the first volume of *The World and the Individual* can be seen, with respect to their distinctive philosophies of time, as partial and reductionist. Each view seizes upon a necessary feature of the nature of time and takes it as a sufficient account of the essence of temporality. It is in his own preferred conception of being—the Fourth Conception or absolute experience, whose logical structure is exhibited in System Sigma in the Supplementary Essay—that Royce relates the contingency of this world to the absolute that is disclosed in the progressively more adequate views of the world.

A key to the success of his argument is his notion of a sense of time that typifies the life of the Absolute: time is a mode of eternity. To deal with temporality in an adequate fashion is to deal with it as a representation and token of eternity: "In defining time we have already, and inevitably, defined eternity; and a temporal whole must needs be, when viewed in its wholeness, an eternal world."[49] The temporal whole, *qua* whole, is simply the same thing as eternity. To the degree that they take on the nature of an organic whole, a whole characterized fully as a system of internal relations, temporal processes aim at fulfillment. Such wholes are realizing purposes, for by definition, a succession of time according to Royce is directed toward a goal. Time has a single direction because it is essentially goal-directed, and the inner meaning of a purpose is explicated in a wealth of successive acts. "Time, as the form of the will, is (insofar as we can undertake to define at all the detailed structure of finite reality) to be viewed as the most pervasive form of all finite experience, whether human or extra-human."[50] A critical realist like Kant would have said here that time is all-pervasive because it is the pure form of intuition that is a first form of synthesis for pure reason. But for Royce, time is the first form of synthesis of practical reason. It is the form of the will, not of the reason. Our purposes, as they seek consummation, lay down the tides and the times of practical activity, as well as demarcate the time spans of different kinds of consciousness.[51]

All of our strivings aim at possibilities that are not yet actual, thus constituting the future. Where these strivings would point toward universally shared consummations, the entire temporal series would be well ordered as a whole. Given the close relationship between time and the will for Royce, it would follow that this well-ordered series, which represents a

confluence of the goal-oriented acts of all persons, is a Eternal Order. It is, at least for the Absolute Experience Royce postulates, present all at once. It is the complete embodiment of all of our acts of will. Just like a symphony that can be present all at once as an aesthetic whole, all times can be present as a single whole.

At the apex of Royce's discussion of an Eternal Order that includes all times as its proper parts is the notion that the eternal present is present in a twofold sense in the same way that the empirical present is a dual present. The eternal includes the sense of a dense series of *discrete* events that really lie outside each other, but the eternal also includes the sense that what is given in consecutive order in independent units is nevertheless *present as a whole.* So the eternal is both changeless as a unity, where all details of reality fall within a single insight, and everlasting as a process, where all passing events are present in their turn, but are past and separate from those events that lie before and after it. John Dewey criticized this double sense of the eternal by attacking the conception of part-whole relations that energized Royce's argument.[52] As we shall see, Royce answered Dewey in the context of replying to the general complaint that time had been turned into something unreal. Mead was to argue that the concept of the eternal present was self-contradictory. But Royce's basic position remained unchanged from the view that the Absolute is the eternal present. It is present in the inclusive, unifying sense, and also present in the exclusive, disjunctive sense. This double sense of the presence of all events is, for Royce, the distinctive mark of the Eternal. It constitutes the *totum simul,* where all time is present at once to the Absolute.[53] All time is present to the Absolute the way the notes and chords are present in a well-ordered rhythm or harmony.

4. PERCEPTUAL TIME, CONCEPTUAL TIME, AND ETERNITY

Conceived time is for Royce an intermediate version of temporality, one that falls between perceived time and time as an eternal whole of all events. Conceived time is also characterized by the relations of before and after, earlier and later, and past and future. For conceived time, as distinct from perceived time, the past extends backward *infinitely* and the future extends ahead *infinitely.*[54] We never experience these infinite vistas of time that are sketched by universal, generalized concepts. But their description, Royce thought, is built up out of experienced times as projections from immediate experience. Conceived or generalized time also overlays perceived time with all of the technical apparatus so serviceable for the natural sciences. This general, more social time is not only infinite,

but is also infinitely divisible. In that numbers can be assigned to the divisions the analytic mind sets up between its parts, time is also measurable. And yet for all of these idealized point-instants, conceptual time is also continuous.[55] Time's divisibility and continuity at the conceptual level mirror time's discrete moments in the unity of perception at the experiential level. In neither case, however, is the present a pointlike entity. The present is always a duality for Royce, a diversity in a unity.

Royce brings the idea of a teleological series to the task of explicating conceptual, generalized time. It is only within a teleological series that facts win their meaning.[56] This allows Royce to differentiate between conceptual time and conceptual space. Time is the field of fulfillment, whereas space is the field of displacement. The one, the temporal order, is irrevocable and irreversible; the other is traversable and symmetrical. Time has its distinctive meaning only when it is perceived and conceived teleologically. Only as will, Royce's basic presupposition still contends, has time any meaning. Ultimately, the will shall be coextensive with time. For the temporal order as actually infinite requires an infinite, absolute will. Temporality, as initially perceived in the present moment and then as more adequately conceived, is fulfilled in eternality.[57]

The temporal order on its conceptual side must be grasped as a well-ordered series.[58] An important concept that applies to well-ordered series is the concept *between*. Distinguishing two events a and b as they arise in experience will cause us to discriminate a third event m which is mediate between them. Other events, such as f and l, will be noted as falling before a and after b. We thus arrive at the conception that a and b are between two other events, f and l, and have another event m between them.[59] The series f–a–m–b–l arises from acts of attention and anticipation and provides the fundamental conceptual order of time. Quantification concepts, providing us with some sort of metric, may then be associated with this initial time series as an interpretation of it. But the initial series—as well-ordered and recursive in the sense of a replication of its basic triadic structure in all extensions of it—gives us, Royce believed, our best understanding of the concept of a well-ordered series. A well-ordered series is illustrated in the life of the will, in the world of appreciation and anticipation. Other kinds of series that arise in what Royce called the World of Description are instances of a less perfect order. That is, topological properties ought to precede metrical properties in understanding the linkage of facts in the world of experience, but the metrical properties are given the greater importance. Whitehead also emphasized topological over metrical properties in seeking to understand the sequences of events given in experience.

The celebrated Supplementary Essay in the first volume of *The World*

and the Individual sets out Royce's most carefully wrought conception of reality as a self-representative system. The results of his investigations into the nature of conceptual time, if fortified with some of the distinctions he drew in the Supplementary Essay, can provide us with a concise summary of his philosophy of time. Our conceptual understanding of the world depends upon the idea of well-ordered, recursive series. More complex conceptualizations will arise as we distinguish series within series. That is, Royce used the idea of a complex kind of series where one cuts across and discriminates between two others. The *relata* in such well-ordered sequences of events are themselves event sequences. "The world thus regarded will consist for us of all these interwoven series, and will constitute a single System."[60] The structure of this system is exhibited in the System Sigma, and is self-representative in the sense that each element in the system neatly mirrors the nature of the whole system internally within itself. Such a system maps itself within itself. We might not grasp the larger timescapes that are reflected within the events of our own lives because of our finite, partial consciousness. Our consciousness of time is quite arbitrary and we are apt to confuse events with some of the resonating aftereffects of those events.[61] Nevertheless, Royce's aperçu has it, despite the distorting effects of particular acts of attention, all orders of events and all events composed of other events will have their being contained within a universal, absolute consciousness whose structure is System Sigma or some other similar, internally related system of categories and relations.

The absolute system of experience Royce described would include the laws of nature, and particular times and places as they fall under the natural laws. Taken as a whole, this temporal order is simply the eternal order. Time and eternity are the same Absolute under two different aspects. The laws of time are exemplifications of the laws and categories of eternity. Present, past, and future are merely selections our finite form of experience makes within an eternal, well-ordered system. Royce does not consider temporality to be ontologically separate from eternality, but merely epistemologically so. The distinction between time and eternity is a distinction without a difference for the fully realized consciousness.

5. RESPONDING TO PRAGMATISM, REALISM, AND VITALISM

Royce's continuing interest in the ways that time and the will prefigure the eternal was made apparent two years after his Gifford lectures, in his presidential address to the third annual meeting of the American Philosophical Association at Princeton on December 30, 1903. The presidential address also showed that he was aware of and open to the new movements in philosophy. The title of Royce's address was "The Eternal and the Practi-

cal."[62] Although developing some of the Gifford lecture themes—that the temporal is dissatisfying, that it arises as the form of the will, and that the dissatisfied finite will tends to evil—Royce also seemed to note that there is a difference between the everlasting or perpetual and the eternal.

In the presidential address, Royce allows that he was once a pure pragmatist back in the early 1880s. Now, twenty years later, he "earnestly insists that knowledge is action, although knowledge is never mere action." To say that knowledge is action is to reaffirm the claim of pragmatists that it is practical. But

> everything is practical; and everything seeks nothing whatever but its own true self, which is the Eternal. . . . The Eternal is not that which merely lasts all the time. Only abstractions temporally endure. . . . That alone is eternal which includes all the varying points of view in the unity of a single insight, and which knows that it includes them, because every possible additional point of view would necessarily leave this insight invariant. . . . The possibility of such an eternal is, of course, the possibility of the existence, in a genuine sense together, as a *totum simul* of the contents of an infinite series of practical and evolutionary processes.[63]

Royce's phrasing, to the effect that the eternal is more than the perpetual or "that which merely lasts all the time," reveals his awareness of the limitations of the idea of perpetuity, and that eternality and perpetuity are different concepts. Some factor is needed to unify the recurrent embodiment of detail, and that principle of unity must be outside and distinct from time. We know Royce sought to find such a unity in the idea of an invariant self, a self which captures—Mozart-like in a unity of insight—all of the oppositions and harmonies of this natural realm. But that he was seeking to move beyond such a formulation, that he seemed to believe that there was work yet to be done on his theory of the relation of the temporal and the eternal —that is, that he still sought some sense of the eternal or absolute that could inspire awe or reverence—is seen in his applying new concepts to the problem in his later work. That he knows where the problem lies can be discerned in some closing words to the 1903 presidential address: "The need for the Eternal is . . . one of the deepest of our practical needs. Here lies at once the justification of pragmatism, and the logical impossibility of pure pragmatism. Everything finite and temporal is practical. All that is practical borrows its truth from the eternal." The truth is a goal of all striving. It does not arise instrumentally in our adaptation to our surroundings, but is progressively discerned as our search for it is steadied through a corporate social will.

In December 1909, Royce read a paper before the American Philosophi-

cal Association in New Haven, that showed his awareness of the criticisms some New Realists were leveling against his views. These views seemed to explain time away and convert all relations into internal relations. Royce ran up his battle standard in the paper's title, "The Reality of the Temporal," and sought to answer the realists by using some of their own armamentarium, especially their theory of relations.[64]

The New Realists, he held, were emphasizing time as a realm composed of novel events related externally as separate occurrences in time. They construe novel events as those "nobody ever saw before and nobody will ever see again." Royce agrees with the view that reality changes in time. Even if there are permanent substances, the accidents of those substances or the relations between those discrete substances are all caught up in change. These changes of accidents and relations are the events of the world, and all fall under general laws. Of any two such events, one is earlier than the other, later than the other, or simultaneous with it. The temporal order, thus, is transitive and nonsymmetrical. Such a transitive, nonsymmetrical ordering of occurrences in the world presents a history of events comprised of levels in time. Overall, then, time is a series of series: "Real processes of the world form an order that one could describe as a series of chronological levels."[65] Royce advises his realist critics that this notion of time as a series of levels is a construct. Time in all of its extensions and dimensions is not a datum, though realists are specially apt to confuse the construct with a datum. The physical sciences, in addition, describe this series of temporal levels in the language of the mathematical continuum. A metric is superimposed upon dimensions by setting up correspondences between conceptualized point-instants and the series of real numbers.

Royce agreed with Bergson that an ensemble of dimensions overlaid with a metric is a construct which subserved our practical interests.[66] It is artefactual. He also agreed with Bergson that it is a fairly useful guide for some of our actions, but doubts that it depicts absolute reality. Bergson, Boodin, Lovejoy: each placed a great deal of emphasis upon the elements of novelty that appear in this mapping of things and events. Once things did not exist. Then they came to be. Now they are irrevocably past. Boodin, Royce observed, emphasized the past, irrevocable side of novel occurrences as they streamed by, whereas Bergson stressed the forward-looking, evolutionary side. But neither approach, Royce was sure, delved deeply enough into the matter, for real novelty cannot be exhibited in a descriptive framework, but must be made manifest in an evaluative framework. From this latter point of view, novelty is to be grasped in appreciative, evaluative terms.

To describe things or events is to present them in general or universal

concepts, and their uniqueness is lost or muffled. Thus, the descriptive approach of the sciences does not suffice. Still less can novelty be grasped in a sensory way as an immediate datum, so Bergson's emphasis on the immediacy of novelty is also groundless. But in discounting novelty as a datum immediately given in experience, Royce has also loosened the hold that the data of experience had on his own early views on the nature of time. At that time, the *datum* of the immediate present provided the ground for *positum* and *postulatum*, from which past and future arise. He now holds that we neither sense the unique present (as opposed to Bergson) nor describe it (as opposed to Boodin). We interpret the novel and the singular as novel and singular. We bring forth the unique with all of its signs as indicators of our own activity. Individuality is neither sensory (or affective) nor descriptive (or cognitive), but rather enacted (or conative):

> How can we appreciate uniqueness, individuality, novelty, whether in the sequence of temporal facts or otherwise? I answer, as I have elsewhere repeatedly offered: Uniqueness, individuality, novelty, can be willed in the case of our own deeds, and can be acknowledged in cases of our interpretation of objects and persons not ourselves.[67]

All events in time are novel to the degree that they are perceived as manifestations of distinct acts of the creative side of our nature, the will. The will and its agency comprised the substantial element in the novelty of events. Royce felt that temporalists like Boodin, Bergson, and Lovejoy missed this element.

For Royce, tides in events are set up by our individual and social acts, and these tides establish the dimensions of time and rhythm in the changing world. It is neither our feeling of immediacy (Bergson) nor our analyzing (Boodin), but rather our acting that takes us deeper into things. In this article, "The Reality of the Temporal," Royce calls such a viewpoint 'voluntaristic idealism'. It would represent a synthesis of his absolutism and his voluntarism, with the new thought currents of the time acting as catalysts for that synthesis. A basic part of the credo of this voluntaristic idealism is given in the words, "the temporal form of experience is to my mind primarily the form of the will. One wills that each new act shall be unique."[68]

These acts of will proceed forward from each other so that each new act departs from a level or degree of achievement already gained. So, too, the ordinal series in the time sequences is the relation of the deed already done to the deed yet to be done. Taken as a whole, the time order is the same as the totality of deeds in time.[69]

Royce had held almost from his earliest published paper in philosophy

that time is the form and order of the will. It follows that his understanding of the nature of time will develop and parallel any changes in his conception of the nature of the will. In the years immediately following the Gifford lectures, Royce's concept of the will did change. That it was modified is apparent in the results of his empirical studies in psychology, in his responses to his critics, and also in his studies in the new logic of relations, especially as set out in the work of Charles Sanders Peirce.[70] In his early voluntarism, Royce's concept of the will stressed the positive or appetitive sense of the will and the achievement of goals, while at the same time neglecting the negative, aversive sense of the will and its avoidance (as opposed to achievement) directives. His early views of time, up to and including the Gifford lectures, reflected that one-sided understanding of the will. An appetitive, goal-oriented view of the will will have as its temporal form a compact continuum with overlapping phases. But a negative, aversive sense of the will with its avoidance directives will have as its temporal form an interrupted series with separate and distinct moments. Royce's investigations in the first decade of the twentieth century began to redress the balance between these two aspects of the will, and his understanding of the nature of time and of the relation between the temporal and the eternal began to develop in the same direction. Where this change in his understanding of the will was supported by a change in his logical point of view —so that the new symbolic logic of relatives began to displace the traditional categorical logic—Royce developed a more empirical and pluralistic approach to the main problems of philosophy.

It was against this backdrop of an enlarged conception of the will that Royce detailed the line of argument summarized in the title of his paper, "The Reality of the Temporal." To take the time order as real is to think of the world will as manifesting itself in past, present, and future deeds. If these deeds are real, then the whole of the time order comprised of them is also real.[71] To be sure, all of that time order is not to be thought of as real at an instant. But it is real, Royce's formula goes, as a time-inclusive totality. Such a whole made up of time's parts is an eternal reality. This absolute reality is not a timeless reality, but is a whole composed of many events, seized as a totality. The eternal is real, not at an instant, but *qua* eternal, and the temporal taken as a whole is precisely this eternal. In short, Royce accomplishes his purpose of showing that time is real by using the concept of the eternal as a middle term. The argument goes like this: Time taken as a whole is the eternal, and the eternal is real, so time taken as a whole is real. This is the sense in which the article affirms "the reality of the temporal." But the argument is valid only if the middle term 'eternal' is used in the same sense in both of its occurrences. Manifestly, that is not the case.

In the major premise, eternal means unconditioned and absolutely transcendent in traditional religious senses. But in the minor premise, eternal means perpetual or unending time. In the major premise, time and eternity are ontologically distinct, whereas in the minor premise, they are the same in their being. In both premises, time can be seen as the form of the will. But in the one premise it is the creative will that separates itself from its creation, whereas in the minor premise, it is the positive, appetitive sense of will that closes upon and remains ontologically one with its desired end. We may conclude, then, that although time may be real as Royce sought to argue in response to his critics, it was not shown to be real on grounds that he adduced. The argument for the reality of time could be repaired only if he could develop a meaning of the concept, will, which could unify the different senses he came to recognize as fundamentally significant.

6. TIME AND INTERPRETATION IN SELF AND SOCIETY

Royce's last significant discussions of the question of time appeared in 1913, in his article "Mind" in Hastings's *Encyclopedia of Religion and Ethics* and in his book *The Problem of Christianity*. Common to both sources is his conviction that the threefold nature of interpretation can throw light on how we should construe the temporal structure of mind in both its personal and social phases. Interpretation, Royce felt, should be interpolated between perception and conception as a mediating concept.[72] According to his reading of the history of the theory of knowledge, it had been mainly concerned with the contrast between the perceptual and the conceptual aspects of experience. The limitations of that old duality, his diagnosis went, could be offset by relating both perceptual and conceptual processes to the intermediate process of interpretation.[73] Perception underlies our knowledge by acquaintance or appreciation, whereas conceptual processes undergird our descriptive knowledge. Interpretation, however, goes beyond both immediate sense data and rational constructs by exhibiting the relations between signs, referents, and interpretants. At this point, Royce's discussion seems to be deeply informed by Peirce's work in semiotics.

To be sure, signs express the meanings of some self. But the fundamental sign process is that of the present self interpreting the past self to the future self. Interpretation is the cardinal act of relating an actual past to a possible future. The relations that arise from such activity, Royce felt, make up the foundational structures of the mind. It is clear that interpretation is a process of orientation, a weighted, fateful expectation of the future.

"When a man reflects on his plans, purposes, intents and meanings, his present self, using the signs which memory offers as guides, interprets his past self to his future self."[74] Taken as a kind of self-conscious awareness, mind is this process of attending to the past so as to channel the future. So taken, mind is a triadic structure: "Every explicit process involving self-consciousness, involving a definite sequence of plans of actions, and dealing with long stretches of time, has this three-fold character. The present self interprets the past self to the future self." The overall triune process is what we mean by interpretation.

Central to the process of attending to the past is the comparison of ideas. Section 3 of Royce's article on mind in the Hastings's *Encyclopedia* is entitled, "Self-interpretation, comparison of one's own ideas, and knowledge of time." Its salient idea is that the comparison of ideas is a manifestation of the growth of self-knowledge in time. The most important way we compare and contrast ideas is to show likenesses and differences between past, present, and future versions of the self. Such comparisons are foundational for all of our cognitive processes. As opposed to the pragmatist who thinks of an idea as an active tendency, Royce's position is to look at the stance of the self behind the idea. He emphasizes the generative power of comparisons between past and present states of selfhood. Without such comparisons "we could never make even a beginning in forming a coherent view of our own past and future, of our own selves as individuals, or of selves not our own."[75] Royce is in effect warning us not to hypostatize the ideas of past and present. If we keep the idea of the past close to experience, we see that the primary datum behind our idea of the past is the idea of a past self, one that is to be compared and contrasted with the actuality of the present self. The past as known is based upon the past self only because the present self takes the stance that those (past) self-aspects are closed, with the flow of self-development proceeding from them toward other anticipated ends. Times that are past times and times that are future times can only be known *qua* past and *qua* future through interpretative acts. "The self, the neighbor, the past, the future and the temporal order in general become known to us through the third type of cognition which consists of a comparison of ideas." Comparison and interpretation are relational activities of the mind, and selves and times arise as embodiments of those relations.[76] There are no external relations between times and selves. Those *relata* are modes of the harmonizing activity of interpretation.

Also written in 1913, *The Problem of Christianity* offers conceptions which develop Royce's views on the philosophy of time by relating them

to the will of the community. Two of the book's chapters revolve around discussions of time and eternity.[77] One of the two deals with the will of the individual insofar as it is the source of some of the structures of time, and the other chapter treats the social will as it shapes time. In his arguments concerning guilt in time and social development through time, Royce believed he was proceeding in a way thoroughly consistent with doctrines that were set out in his Gifford lectures.[78] But in *The Problem of Christianity*, Royce relates his discussion to the idea of interpretation as he did in the article on mind, holding that our notions of past, present, and future are cast in a new light when related to the process of interpretation. His remarks about Peirce notwithstanding, the best single locus for this side of his thought is the voluntaristic idealism of Berkeley.

In some of his earliest speculations about time, Royce bespoke the changeless, irrefragable character of the past. This property of the past is further elaborated in his analysis of time and guilt in the context of Christian thought. The irrevocable nature of sin is pointed up. The sin is done; the deed is past, and cannot be called back. It is the "hell of the irrevocable" that we have entered.[79] The guilt for such changeless acts will be everlasting, as enduring as time. It must always be the case, Royce believed, that we have introduced evil consequences and a false sense of trust at actual times and in sundry places. By this means, a permanent disfigurement is laid across any number of good deeds we may later do. The past sin causes a deviation from our intent to enter into a better community, and later evil deeds will simply act as multipliers of our waywardness. The sin is set because the past is set. If my present self interprets my past guilty deed to an anticipated future condition of my own self or society, the guilt will be invigorated and multiplied because its effects channel my future acts. But even if I abjure the past false act as I interpret the past to the future, the future will not be as vigorous as it otherwise would be. The future will not be as invigorated from acts interpreted to it, $a, b, d,$ and $e,$ with the sinful act c' abjured and now lying fallow, as it could be from $a, b, c, d,$ and $e,$ where c would be the good and right act. That is, whether compounded or avoided, the commission of c' has weakened or decommissioned the future through our skewed anticipation of it and interpretation of the past to it. Guilt-commissioned time is thus endless time, and guilt-laden past time is inexpungible.

Royce wanted to extend his analysis of the self and its temporal structures to encompass the structure of society. Reaffirming a tradition in Western philosophy whose first careful elaboration was voiced in Plato's *Republic*, Royce held that the social structure and the structure of the self

are analogous. The analogy, he thought, is "extremely familiar." The community, like the self, is a special embodiment of a given level of a temporal process. "A true community is essentially a product of a time process. A community has a past and will have a future. Its more or less conscious history, real or ideal, is a part of its very essence."[80] The time process is a necessary feature of the pluralistic "self" of the community. All triadic structures of the individual self are simply replicated at the level of social life. The deeper and richer the lives of selves or communities, the deeper and richer their pasts, and the more extended and hopeful their futures. The community is also a structure of memory and expectation. And just as the temporal process with its five primary marks[81] characterizes the structure and order of the self, so too does the temporal process with its superadded interpretive aspects underlie communal life. "The time-process, and the ideal extensions of the self in this time process, lie at the basis of the whole theory of the community." Whether brought into fine focus in the individual psyche, displayed with a rougher grain in nature, or writ large in the life of a community, the Absolute Will exhibits its essential nature as a unity-in-diversity. "The most general distinction of past, present, and future appears in a new light when considered with reference to the process of interpretation. . . . This analogy between the relational structures of the whole time process and the relations which are characteristic of any system of acts of interpretation seems to me to be worthy of careful consideration."[82]

The relations of time to eternity are also extended by means of Royce's analogy so that they reach into the very essence of communal life. The whole of communal time processes is not a timeless whole. In this respect, at least, a property of a part—e.g., its temporal character—is also a property of the whole itself. Whether in the life of the individual, in nature, or in communal life, these temporal processes admit of inclusion within a single series of temporal levels. "The very being of the universe consists in a process whereby the world is interpreted—not indeed in its wholeness, at any one moment of time, but in and through an infinite series of acts of interpretation. This infinite series constitutes the temporal order of the world with all its complexities."[83] Royce evidences here his use of the system of Western philosophic ideas that Arthur O. Lovejoy christened "the great chain of being." Temporal processes which reflect at different levels the same basic structures cascade forth in a procession of being. Recursively, the complex relations holding at any level of the series can be defined accurately in terms of simplified versions of the relations at some more primitive level of the series. For Royce, the most transparent versions of the relations that characterize all real processes occur within the actual

self as it interprets its past actions to its anticipated future. At its best, this actual self is a social self.

7. CONCLUSION

The temporal order is the exteriorization of the life of the will. That leit-motif runs through the entirety of Royce's published views on the nature of time and its relation to eternity. For any sequence of natural happenings or human actions, the past is being projected into the future by means of interpretation. "If we consider the temporal world in its wholeness, it con-stitutes in itself an infinitely complex Sign. This sign is, as a whole, inter-preted to an experience which itself includes a synoptic survey of the whole of time."[84] The idea of an infinitely complex sign which contains an adequate register of the whole of time is the form in which System Sigma of the Supplementary Essay guides the later phases of Royce's philosophy of time, and provides the best linkage between the purposes of a finite and an absolute will. The key to understanding the world as real is the idea of well-ordered relations in time. These temporal relations, in turn, are ex-pressions of the will as it clarifies to itself its nature and purposes. A social will, as a triune process, is the ground of the world as real.

In tracing some consequences of his view of time in relation to the Ab-solute, Royce most fully discloses both the intent and the limitations of his views about the nature of time. He criticized Aquinas's view that there is a gulf between eternity and time. Royce would have none of such an on-tological separation between eternity and time. He believed that the *totum simul* concept which Aquinas had accepted from Boethius was fundamen-tally compromised if time was not included in eternity. Time would be in-cluded in eternity if the distinctions between past, present, and future were included. And Royce did maintain that those modes of time are with-in eternity.[85]

But Royce talked about eternity in two different senses, and mingled them for the most part. One is the sense of everlastingness, the other, the sense of a timeless origin or first cause which engenders time and every-thing else that is real. The former sense, strictly, would be called the per-petual and the later would be called the eternal. Thomas Aquinas and other Christian philosophers who work with the idea of creation accept a basic dualism between creator and creation. The concept of creation requires that there be a real separation of being between the originating source and the products arising out of the agency of that source. Royce's criticism of the first form of Being in his Gifford lectures, i.e., realism, and its attendant

ideas of independence or separation prevented him from seizing accurately upon the distinction between the perpetual and the eternal.

Fundamentally, Royce's theory about the relation between time and eternity views time in relation to perpetuity. In failing to capitalize upon the authentic features of real separation in the domain of existence—as we saw achieved for example in William James's views—Royce ends up with a one-sided conception of time. Despite his asseverations in the 1909 paper, "The Reality of the Temporal," time has only a limited kind of reality for him, that of a mode or aspect. In making time less than it is, he also made more of time than is warranted. He diminished time by making past and future all of a piece, with the differences between the two turning solely upon the question of perspective. But he also made of time more than is warranted by including all of past, present, and future, *qua* past, present, and future, in an absolute experience. Royce's concept of the Absolute differs from the concept of the creator present in classical Christian philosophy, in about the same degree and for the same reasons that the concept of the perpetual differs from the concept of the eternal.

Royce is correct in judging that "all the questions as to our deeper relations to the universe are bound up with this problem of Time and Eternity."[86] But in perpetualizing time, he stopped short of a full analysis of the relations of the temporal and the eternal. Only in the writings of his last years did Royce begin to develop a more adequate concept of eternality. The movement is first adumbrated in the more realist turn in his logic, and in his growing attention to the aversive aspects of purposive activity. If time arises as the form of the will, then any change in his concept of the will can be expected to redound to his notion of time. In most of his philosophical production Royce did have a one-sided conception of time, because he had a one-sided conception of the will. Both Peirce and James had a more realistic understanding of the full nature of purposive activity, as aversive and appetitive, and their philosophies of time also prove more adequate.

Santayana and the
Temporal Compulsion

Belief in time is, I think, the deepest belief we have.
Three Proofs of Realism

Time, the right time for each thing, was the most sacred of the standards
one had to live up to.
The Last Puritan

PLACED together, the above state-
ments underscore each other. It is hard to tell which is the sounding and
which the echo, for the superlative degree of each increases the expressive
weight of the other. Taken together, they are indicators. The forward stride
of matter, matter's haste to change its current style, the tides of nature
which run deep into the psyche to erase some habits and deposit others:
these themes find their index in that doublet. Moreover, those superlatives
can remind us how much of Santayana's philosophy is a gloss on his theory
of flux and time.

An overview of that theory would, I think, go as follows: To believe in
time is to accept the passage of all things. Their passage is as real as their
permanence. Things arise that were not. They gather together an inheritance from the dispersive stages of other things. They achieve a certain
presence or posture. Thus they have their seasons, their special kinds of
fulfillment. But matter is in haste. Its whole force overpowers the realization in any part of it, jostling that part forward, leading it to eccentricity

and forgetfulness. And so all things pass on. Now they are, but there will be when they are not. Things will unhinge and disperse, and their transitive members will become aspects of new existents battling for actualization.

Given this state of affairs, man's acceptance of his essential impermanence would be his most natural posture. Disengagement or detachment from spurious forms of permanence would be the normal attitude. Certainly Santayana's own efforts at detachment are familiar enough. So the fact of his detachment becomes less important than its nature. He was seeking withdrawal, but not from the material conditions of life. His spirit, though perhaps fatalistic, was not anchoritic. He felt that this world was his host. "Matter," he conceded, "has been kind to me, and I am a lover of matter."[1] Rather, he was seeking to excise the conventional mental perspectives of his society. He was withdrawing from its subjective norms and flagrant moralizing. Thus his detachment was a purgative, a way to clear his vision so that the regularities of the material world could be spied in their native forms.

This point about the nature of Santayana's detachment has been missed by some who knew him personally and who highly valued his work. Professor Horace Kallen, for example, has said, "Santayana's condemnation of what he called the Hebraic tradition was part and parcel of the intellectual rejection of a world of flux and change and drama and salvation, in favor of the well-ordered Hellenic world."[2] Santayana did reject the drama and salvation of both the Hebraic and Christian traditions which, he believed, paraded without regard a moral subjectivism. Yet he was not discarding the flux and change, the bedrock temporalism of those traditions. Moreover, though Santayana did accept the well-ordered aspects of the Hellenic world, he also affirmed its Dionysian and telluric parts. How deeply Santayana's views are invested in flux and change is apparent in the value he places on the doctrines of Heraclitus, and in the way he uses Heraclitean conceptions to revise the materialism of Democritus and Lucretius.

I. SOME HELLENIC ANTECEDENTS: LUCRETIUS AND HERACLITUS

Behind the philosophy of William James and Schopenhauer, and confirming Santayana in his choice of idiom more than did either of these two moderns, were the Greek and Roman naturalists, the Ionians, and even certain nuances of Eastern philosophies. "The more I retreated in time, and the farther East I looked, the more I discovered my own profound and

primitive convictions."[3] Lucretius played a central role, both as spiritual mentor and instructor in philosophical atomism: "The great master of sympathy with nature, in my education, was Lucretius." Santayana memorized the great passages in Lucretius.[4] Once having learned them, he etched them even deeper into his sympathies through repetition, and by checking them against what he took to be the dramatic extravagances of the moral world of Christianity. "I recited my Lucretius with as much gusto as my St. Augustine; and gradually Lucretius sank deeper and became more satisfying."[5] That material nature is fundamental—as ground and source—is the lesson Santayana learned from Lucretius.

But what is important in material nature—flux and cadence—is the lesson that came from Heraclitus. Santayana believed that all worthy speculation about nature is born of the profound Heraclitean insight that "all things change; existence is a perpetual, irrevocable flux."[6] Things change, and a form and order determine the nature and direction of the change. In a letter to B.A.G. Fuller in 1918, Santayana judged as correct the Heraclitean belief that Dike (Justice) "presides over" the passage of things.[7] Flux, but with regularly fixed cadences; flux, but such that it included logos as a pacing feature of itself: that is the idea of material nature Santayana received from Heraclitus.

That the Heraclitean doctrine was used by Santayana can be seen in the way he revised Democritus and Lucretius. Existence is dispersive, but atoms are not basic to it.[8] His rejection of atoms does not proceed from the vantage point of modern physics. Rather, the Democritean definition of atoms simply went beyond what is experienced. To conceive of them as autonomous centers of existence is to import a subjective perspective, based on the moral necessities of the animal psyche, into the deepest strata of nature. The Heraclitean intuition is at least as sound as the Democritean.[9] The palm, indeed, goes to Heraclitus. On matters concerning the nature of physical substance, Santayana held that Heraclitus "represented Greek genius in its fullness."[10] We do experience that things have a certain staying power, but we also experience things changing. Moreover, this dual experience of constancy and change must itself ride on the tides of nature.[11] Elements that are as eventlike as they are atomlike must be the valid isolables in the study of nature. Tropes, or perhaps primitive complexes of permanence and passage like tropes, are the seeds of things. Thus, the cosmology of Santayana, the one supporting the overview given earlier, is woven from Heraclitean and Democritean (Lucretian) strands: discrete, externally related, changeful units pacing each other into and out of times of realization. This is the general concept of matter's interior

mechanism which Santayana worked toward and which, once framed, helped regularize his descriptions of the other realms of being.

2. THE MATERIAL FLUX AND ITS DISTINGUISHING MARKS

Taken as a token for the changeful stress of nature, "flux" refers to the compulsive twists and turns in the operations of material substance. Matter tries first one form and then another, dropping each in haste. The haste to change forms, Santayana says, is the "whole reality" of matter.[12] Accordingly, it is the basis of the temporal compulsion of all of existence. Existence is a fluxing, a continuous moving and passing by. Its parts do not merely repeat each other; they really succeed each other. In a letter to Logan Smith in 1919, Santayana asserts that "existence is fundamentally in flux—that is a conviction and expectation to start with."[13] There is, to be sure, more to existence than mere flux. Its other tokens are external relations and irrelevant jostlings, with each thing being pushed and constrained by other things.[14] Still, flux is a necessary condition of existence, indispensable to it and, taken as equivalent to transition, even the salient mark of existence.[15] Flux, then, seems to be *primus inter pares*, the most honorable of three ancients who control the surge of existence.

Flux cannot be defined by genus and differentia but can only be described in its relations. It cannot be synthesized under any essence, and so must simply be endured.[16] But Santayana does supply a metaphor for suggesting what the flux most resembles. It is like the will, and shares the compulsion typical of the will. The will of Schopenhauer's philosophy, he says, "was a transparent mythological symbol for the flux of matter."[17] Metaphors to one side, flux is a principle of existence, and thus is closely related to substance. According to Santayana, substance is a condition of flux, and is also internally in flux, but substance is also a principle of individuation. Substance determines which essences are exemplified, and is a condition of the external relations holding between existents. Thus, it appears that substance, which is also called a principle of existence, is not a fourth principle in addition to the three already cited, but is instead a name for the combination of the first two: the surging flux, and the permanence of its phases, i.e., their real externality.[18]

The flux shows that substance is generative.[19] Without flux, substance would be inactive. But it is active, pushing new things forward, and selecting new combinations as eruptions and effluences of itself. Because it is in flux, substance is at the base of physical time.[20] It underlies physical time because the flux of material substance is not only generative but also vectoral. Its direction reflects a prior composition of material forces, with

a single direction: forward.[21] The flow of things cannot reflux. The stride of existence is away from what has become actual, through what is still possible, toward what is achieving a finished (and fatal) status.

When nature arrives at finished states, the flux has slowed enough to allow things an attitude of temporary repose. But material substance is still quietly at work during these times of apparent rest. Nature's infinitesimals are still units of action. There is "an infinite, ceaseless, infinitesimal flux of matter" behind all things. Insofar as nature's causation is "crawling work," the infinitesimals that mark its passage are traversed on all fours. They are qualitative units, possessing breadth and resistance. At every point "there is a rising, a bursting, and a lapsing stress." Thus, the infinitesimals of the flux of matter are more like drawn bows or pent-up streams than like the points of mathematical space and time. That portion of the flux present during one of these thick natural points or cresting moments is called a 'trope' by Santayana. "Tropes of some kind [are] the minimal units of a flux."[22] This means that to speak of the events into which nature is periodized is to identify units of action. During these intervals of poised stability, the material flux is marking time. Everything flows, but not excessively. The material world is not too fluid; it has "islands of relative permanence."[23] These special patterns or collocations are changeful, but at a different rate than the flow of substance itself.

3. PHYSICAL TIME AND NATURAL MOMENTS

It is clear that for Santayana, time did not always exist. The prior condition was a flow of substance that did not run in tides. Arising from the flux of matter, time itself is an event, a happening. It is an *"eventum* created by" material conditions.[24] It is a product of matter's fecundity. Physical time and physical space are results: "Interaction and genesis involve this sort of space and time, or create them."[25] Chronos had parents. Time was born, and substance and flux are its progenitors.

Physical time is not the same thing as absolute time. Absolute time is a creature of sentimental human perspectives. It is the time that would triumph over all, including substance. Physical time is changeful, having many faces and knowing many cadences. But absolute time is a static thing, empty, directionless, deaf to any tocsin, a figment born dead. According to one of Santayana's definitions, physical time is an "irreversible order in lapsing events."[26] There has come to be a before and an after in the deployments of substance. According to a second definition, physical time is "an order of derivation integral to the flux of matter."[27] The two definitions complement each other. The first stresses the asymmetry of the rela-

tion of natural temporal sequence; the second emphasizes the genetic properties of apparentation and inheritance proper to each element in the irreversible arrangement, thus defining a successor. These definitions hedge in the more relaxed choice of terms where Santayana simply says that "physical time is another name for this native instability of matter."[28] The appearance of time means that efficacious tides have risen in material substance. There is more activity than mere eddies that recur and do no work. Moreover, the tides augment and becalm each other, constantly raising new complications in the flux of existence.

Physical time is unidirectional in nature. It is a "genesis involving inheritance." Dramatization at the level of the psychic flux might seem to belie the irreversibility of physical time. At that level, a person might believe that there are "reversible circuits" in time.[29] But at the level of the flux of matter, each moment in physical time has its seeds and its consequences. These moments are no more interchangeable in their generative order than father and son are interchangeable. We verge here on a premise that supports Santayana's belief that irreversibility is a property of physical time. The premise, moreover, plays about the same role in his materialist philosophy that the idea of entropy plays in the contemporary scientific world view. If time were reversible, there would be no genesis.[30] That is Santayana's key premise. But clearly there is genesis. Hence, the conclusion: time is irreversible.

Many of the properties Santayana ascribes to the flux and to physical time also hold for the units or parts within them. Natural moments and tropes can, indeed, be perceived as cameo versions of the material flux and its natural tides. That natural moments and tropes are closely akin can be seen by comparing them under four headings which are derived from the earlier analysis of flux and time: First, each is primitive in the unending stream of existence; tropes are the "minimal units of a flux," natural moments are the "ultimate elements" of existence.[31] Second, each is an ordered portion of matter that is graded by essences; tropes handle essences in sequence, and "a natural moment is a realized essence."[32] Third, both have features of permanence and externality. "A trope is a recognizable sequence of distinguishable elements"; "a natural moment has an irreversible polarity."[33] Finally, they are closely related to events: a trope is the form of an event,[34] whereas "a natural moment marks the existential emergence of a new form." Given these similarities, natural moments and tropes cannot properly be separated. To the extent that they can be distinguished from each other, they differ as do form and matter, or as structure and content differ. Events, Santayana asserts in his exposition, are composed of natural moments. Thus, tropes are forms of events, and natural

moments are the contents of events. This contrast between tropes and natural moments would be a distinction without a difference, inasmuch as it is based on the form/content distinction, one which does not touch the inner mechanism of things.

4. PRESENTNESS AND CRITICAL INSTANTS

Santayana's philosophy of natural time reaches its most perfect expression in his theory of presentness or critical instants. Nature compulsively fluxes, always waxing and waning. But she also impulsively strikes postures that perhaps fortuitously require that no further exertion of force be maintained. Her effluences, then, are not just a flaring up and an extinguishing; they have relaxed into a steady state of emanation. This steady state is called 'presentness' by Santayana. "Presentness, taken absolutely, is another name for the actuality which every event possesses in its own day, and which gives it its place forever in the realm of truth." It is a span that overlaps its stressful evolution on the one side and its precipitous devolution on the other side. It is an interval for inner windings, an involution. "Nature is full of coiled springs and predestined rhythms."[35] This image of coiling or winding is also applicable to levels of nature where psyche is found. In a letter to C. J. Ducasse in 1928, Santayana states that "the animal organism is wound up."[36] Unwinding or devolution sets in when the forces bearing against the steady state of a thing interfere with its equilibrium, and thus trigger the irreversible sequential movements for which the winding provided the potential.

Each thing, each concrete phase of matter, arises from this tension between opposing phases. Santayana's thought reflects the Heraclitean conception of material substance, that strife is the father of all things. For Santayana, each concretion is constituted by such a tense equilibrium.[37] Each object is a relatively steady state in nature, a balance where its ascendent and descendent sides hang poised in a state of polar tension. But the balance obtrudes only for a time. The natural justice in all things weighs the claims of the whole of nature against the claims of this impertinent part. Dike's verdict never changes. The part is found wanting, and the sentence is always capital. The concrete thing passes on. Its special act of equilibrium, its presentness, is no more.

The foregoing account examines what Santayana called the absolute or transcendental sense of presentness, where time is dramatized. But he also gives to presentness a relative or natural sense. In this second sense, "presentness is rather a name for the middle position which every moment of existence occupies between its source and its result."[38] Santayana's

phrase "critical instant" has about the same meaning as this latter sense of presentness: relative presentness. Professor John Lachs has judged that the "theory of critical instants" appearing for the first time in some of Santayana's previously unpublished essays is a "new view."[39] It may be, however, that critical instant is simply a new label for Santayana's staple doctrine of relative presentness in *The Realm of Matter*.

Like relative presentness, the concept of the critical instant is a triadic notion. It refers to the time where one event ends, another begins, and a third event is overlapping the other two. A critical instant, for example, would be that interval encompassing the crest of a thrown ball's motion, when its straightforward flight would be most noticeable. The essence of the event, its lateral passage, would be most transparently displayed then. But the actualization is not perfect. "No event at any instant realizes the whole essence of that event."[40] The thrown ball rises and drops during its essential forward movement. The flux could not have an island of eternity, an essence, perfectly given in it and still remain what it is, febrile and generative. The temporal compulsion is the unremitting forward momentum of existence. Each thing must seek its own special poise or equilibrium, striving for a ripe presentness or *kairos* when it most truly reflects its special nature to itself. To achieve the existence proper to it, each thing must have its critical instant, its relative presentness, a threefold state of staying which is also an arrival and a departure. A similar idea is used by Whitehead; each actual occasion limits itself by mirroring inward the special conditions and relations to which it conforms.

5. TEMPORAL LEVELS AND TRANSCENDENTALISM

For Santayana, existence has a linear momentum upward which complicates its linear momentum forward. Nature is a hierarchy, an upward-flinging as well as a forward-thrusting. But it is not under the same compulsion in both directions. Matter has to flux to be what it is, but it does not have to produce life, and life is under no obligation to produce spirit.[41] Still, the upward complication does exist. Nature has the hierarchical habit. There is a "natural hierarchy" present among the realms of being in which substance is displayed.[42] This notion of a natural hierarchy means that substance is more faithful to some forms than others.[43] The hierarchy simply reflects the different gaits or cadences of flux and time. Santayana's view is consistent with Royce's conception of a hierarchy of time levels.

The infinitesimal unit events of nature mentioned earlier are not only thick, but some are also storied. The flux of matter involves a morpho-

logical flux which arises out of it and which depends upon it in the sense that accidents depend upon substance. This morphological flux is a changing pattern of relations which holds between the discrete items which have arisen in the flux of matter. This second, morphological flux is, in turn, the seat of a third flux. At this third level of the flux of matter, certain morphological units experience the discontinuities of existence.[44] Such an experiential center is called a psyche, which, in turn, is a special kind of stacking of tropes.

The flux of existence has three gaits: (1) the ordered, unidirectional, generative flux of material substance; (2) the morphological flux; and (3) the psychic flux. "The flux of matter is the ground of the morphological and of the psychic flux."[45] The latter two are epiphenomena of the first. The ground of all temporality—the material flux—in no way depends upon the psychic and the morphological kinds of flux for its own existence. There would be material tides or times whether or not there were psychic or sentimental times. A cardinal error of metaphysical idealism, we might interpret for Santayana, is the belief that *all* of the natural flux is three-storied, or triple-gaited, and that the psychic level is a cosmic necessity, posited within or hidden behind the native flux of matter.

It is clear that Santayana saw himself standing at different levels, discussing a topic first by using a set of concepts appropriate to one kind of natural cadence, and then using notions proper to another level. Evidently, he attributed some of the criticism of his philosophical style to his multi-level approach to things. In a letter to Logan Smith in 1919, he wrote: "There is a real vacillation or incoherence in my expressions, because I take alternately and without warning now the transcendental and now the naturalistic point of view; i.e., I sometimes describe the *perspectives* of the senses and imagination, and sometimes the natural sequence or relations of facts."[46] With this warning from Santayana to guide us, we may keep temporal levels distinct by saying that time's *qualities* are spiritual—and thus, transcendental—expressions of those convulsive epicenters of matter called psyches or minds. But time's *properties* are factual and natural, measured by the crossing tides of material substance. Physical time is what arises from our adopting the natural stance, whereas sentimental time is how the flux of things looks from the transcendental, perspectival vantage point. Santayana was content with a dualism of perspectives that did lead to the "vacillation or incoherence" he noted in his views, but it was typical of Whitehead's second major approach to the problems of time that he overcame the dualism by appealing to the value-creating activity within actual occasions.

6. INTENT AND EXPECTATION

The most constant of nature's habits are found in the deeper strata of the material flux. Gaits are established in matter's movements which thereafter provide the cadence for some of the sequences displayed in the upper, more occasional strata. According to Santayana, this dependence of the mind upon material substance is revealed in what we call intent. "Intent is action in the sphere of thought; it corresponds to transition and derivation in the natural world."[47] Given the roles played by transition and derivation in the material flux and physical time, we can surmise that intent and expectation play a similar role for sentimental time. For Santayana holds that intent is a material fact displaying the same structure as many other lower level material facts. "The fact that intellect has intent, and does not constitute or contain what it envisages, is like the fact that time flows, the bodies gravitate, that experience is gathered, or that existence is suspended between being and not being."[48] The facts differ when nature transposes from one key to another, but the rhythm of her habits of passage remains the same.

Intent and expectation are akin. Expectation would be the awareness of intent's leading edge. Santayana has it that expectation is found in our "readiness to meet the unknown at a moment not predictable."[49] Both intent and expectation display the temporal compulsion of material substance at the level of the human mind. Expectation thrusts the mind out of its presentness toward some future equilibrium, casting at the same time a shadow backward into what will become the past when preparatory circumstances have been aligned with that future equilibrium:

> The compulsion to expect a future cannot be either empirical or logical; it is clearly physiological. A hungry and watchful animal is prophetically organized, he is ready for more. . . . instinct and intent are accordingly deeper than memory and underlie it: the projection of memory into the past, by which it becomes a sentimental perspective, is itself a sort of inverted expectation; we remember by imagining what we should find if we could travel backward.[50]

Santayana's doctrine is that the axis of memory and hence of experience is determined by intent and expectation. Appetition is the ground of our cognition, and is itself the outgrowth of matter's haste to change its forms and move on. The main implication is that all of our human perspectives and projections are generated out of the intent and expectation of the psyche. Santayana's view here seems to proceed in channels first laid out in the teaching of James and Royce, his professors at Harvard.

A difficulty is that there are many such psyches, each of which takes its alignments of experience as paradigms for all the others. Each posits temporal perspectives which radiate out from its special station amid the flux.[51] But the idiomorphic taint can be removed by checking sets of perspectives against each other, for what is common to several is a revelation of nature's own cadence. Natural reason can thus discover the more essential regularities by comparisons of perspectives. "It is only reason that can discount these childish perspectives [of the interested animal], neutralize the bias of each by collating it with the others, and masterfully conceive the field in which their common objects are deployed, discovering also the principle of foreshortening or projection which produces each perspective in term."[52] The projections of the animal psyche include those which comprise its sense of time. Sentimental time, Santayana says, is a "specious private perspective," a local emotional and moral perspective.[53] Nevertheless, all of the perspectives of the animal psyche, including those of sentimental time, can tell something about the transitions and sequences in those steadier states of the natural world from which the psyche arose. But they tell it badly, and improve their accounts only through recourse to that kind of colligating activity called natural reason. This requirement of interperspectival comparisons makes Santayana's realism critical, and his doctrine harmonious with James's historical deduction of the category of time.

7. SENTIMENTAL TIME AND SPECIOUS TIME

Time in both its physical and sentimental versions is a creature of a particular stratum of nature, a keeping of accounts of the pace and passage of things at a certain level of the natural hierarchy. Physical time is born of the flux, and sentimental time is born of intent. These progenitors, flux and intent, present different faces of the temporal compulsion. But the human spirit ascribes to the intentional forms of its pacing activity a kind of permanence they do not possess. It creates the vistas of sentimental time "in its effort to dominate and synthesize the flux of things." Still, the spirit is a child of matter, and receives parental advice from it. Matter signals its deployments across the inner distances of nature's hierarchy, and sentimental time is the spirit's prodigal way of recording what its forebear intoned. Sentimental time, accordingly, is not simply a free creation, but it is also a resonance. It is an echo of physical and natural time. Sentimental time, thus, appears to have a two-fold nature: it is veridical insofar as it echoes physical time; and it is illusory insofar as it reflects the pretentious intent of the spirit, spirit's attempt to dominate the material substance

from which it arose. Even so, this duality of sentimental time is a natural duality. "The sentimental perspectives of time are the only available forms in which a physical flux could be reported to the spirit." The spirit is too occasional, and too frenetic in its occasions, to have a direct purchase upon the processes in the lower strata of the material flux.[54]

The temporal compulsion at the level of sentimental time is apparent in the insistent presentness of 'now'. 'Now' is the most objective term in sentimental time. It is poised at the overlap of fancy and action.[55] The other modes of sentimental time fall on either side of this juncture called 'now'. 'Now' would be the sacramental interval during which there is a marriage between impulse and ideation. On the one side, the 'now' leans into the future (and that side is fancy or ideation), and on the other side it is tugged by the past (the side of impulse and action). "Not yet," "soon," "just now": these are tokens of the felt time of fancy, whereas "always" and "never" are conditioned by the relations in physical time.[56] Clearly for Santayana, some modes of sentimental time are more dependent upon physical time than others.

Sometimes he speaks of specious time instead of sentimental time. These expressions mainly refer to the same subjective sequences, but differ in the way those sequences are weighed by the psyche. The more pejorative of the two expressions is 'specious time'. Sentimental time is veridical to the extent that perspectives are collated and fancies curbed. But 'specious times' refer to occasions where the spirit takes its perspectives as determining the flux itself. On such occasions its emotional locality causes its claims to be inflated. Thus, specious times cannot be collated. They are incommensurable with each other except emotionally.[57] They are not corrigible through symbolic references. But because of the staggering number of such specious occasions, it is doubly important to correlate them. Indeed, Santayana holds that there are as many specious times as observers or observations.[58] If sentimental time arises from our normal madness, specious time would come from our playing at utter normality, as if the axis of reality were a projection of our own special intentions.

8. CONVENTIONAL MOMENTS

Conventional moments are the phases or intervals into which sentimental or specious time is resolved, analogous to the way physical time is divided into natural moments as its least units. The conventional units of sentimental time are as limited in extent as the moods and motives from which they grow. "Each passion or interest in a man's life is called a conventional moment."[59] Unlike physical time, where there are external relations be-

tween members of a generative series, so that real work marks the passage from one natural moment to the next, sentimental time has internal relations between many of its members. Thus, conventional moments fade into and qualify each other in reciprocal fashion, and even the sequences between them seem reversible. That the members of the series of conventional moments seem to fade into each other is due to the fact that these moments are being synthesized within the perspectives of the spirit. The here and the now of the spirit's making provide the most pressing locus for blurring conventional moments into each other.

The main types of conventional moments are the future, the past, and the specious present. The necessities of animal life, and the times of critical passage in it, establish the forward and backward directions in time. Santayana believed that splitting time in half, into future and past, is part of "the normal pathology of an animal mind."[60] For him, normal madness is not a condition to be despised. Rather, it is a reflection at the level of human life of matter's compulsive haste to change its forms. Nevertheless, animal requirements lie behind the fearful glance forward and the circumstantial glance back. Such watchfulness provides the main justification for the subjective contrasts of past and future. Santayana does use the terms 'past' and 'future' in a natural mode of describing the real states of passage in things, because the intent of the spirit is an effluence of the material flux and carries the marks of its origin with it.[61]

Santayana believed that we constantly rework or edit our past. The picture we frame of the past changes, growing progressively less like its original.[62] This is because the present is not a knife-edge present, but a specious present whose scope is set by the shocks of animal existence. Santayana defines the specious present as "the vaguely limited foreground of sentimental time."[63] Vistas forward and horizons background flow away from the specious present, fading away into the flux that gave birth to all of time. The other conventional moments, past and future, are thus wedded to and overlap with the specious present. Where all three moments are taken together, they still only indifferently and fortuitously reflect the real passage of things in the operations of material substance.

9. CONCLUSIONS

Santayana's philosophy of time is quite comprehensive. In many respects, his discussions square with more recent specialized investigations in several fields: (a) His temporal hierarchy is consistent with present-day interpretations of the doctrine of evolution. (b) The analysis of the flux of material substance he offered fits rather well with the scientific world

view of contemporary physics. (c) His portrayal of the psychic flux, aside from its materialistic presuppositions, is consistent with many phenomenological and psychiatric studies of the structuring of man's consciousness of time. But (d) there is an important lacuna in his philosophy of time concerning the existence and nature of social time.

(a) The doctrine of evolution is taken broadly here. Thus, there have evolved, from some primal energy state, levels of organization that range from stellar and physicochemical at one end, to organic and cultural at the other. Each level has processes and pacings peculiar to it. The stages are distinguished from each other by degree of complexity and by rate of energy exchange. In such an evolutionary scheme, time is conceived as a function of force fields, and of exchanges between them. In marking off the major stages of evolution into the cosmic, the physical, and the psychosocial, Julian Huxley has presented a philosophy of evolution whose structure is quite similar to the temporal levels found in the philosophy of Santayana.[64] Passage between the two theories of the material world is quite straightforward.

(b) Like recent physics, Santayana has introduced event and change into the innermost nature of matter. Defining material substance as a dual condition, a balance between transcience and permanence, is much like saying that matter and energy are interconvertible. For both positions, the ideas of force, event, work, unidirectionality, and so on, are fundamental. They would differ on at least one important point, however. If, among the varied senses of the concept of entropy, emphasis is placed upon the limiting case, where entropy has increased to that point where no more energy exchanges take place, we are then dealing with the marginal conception that the universe could in fact run down. Santayana would take exception. His material substance will always work. That case to one side, both positions accept as fundamental the irreversibility of natural process.

(c) Santayana's view that intent and anticipation provide the axis of the mind fits quite well, not only with the views of James and Royce, but also with Edmund Husserl's conception of internal or psychic time. Common to both positions is a doctrine that intentionality is a cardinal mark of the spirit and organizes experiences in terms of ideal objects or essences. The pacing of experiences, one's internal time consciousness, results from such intentional activity. Moreover, Santayana's doctrine of psychic time is similar in some ways to contemporary applications of phenomenology in psychiatry. In the analyses of Eugene Minkowski in *Lived Time*—concerning the structuring of time in different mental disorders—we see how one's direction in time is determined by one's *élan* or intent, the urge to become. Although Minkowski is influenced by Bergson's views of time,

his ideas mesh fairly accurately with Santayana's exposition of sentimental time.

(d) But Santayana had little appreciation of society's role in determining psychic time. Natural reason does provide a colligating activity between the multitude of temporal perspectives. He held that there are as many perspectives as there are observers, but this is a mistaken view. The work of Karl Mannheim especially has shown how one's expectations, and hence one's time sense, are notably a function of one's position and role in society. The sociology of knowledge shows that various social strata experience time differently, organize their activities differently, march to different rhythms. The idea of temporal levels in social consciousness would fit quite well with Santayana's general analysis.[65] His own investigations into time, however, simply never entered that area. His detachment from society perhaps left him with a blind spot concerning the way societies and class levels in societies determine the time sense of their members.

Dewey and the Temporalizing of Time

$\mathbf{T}$ HE most influential American philosopher during the early decades of the twentieth century was John Dewey (1859–1952). Although perhaps *primus inter pares* in the decade preceding the First World War—when the spirited dialogues between Idealists and Realists dominated Anglo-American philosophy—the decades between the First and the Second World Wars found him holding the center. Taking as fruitless the debates concerning the existence of entities transcending human experience, and concerning the manner in which such privileged objects or beings could be known, he came to deny altogether the existence of transempirical, nonnatural beings.

Important among the implications of his progressively stronger turn toward the natural and the experimental was his eschewing the eternal in favor of the temporal. He thought that philosophy should reconstruct its goals and come home to its proper business in this world. If Santayana could judge that Dewey's philosophy was all foreground, Dewey could reject as irrelevant the foreground-background, temporal-eternal distinctions. What we have, his alternative view went, was a dynamic natural and social experience of varying depths, but containing nowhere a static, eternal deep. Experience, so construed, is not a veil that conceals reality but a probe that tests it. Affairs and processes have different spans of endurance, and each will wane sooner or later. Everlasting forms or substances? No. *Secula seculorum*, with the tooth of time sunk into even the most enduring natural complexes? Yes. That was Dewey's doctrine of nature-in-passage when it reached its maturity. It is our task now to trace

the stages and plot the horizons of his developing conceptions of the nature of time.

Dewey's mature view of the nature of time and temporal quality was preceded by two or three phases of his understanding of the temporal aspects of experience. He was aware of the series of changes wrought in his own philosophy because of his involvement in new social and professional situations. His intellectual biography was not a unified whole:

> I seem to be unstable, chameleon-like, yielding one after another to many diverse and even incompatible influences; struggling to as- similate something from each and yet striving to carry it forward in a way that is logically consistent with what has been learned from its predecessors.[1]

We can, in what follows, identify some of the influences on Dewey's phi- losophy of time, and examine his tendency to carry forward some of his earliest judgments into his more complete theories. The theme of time in terms of temporal quality and temporal order arises in his psychology, logic, epistemology, and metaphysics. As his views developed in those substantive areas, so too did his ideas about the nature and modes of temporality.

I. SKEPTICISM ABOUT ETERNITY AND MERE SUCCESSION

A lifelong concern with the problems associated with change and time is presaged in the first article Dewey ever wrote, "The Metaphysical Assumptions of Materialism" (1881). His method of dealing with the as- sumptions is explicitly analogous to Hume's skeptical method.[2] Dewey proposes to overturn materialism by showing that monistic materialism is either self-contradictory or circular in its arguments. It seems self-contra- dictory in denying at the level of appearance what it must affirm at the deeper levels of substance, namely, the existence of mind as a cause. That is, for mind to appear, there must have been present in matter, from the very first, tendencies that are actualized in what we call qualities of mind. But this is to ascribe mind to matter *ab initio*. On the other hand, material- ism begs the question by concluding that experience gives us knowledge of causation, for causation must be assumed in order to make experience trustworthy.

In the course of his analysis of materialism, Dewey criticizes the con- ception of time held by materialists. He discounts their view of time as an endless succession, by appealing to the Kantian-Hegelian view of time which emphasizes its ideality. Materialism, his argument goes, affirms the

possibility of an ontological knowledge of material substance apart from the mere succession of phenomena in which it appears. Thus, materialism denies that time is a necessary form of all intuition of being. His criticism of materialism includes just this point concerning the possibility of a nontemporal intuition of reality that is not in any way bound up with successiveness.

If the materialist theory is true, that fact must be consistent with our knowing that it is true. But on what grounds is such knowledge available? Certainly not on materialist grounds, for all that materialism allows us is a succession of phenomena with no intrinsic connectednness between earlier and later phases. Or else it allows the coexistence of conscious states with nothing to blend or configure them into a significant whole: "Successions of consciousness irrelated, or related only in time, can but give knowledge of phenomena similarly related. . . . To have real knowledge of real being, there must be something which abides through successive states, and which perceives their relations to that being and to itself."[3] Thus, the power of active synthesis needs to be introduced *petitio* by some sleight-of-hand. Materialists accomplish this by using an empirical concept of causation which includes experience as *already* organized. But for Dewey the embryonic idealist, the organization of experience includes the category of causation as a necessary condition of knowing as such. Reason brings this requirement to experience and does not read it out of experience in the empiricist's sense. If he is consistent, the materialist can only appeal to mere "irrelation or relation only in time."

Dewey's use of this formula in his criticism of materialism shows that he views mere succession as bare antecedence and consequence. To upgrade bare serial connectedness into integral connectedness is to harness active relations like efficacy and dependency, ideas he would clarify only in much later studies. Materialism is driven to assume active, synthesizing relations and powers in such categories as causation and reciprocity. Because it assumes these powers of mind in accounting for the reality of matter and its modes of operation, Dewey maintains that materialism self-destructs.

Another "trial run" publication by Dewey appeared in 1882, entitled "The Pantheism of Spinoza." He used the same methods of criticism in evaluating pantheism that he used in disposing of materialism: he argued that pantheism is encumbered by antinomies or by *petitio*. The problem of philosophy is "to determine the meaning of the Actual." In showing how Spinoza fails to deal with this problem, Dewey advises that we can begin "with no better thought than that of Kant."[4] He has in mind Kant's criticism of dogmatic approaches to metaphysics. He will, accordingly, try to

draw valid conclusions from Spinoza's premises, which will contradict Spinoza's own chosen conclusions.

The main contradiction Dewey elicits is that finite things cannot exist as modes or accidents of God or Substance. Finite things, Dewey proceeds, cannot be modifications of eternal or infinite things, or somehow arise from such eternal things, unless we assume the existence of something noneternal and time-bound that connects the eternal to that which arises out of it. For the eternal cannot itself produce change.[5] But to assume such a finite agency at the beginning is to engage in *petitio*. Temporality may be consistent with eternality, but it does not thereby arise out of eternality or follow from it. Spinoza still has not *shown* that there are finite, temporal things, so Dewey concludes that "Spinoza is a juggler who keeps in stock two Gods." One of them is infinite, absolute, and eternal. The other is a composite image of the finite, the changing, and the relative. To extract the temporal and the finite from the eternal and the infinite, you must lodge it there in the first place, giving us *petitio*. Alternatively, if we compare the two necessary original conditions, the two Gods, we discover self-contradiction.

Dewey's method of analysis in these two early articles shows that epistemological problems are central, that solving them is a means to the end of the true characterization of the actual, and that they cannot be solved without clarifying issues that are caught up in our experience of things under the conditions of time and space. Dewey's conclusions in these exploratory articles are limitative, not substantive. The real or the actual cannot be a monistic, material substance, and it cannot be an eternal, changeless substance. Later in his career, on other grounds, and in his most important works of the 1920s and 1930s, Dewey denied that there *were* eternal, changeless substances. These first epistemological sallies helped pave the way toward such metaphysical positions. Dewey was sharpening his analytic tools with exercises in Humean and Kantian skepticism. The conclusion is that there can be no ontological knowledge of the Actual. Actuality is to be known under the conditions of time and space.

An emphasis upon time and space as forms of intuition was also registered in some of Dewey's psychological writings which appeared after he had joined the faculty at the University of Michigan. Temporal form and temporal content differ. In "The New Psychology" (1884) he questioned Mill's principle that the psyche is "never the same . . . in two moments of the same life."[6] Psychical life is a shifting scene of continuous processes proceeding at different rates of change. Based on this viewpoint, and consistent with the work of G. Stanley Hall which stressed a latent dynamism in the psyche, Dewey criticized the reigning psychology of introspection,

which is caught up in a study of shifting phenomena. It is defective because it "can deal only with the immediate present, with the given now."[7] This holds despite the fact that introspection, he believed, presupposes a kind of psychostatics. But the supposition is bound to totter and fall because we can "nowhere find spiritual life at rest."[8] For introspection to work as a sound method, it must presuppose ontological knowledge of a changeless psyche behind the shifting temporal and spatial panoramas of the finite self. Dewey's criticism of the old psychology relies on the methods of showing *petitio* or self-contradiction, the same methods he had worked out in his first writings in metaphysics. Significantly, the contrast between change and stability, between the actual temporal processes of the psyche and the presupposed changeless ground of the self, provides his point of attack. His search for an adequate methodology is coming to hover in the area of temporal and spatial forms of intuition and our understanding of them.

In two writings in 1886, Dewey treated time dynamically, as something that has come into being. He advanced from the Kantian conception that time is a necessary form for all empirical intuitions, to the Hegelian view that time is an organizing medium that itself arises out of more fundamental processes that are not temporal. In "Soul and Body" (1886), Dewey stated that he shared with a critic of some of his work the belief that time, as part of the enabling conditions for knowledge, is more than just a means to the end of knowledge, but is in some sense an end result of other activities. "We both admit that the becoming of certain definite forms of knowledge, say Space, Time, Body, External World, etc., etc., may (in ideal at least, if not yet as a matter of actual fact) be accounted for as the product of a series of events."[9] Dewey as idealist thus began to speak of time as both a process and a product. Time is a kind of process, yet it arises out of happenings or events. He continues his remarks by distinguishing between time and space as ideas, and time and space as forms that have arisen: "It is indeed the business of the psychologist to show how (not the ideas of space and time, etc., but) space, time, etc., arise, but since their origin is only within or for consciousness, it is but the showing of how consciousness specifies itself into various given forms." Thus, time is a mode of consciousness.

In "Psychology As Philosophical Method" (1886), Dewey repeated the assertion that time is "only within or for" consciousness. Where time had earlier been presented as both process and product, it is now referred to as both form and function. "Time is not something outside of the process of conscious experience; it is a form within it, one of the functions by which it organically constitutes its own being."[10] Interestingly, the three clauses

in this sentence recapitulate emphases about the nature of time that appear, respectively, in Leibniz, Kant, and Hegel. Like those German philosophers, Dewey is treating the psyche as a center of power or force; time is one mode of the actualization of that self as it passes from a formal ideality to a real individuality. This approach shows up in some of Dewey's last statements about time, when his naturalism and instrumentalism were at high tide. But in these articles published in the 1880s, Dewey's idealistic approach can hardly be distinguished from that of Royce: for both philosophers, time is closely associated with the purposive realization of the psyche.

The self is temporal, a kind of being which realizes itself in time. We cannot, from a psychological point of view, have knowledge "about any consciousness which is out of relation to time."[11] The self Dewey characterizes in this way is not a changeless, substantial self hidden behind a shield of phenomena. Rather, it is a dynamic being, one which changes and grows. The self construes its own nature as a unity, but not as an identity. Its unity is related to its continuity in time; its singularity (whereby it differs from other individuals) is related to its existence in space.[12] The principle of individuation, as that principle applies to selves, is space/time and the manner in which selves are embedded in it.

In these articles, written while he was at the University of Michigan, Dewey took time and space as forms of intuition, more as psychological product than natural process. They deal more with things *presented* as existing than with meaning. The fact that experience could extend beyond mere sequence in time and coexistence in space and present us with meaningful objects and events would require a more active, ideal element.[13] Dewey was aware of dualisms here that needed to be overcome, the dualism between the physical and the psychical, and between existence and meaning. The impetus to overcome such dichotomies, he thought, arises primarily in the field of practical, moral experience. In "Ethics and Physical Science" (1887), he argued that the mechanistic approaches of the physical sciences and the topological approaches of the sciences of mind are so diverse that a reasoned morality almost becomes impossible:

> We are sure that an interpretation of reality which confines it to the coexistences of space, the sequences in time, and the reign of mechanical law, is fatal at once to the categories of morals and to the attitude of the practical life of morality.[14]

The world of science is a phenomenal world. It offers a view that is not yet organized teleologically. "In a threefold way . . . the world of science is not a whole; it is only a world of *progressus ad infinita*, whether of space, of

time, or of causes." We cannot have ethics without a teleological perspective. Inasmuch as the physical sciences fall short of such an organizing perspective, those sciences cannot provide a cognitive basis for ethics. "We cannot admit the claims of physical science to be the founder of the ethical systems of the coming man. We have to deny it, because ethics deals with an end, and there is no place for an end in nature as confined to space and time."[15]

Dewey was siding with Leibniz's organicism against Newton's mechanistic science in setting off these different implications of our assessment of time and space. There is no question that James's *Principles of Psychology* (1890) influenced Dewey's thinking about the nature of space and time. But in 1888, Dewey had already finished his meticulous, enterprising study of Leibniz's *New Essays* before he came under the influence of James's psychology. James's discussions on time were read by a Dewey who had already appropriated Leibniz's doctrines. Dewey was prepared both by Leibniz's organic philosophy and by James's empiricist and realist constructions to move outside of the idealism of Hegel and Kant.

2. TIME AND ACTIVITY: A MIDDLE ROAD

Dewey's idealism was quite pronounced in the 1880s. He held that Christianity and Hegelianism were identical. He was teaching Kant, Hegel, Green, and Caird on Kant.[16] He was continuing to explore the problems of philosophical method that appeared in his initial writings and in his Ph.D. dissertation on Kant. But where the idealists emphasized formal and transcendental logic in handling methodological questions, Dewey began to pay increasing attention to a psychological approach to answering such questions.[17] He had learned the lessons of Part II of the *Critique of Pure Reason*, where Kant had distinguished carefully between mathematical and philosophical method, and had thus helped free methodological issues in philosophy from their entangling alliances with Cartesian rationalism. With the belief that philosophical method could not parallel mathematical method but must be something more topological like psychology, Dewey turned back to Kant's great predecessor, Leibniz. In the course of reexamining Leibniz's philosophy, he gave full attention to Leibniz's views of time, space, and causality.

Leibniz, Dewey held, was the greatest intellect since Aristotle.[18] He was the harbinger of the modern world. The unity of the *content* of his philosophy, stressing organism and harmony, and implying the essential interconnectedness of different parts of an active processual whole, constitutes Leibniz's great glory as a philosopher.[19] Contrariwise, Dewey

thought, the *logical* unity of Leibniz's method excluded process and mediation. This opposition between subject matter and method was fundamental in Leibniz's work, so one must disentangle the real substance of his thought from his method. If we approach Leibniz's idea per se, independent of its scholastic method, we find a Leibniz who holds that reality is activity, and substance is action.[20] We are presented with a radical dynamism. We can ignore his formal principles of method (identity and contradiction), and concentrate on his real principles (sufficient reason and continuity). What we find Dewey attempting as he exposits Leibniz's philosophy is to correct and reconstruct it with proper emphases that would bring out its living message.

Continuity is especially revealing in the activities of living beings. Indeed, life is the most important of Leibniz's categories, "the alpha and omega of his philosophy." Leibniz thought that the relation between the individual and the universe was the nerve of the philosophical problem.[21] The unity between the individual and the world had to be a spiritual unity, mediated by the category of life. It could not be a material unity, for the nature of matter is to be infinitely divisible. A material, natural world is a world of space and time. In this natural realm of space and time, we can find no unity within which to rest, for what exists in nature is relative to time and space and quantity, and anything that exists in spatiotemporal relations is subject to a metric.

Monads are the basic elements of reality. They can only be thought. Inasmuch as they are not sensible, they are not imaginable and thus are not conditioned by space and time. According to Dewey, not being imaginable and not being conditioned by space and time are strictly correlative expressions.[22] In his exposition of Leibniz on these topics, Dewey aligned himself with Leibniz against Locke, who had derived the features of reality from empirical intuitions and had thus made too much of space and time as features of reality. Time and space, for Leibniz, are secondary and have pure energy or spiritual activity as their absolute ground. The living activity of monads that gives us an image or reflex of diffusion and extension is perfect continuity.[23] Behind extended substance and sequential phenomena is continuous force or power.

As Dewey interprets Leibniz, time and space are not products of active force. Rather, they are a medium through which force is deployed as it enters into the realm of bodies. Both Plato and Leibniz have intermediary offices between the rational and the sensible.[24] For Plato, mathematical or geometrical relations provide linkages between Ideas and phenomenal objects. For Leibniz, space/time relations oversee the passage from the domain of monads to the sphere of sensible bodies. Although Leibniz's

theory was suggestive to Dewey, as we shall see, it was a theory Dewey rejected in the end. For inasmuch as he only accepted as a temporary convenience the distinction between the sensible and the intelligible realms, he also would have no reason for assigning space and time mediating roles between the realms either.

The most interesting part of Dewey's analysis of Leibniz's theory arises as he traces Leibniz's distinction between space and time on the one hand, and extension and duration on the other. In his *Essay*, Locke handled space and time as species of extension and duration. In *New Essays*, which was Leibniz's dialectical exposition of Locke's *Essay*, Leibniz sets out a theory where space and time are of a higher order than extension and duration, and not subordinate to them. As Dewey presented Leibniz, space and time are "innate ideas."[25] They are the offspring of intellectual and spiritual activities. Extension and duration, however, are sensible experiences, not intelligible. Extension and duration are not rational, clear and distinct, and eternal; rather, they are phenomenal, confused, and evanescent. Dewey sided with Leibniz here, giving to his own developing view an impress that appeared again and again, especially in his late study, "Time and Individuality" (1938).

Extension and duration are qualities; space and time are relations.[26] Extension and duration are objective predicates of things and events; space and time are relational predicates bearing on the connections between things. Extension and duration have to do with the mass, the continuation, or the repetition of some substance; space and time give the measure of mass, the law of continuation, or the order of the repetition. Although extension/duration apply to what is actual, Leibniz took space/time as applying equally both to the actual and the possible. That is, space and time present the necessary conditions for any possible order of existents, whether or not that order is actualized. This makes space/time *relations* intrinsic in actual fact, which the empiricists stoutly denied. In this respect, space/time relations are closer to eternal truths than to temporal facts.[27]

In *New Essays*, Leibniz's critique of Locke would have provided Dewey with a picture of a world dynamically alive, even had Dewey found it nowhere else. Leibniz's metaphysics emphasized the ideas of living force, organicity, activity, and individuality, ideas that served as lessons to reinforce some of the teachings of William James's *Principles of Psychology*. Taken together, the work of Leibniz and James led Dewey to give greater consideration to psychological method as the correct approach to philosophy. Some of the first fruits of this assemblage of ideas stressing activity, organic relatedness, and true individuality matured after his move from

the University of Michigan to the University of Chicago in 1894. It is almost as if the change in Dewey's thinking needed confirmation from a richer mixture of social and professional relations, with all the attendant stimuli, in order to divert a stream of tendency into clearly innovative channels.

At about the same time that he undertook his Leibnizian studies, Dewey was carrying out the inquiries that appeared in his book *Psychology* (1887). In this volume, he treated space and time from an idealistic viewpoint in transition, a viewpoint that introduced themes from the work of physiological psychologists like G. Stanley Hall. Dewey argued that actual knowledge deals with objects in relations. It is concerned "with a universe of things and events arranged in space and time." That is, actual knowledge never deals with isolated, particular entities. As we come to know, we are tracking things that are already given in space and time. Experience, he added, never gave us "any breach in continuity," so anything experienced as known is a *relatum*, something already associated contiguously with something else. Space and time, moreover, are the two kinds of contiguous association, the minimum conditions of continuous experience.[28]

Now this space and this time are not separate kinds of data that appear in experience. They are forms of association that mold our perceptions. Things and events, when first perceived, are perceived as existing in space and connected. But understood as parts of a world *not* ourselves, things and events are taken as separate particulars. For Dewey, the perceived world is a present world, one given in space. This sets it apart from the remembered world, a past world, one existing in time. Dewey is allowing here that space, as a form of association in the psyche, is "more ancient" than time. Memory is built up out of perceptions, and the form of memory—time— presupposes the antecedent organizing activity of the basic form of perception. As memory is related to perception, so too is time related to space: "The relations of time ... which connect events with each other and with the self, are developed." Time, it appears, is subsequent to and attendant upon space. Time relations, Dewey added, are of two kinds, succession and duration. The difference is that succession refers to change and duration refers to extent.[29]

The influence of the new physiological psychology is also shown in the manner in which Dewey relates space and time to specific channels of perception. Space is fundamentally considered in conjunction with the sense of sight, and time is related to auditory sensations. Sounds in sequences give us rhythm, and rhythm is the foundation of psychic organization. We can, he held, hardly overestimate the importance of rhythm in the psyche.[30] Its role there is a reflex of connectedness in the outer world. That is,

rhythm is to psyche as periodicity is to the physical universe. Rhythm is the native form of all apperception. "In rhythm every sound points, by its very structure, both to the past and future. Rhythm . . . meets the requirement of perception of succession in time: permanence amid change. . . . It is only because of this that time relations are perceived."[31] We have already seen that Josiah Royce gave special attention to the importance of musical rhythm in understanding the nature of time. Dewey's views neatly parallel Royce's on this point.

The most significant passage on time that Dewey wrote during this early period is one wherein he held that time is involved in both unity and difference:

> The relations of time, which we have seen to be characteristic of memory, repeat the evidence of the existence of both the identifying and the discriminating activities of intelligence. All *times* are regarded as constituting one time; any point of time has no existence, except as in relations of before and after to other points. It exists only by virtue of its relations to them. It is the continuing of the previous time and the passing into the next time. Time, in short, is one or continuous. But we must recognize, also, that time is discrete. Each point of time is outside of, external to, every other point. The essential trait of any given period of time is, in fact, that it is not any other period. We discriminate events as particular by referring them to some time, as we do objects by referring them to some place. Time as a whole appears, also, external to, and unconnected with, the self. The self in memory appears identical with itself and permanent, while time is always changing. But that time has less of the element of externality than space is evident from the fact that the mind regards its own experiences as happening in time, while it never thinks of supposing that they occur in space. Time presupposes, in fact, a certain degree of internality, or intimate connection with self.[32]

The passage is significant in emphasizing some notions about time that Dewey had dealt with from the very first, only the problems have been transposed. Terms like 'the eternal' and its relations to time, or 'matter' and the sheer successiveness of events have been inverted into the language of experience and relations within experience. We should note these things about the passage: (1) Dewey stresses the importance of the before-and-after relations in constituting time. (2) He relates the unity of time to the idea of a dense continuum, whereas the diversity within time is connected with discrete or atomic periods of time whose extremities are points that occur within the continuum. (3) The mind in one of its aspects, the self, seems atemporal, whereas in its other aspects it is temporal, hav-

ing experiences in time. (4) Finally, Dewey says that time *is not* connected with the self, but also that it *is* connected with the self. Clearly, this passage—which appears as the concluding section of chapter six in *Psychology*—presents us with a roster of problems about the nature of time. The main point, however, is that if Dewey had hoped to avoid the difficulties concerning the notion of time that he had discerned in the extreme positions of Spinozistic monism and materialism—by taking a mediating position which rooted time in the activity of a cognitive or psychic center much as Leibniz did—then those rejected extremes would have to be dealt with again in the context of a philosophy of experience where they had revealed themselves with new vigor. Having discharged Spinoza's notion of eternal substance, Dewey must now be prepared to discharge the notion of something timeless about the self. Although his ideas about time eclipse idealistic approaches to some degree, he is still willing to summarize his ideas using a favorite idealistic formula: time involves unity and difference. Halfway through his tenure at the University of Michigan, his views still reflect the critical idealism of the German and Scottish schools, notably the work of Kant and Caird. But his restless idealism is revealed in his reference to his own philosophy during this period as "experimental idealism."[33]

3. EVOLUTION AND TIME

At the turn of the century, Dewey's philosophical views were in ferment. Themes arising from his concern with a functional, behavioral psychology began to appear in his logical studies. The spirit of William James's psychology and Charles Peirce's methodology broods over his work now. With Peirce, Dewey also explored the idea that thought arises in the tension between an inhibiting doubt and an assuring belief. Indeed, Dewey's essay of 1900, "Some Stages in Logical Thought," seems almost a mirror image of Peirce's 1877 paper, "The Fixation of Belief," but it also reflects most astutely the influence of a functional psychology.

The new emphasis in Dewey's essay on the evolutionary phases in logical thinking (1900), is a redressing of the balance between reason and experience in favor of experience. Facts and contingencies sounded only minor notes in the transcendental logic of Kant, Hegel, and Caird in which Dewey had been trained and which he was still teaching at Chicago. In the received logic, facts and contingencies were virtually expendable, or at best afforded a "redemption by grace" through the higher sacrosanct truths. But a spirit which values observed things and events begins to correct Dewey's idealist logic. Facts are not to be taken as illustrations of

higher truths but as phases of spatial and temporal relations. Moreover, laws that govern the realm of fact are immanent in that realm, and provide an account of spatial and temporal ordering amidst those discrete, contingent facts.[34]

Dewey identified four stages of thought. At the first stage, ideas are taken as fixed and static. The second stage is a corrective to the first, and deals with ideas as "essentially subject to change."[35] It humanizes ideas and deals with them as artifacts in some respects. The third stage, representing a synthesis in a dialectical process, is where ideas are stabilized anew by securing them in deductive patterns of reason. But the last stage goes beyond the proving of ideas to the inference of new ideas that relate to the ordering of facts in the spatiotemporal domain. The fourth stage shows that logical thought for Dewey is balanced in favor of future experiences, and not directed toward past experiences that are simply thought of as given.[36] Each fact observed and inferred is a harbinger and a gateway to new realms of fact lying beyond it. That Dewey foretold lines of argument that would not reach fruition for two decades should not obscure his call for a logic that will reassign the key notions of concept, judgment, and inference to the domain of changing circumstances.

The significance of this accent upon facts embedded in spatiotemporal relations was, with the wisdom of hindsight, emphasized by Dewey several years later after he had been at Columbia University for a decade. In 1917, "Some Stages in Logical Thought" (1900) was reprinted, along with several other essays on logic from his Chicago period, in a new volume, *Essays in Experimental Logic*. The special introductory essay that he wrote for the new volume opens with these words: "The key to understanding the doctrine of the essays which are herewith reprinted lies in the passages regarding the temporal development of experience." What had been one emphasis among several others in the original essays is now offered as the key to unlocking their doctrine. Logic must be recast in terms of its historical development across time.[37]

However, it became clear, mainly in retrospect, that a stress upon the temporal categories of experience was emerging in Dewey's thought and was increasing to a degree that it would reappear as an emphasis in his ontology. Several years after he had arrived at Columbia, some of Dewey's philosophical critics still perceived him as an idealist.[38] But it is quite clear that during this period, Dewey was molding anew the fundamental ideas of space, time, process, and development. His growing naturalism was fortified by some of his new colleagues at Columbia, especially Frederick J. E. Woodbridge. In the Winter/Spring term at Columbia in 1909, Dewey gave a series of lectures entitled "Charles Darwin and His Influence on Science." One of those lectures, "The Influence of Darwinism," became the

opening chapter of his *Influence of Darwin on Philosophy* (1910), and set the tone for the entire book. If Dewey was to make good the promise of his new initiatives in logical theory, then he needed to relate the changes in logic to actual practice in the experimental sciences.

Darwin's work provided Dewey with the vehicle for passing from a functional logic and a functional understanding of mind to actual scientific practice. It gave body to the vague perception of the importance of organic modes of thought, which Dewey had first imbibed from Thomas Huxley in his senior year in college and which he remembered fondly in later years.[39] His studies in the philosophy of Leibniz only confirmed for him the significance of organic modes of thought. But no living connection between those biases and the contemporary scientific thought of his time could measure up to the linkage he found in his studies of Darwin. Dewey used Darwin's work as a *speculum maius,* as a body of investigations which reflects back into consciousness the growing maturity of an alternative logic and metaphysics. He read off those reflected marks a set of lessons which departed radically from the traditional Hellenic atemporalism and acosmism that continued to vex Western thought. The very phrase "origin of species" was taken by Dewey as a register of a changing intellectual temper. For a species, as the biological surrogate for *eidos,* was by Greek standards static and changeless, an entity that was indifferent to its appearance at this place or that. "We live," Dewey concluded, "in the twilight world of an intellectual transition." The universe could now be regarded as open and subject to modification, caught up in change and development and hazardous endings. This new universe was boundless in time and space. It is not a finished whole at all, but at best a statistical whole that reflects myriad local changes and different time frames.[40]

This new world is no longer the intellectual world of changelessness where the causal relation is but a species of the relation of ground to consequent. It is a world of real change known through the use of practical reason. Such practical thinking is experimental and tentative. It looks to the future, and to the past for help in the future.[41] Its significant relations are contingent and not necessary. Thus, it seems that the fourth stage in the growth of logical thought—the stage Dewey had spelled out in his 1900 essay on logic—reappears here as a distinct line of argument. Experimental reason that tilts toward the future is reaffirmed, and is fortified by developments in the life sciences. Meanings are no longer static subsistents, but are experimental conceptions that happen. They arise temporally, Dewey judges.[42] They are immanent in a world of change and are not instances of an *eidos* that ingresses from another domain. Rather, meanings egress from the web of happenings. G. H. Mead also stressed this approach.

That Dewey was increasingly aware of the need to rethink time in

terms of individuals, contingencies, and features given directly in experience, and not as a shadowy image of eternity nor as a subjective condition for experience, can be seen in his studies on metaphysics and logic in 1915–16. The occasion for a paper on metaphysics, "The Subject-Matter of Metaphysical Inquiry" (1915), was to evaluate some themes current in the biological sciences, especially where vitalist or biocentric forces might be seen as characterizing the fundamental world process. To attribute vitalistic traits to the basic constitution of the cosmos is to conceive ultimate reality temporally, for vital processes are not static or homogeneous through time, but are changing and developing. Unique existences; interactions between changing systems; evolution of traits: these typify the way living things work. Dewey is in fundamental agreement with biological sciences that resist reductionist efforts to dispel heterogeneity, diversity, quality, and other marks of living systems.[43] The conclusions Dewey reaches in this metaphysical excursus reaffirm the views he consolidated in his studies of Darwin's work, but push them a step farther. He now held that the evolutionary approach requires the notion that time is a primordial something, a real objective given: "The chief significance of evolution with reference to such an inquiry seems to be to indicate that while metaphysics takes the world irrespective of any particular time, yet time itself, or genuine change in a specific direction, is itself one of the ultimate traits of the world irrespective of date."[44] Dewey never wrote a metaphysics in the generally understood sense, but this trait of temporalism would have appeared prominently had he written extensively in that area. For, once this note of radical temporalism is sounded, it appears frequently in his best philosophical productions.

4. TIME, EXPERIENCE, AND THE PROCESSES OF NATURE

A manifesto for radical empiricism—where Dewey has broken away from perennial Western philosophy with its substantialist motifs and its yearnings for the eternal—is set out in the lectures Dewey delivered in Japan immediately after the First World War. Given in the spring of 1919, the lectures were published in 1920 under the title *Reconstruction in Philosophy*. These addresses provide an admirable summary of the themes Dewey elaborated across two decades. But they also reveal new lines, perhaps in response to the stimulus afforded by the new cultural setting and by the need to be nonparochial or non-Western in decisive respects. Included among the postulates that control the reconstruction in philosophy Dewey espouses, is his conviction that biology provided new foundations for psychology. This meant that the psyche is a mode of continual readjustment

to its environment and its sweep of happenings. Experience, accordingly, is a doing. It is experimental and not merely empirical.[45] An adequately reconstructed philosophy must reflect such a change to a noncontemplative, operative view of adjustment to things and events. The ideas of space and time Dewey sets out in *Reconstruction in Philosophy* reflect this experimental, organismic approach.

An empirical view of time would exhibit what is now given in the present or what was already given in the past, but an experimental view underscores what will occur in the future: "A logic of discovery . . . looks to the future."[46] This inclination of experience toward the future finds the imagination embodying new conditions there. Progress, the great liberal idea, is strengthened by placing the desiderata of humans in their future conditions. Such approaches in epistemology and in ethics, Dewey thought, place philosophy on a new foundation. The older Greek foundations are shaken when process and change come to be considered as fully real. Time, change, and movement are no longer stigmata, but are the marks of an open universe:

> Instead of a closed universe, science now presents us with one infinite in space and time, having no limits here or there, at this end, so to speak, or at that, and as infinitely complex in internal structure as it is infinite in extent. Hence it is also an open world, an infinitely variegated one, a world which in the old sense can hardly be called a universe at all; so multiplex and far-reaching that it cannot be summed up and grasped in any one formula. And change rather than fixity is now a measure of 'reality' or energy of being; change is omnipresent.[47]

The main Hellenic tradition notwithstanding, acting now takes precedence over knowing. No longer, Dewey thought, can we construe reality as immutable and timeless. A reconstructed view based on the new natural and biological sciences will secure the idea that process is fundamental.[48] Heraclitus, not Parmenides, will be the patron saint of the modified world view.

With a balance of view and comprehensiveness of expression regarding the nature and significance of time, Dewey's Carus lectures, published in 1925 as *Experience and Nature*, carry through the intended reconstruction of philosophy along several lines. The scope of his treatment is accompanied by a penetration of idea toward novel doctrines. Behind time as an order he discerned time as a primitive quality.[49] Time and reality with it are thrown fully into process. The temporalization of time is carried to completion, and the implications of such a temporalization are explored.

Dewey believed that to understand objects, events, and psyches properly, we must deal with them as we find them given to us: as actual. Our understanding needs to proceed on three fronts: We must first discern the aspects or factors that, in their development and interplay, make sense of the world as it is presented. Metaphysics is the theory of our surrounding existential world understood in this manner. But we also want our theory to account for things as they seem to be. So in the second place, we need to show how the misapprehension of the real factors of existence lead to false problems in modern philosophy. Third, we should be able to show how the fallacious constructions of discredited philosophies do in fact arise out of unnoticed developments of the real factors or elements of our correct theory. Dewey's theory of temporality in *Experience and Nature* proceeds under the control of these three considerations.[50]

Existence, Dewey thought, is both hazardous and stable. Although it is precarious and threatening in some respects, it is enduring and satisfying in other ways. The world as it is given to us is the union or overlapping of these two factors.[51] Existence may be aleatory, but it is also under constraints; it is both tychistic and determined. Insofar as we attend to the hazardous features, we see the world as incomplete, characterized by breaches and discontinuities. But as we attend to the recurrent factors, the discontinuities appear to fade away. The discontinuous versus the recurrent; the contingent versus the necessary; the hypothetical versus the apodictic; for Dewey, these are complementary ideas. They are pairings, where neither member can be properly understood in isolation. "A world of 'ifs' is alone a world of 'musts'—the 'ifs' express real differences; the 'musts' real connections."[52] Understood in such a manner, the world is a world of processes and histories. Erwin Edman saw and especially valued in Dewey's views this idea: To be is to be eventual.[53] To exist is to exist as an event, as a complex possessing both processual and structural aspects. But inasmuch as structures exist, they are also eventlike. Dewey treats structures as characters of events. What we call essences or structures are not subsistent, impervious to change, but are fully immanent in the realm of happenings.

Existential changes or processes proceed at different rates. The rate of change in a process is a function of the exchange of properties with other interweaving processes. A structure is "an arrangement of changing events such that properties which change slowly, limit and direct a series of quick changes and give them an order they do not otherwise possess."[54] Slowness and quickness are not intrinsic, measured against some fixed standard, but are arrived at immanently in a given context. The subordinate process, the slower, is given its pace by the faster. Thus from the events and affairs

of varying complexes, the basic aspects of change and structure emerge. Structure is a slower, more enduring change which circumscribes the more unstable forms of passage. On one of its sides, an event is a process or a changeling, a transitory complex of chance and instability. But all that is, is eventual. The structural, more enduring forms of change enter into other changes as instrumentalities.[55] Thus, they are the efficient bonds that lead the intensive and immediate aspects to recur.

Perhaps the most important pair of terms in Dewey's metaphysics of time are 'temporal quality' and 'temporal order'. These expressions are not complementary factors in the real world, as hazard and stability are complementary. Rather, temporal quality is a more fundamental aspect, and temporal order is secondary and derivative:

> Temporal quality is . . . not to be confused with temporal order. Quality is quality, direct, immediate and undefinable. Order is a matter of relation, of definition, dating, placing and describing. It is discovered in reflection, not directly had and denoted as is temporal quality. Temporal order is a matter of science; temporal quality is an immediate trait of every occurrence whether in or out of consciousness. Every event as such is passing into other things, in such a way that a later occurrence is an integral part of the *character* or *nature* of present existence.[56]

Dewey's assertion that temporal quality, an undefinable something, is a feature of all occurrences *whether in consciousness or not* is a complete rejection of idealistic accounts of time. It is a piece of realistic metaphysics that sets temporal qualities into nature itself.

Modern epistemology had gone astray, Dewey believed, through its adherence to the dogma "which denies temporal quality to reality as such." Indeed, temporal order was ascribed to reality by some investigators, but that is quite different. For temporal order is itself timeless, a creature of science. "All relations, all universals and laws as such are timeless. Even an order of time as an order is timeless, for it is relational."[57] We are thereby led to the dogma of a timeless reality because we see things telically. This would account for Royce's mistaken approach to time, Dewey would probably judge.

It was in the context of discussing the nature of reality as temporal that Dewey came to some of his clearest affirmations of a naturalistic metaphysics.[58] The real metaphysical question is now taken by him as fully displaced into the realm of events, of temporal quality. According to Dewey, the problem of metaphysics, the existential problem, is this: "It is whether existence consists of events, or is possessed of temporal quality, character-

ized by beginning, process, and ending."⁵⁹ The question of temporal order, dealing with the descriptive matrix supplied by science, is not registered in this statement of the metaphysical problem. This kind of temporal feature is an affair of the mind, a product of meanings not themselves a part of the natural order of events.

Dewey answers his basic question in a way that seeks to preserve both alternatives. Nature is an interwoven complex of temporal elements. Each element has its own quality. Nature is a whole, but it is a pluralistic whole having internal distinctions, and is not monistic, like some block universe. It is an affair of affairs. Beginnings of some events may accompany the apogee of others. The endings of events may dilute the rising tide of others. But there is no one beginning, no absolute beginning for all of nature. The teleological consciousness, however, inspired by religious and aesthetic motives, reinforces such a conviction of a single origin of all that is. "In the degree . . . in which the mind is weaned from partisan and egocentric interest, acknowledgement of nature as a scene of incessant beginnings and endings presents itself as the source of philosophical enlightenment."⁶⁰ If we hold, however, to the dogma of a timeless reality from which all process takes its departure, we will be led from a false metaphysics to a false epistemology. We will have a view of experience where we substantiate the eventual and temporal qualities into clearly demarcated beginnings and endings.

Both matter and mind can be thought of as characters of natural events. They are phases of an operation, and are not themselves entities at all. "Nothing but unfamiliarity stands in the way of thinking of both mind and matter as different characters of natural events, in which matter expresses their sequential order, and mind the order of their meanings in their logical connections and dependencies."⁶¹ Dewey's view is that both mind and matter are features of the natural order. They are immanent in the constellations of processes and affairs that is nature in the making. Indeed, those processes and orderings we call 'matter' are the more enduring features. But matter is not something that causes changes or processes. Rather, the more deep-seated rhythmic orderings that endure through successive states so as to guide future interactions are the things we come to call 'matter'.

Those events whose rhythms connect with the circumstances and affairs of our own lives take on a kind of symbolic reference, and such references provide a network of meaning. Although we tend to objectify the events in terms of their meanings for us, the events and their rhythms are not, in their continuing effects, merely to be limited to their bearing upon our own future prospects. We name events because of the way they con-

strain our lives and add a rhythm to them, yet such a naming is proleptic.[62] We construe it in terms of the way it specifies our lives into orders and rankings so as to bear on our future prospects, but such a construction is the nerve of our dealing with events in a one-sided, fallacious way. The fallacy is hypostatization.

5. TIME AND RHYTHMIC ENDURANCE

Dewey's views on time in *Experience and Nature* raised a standard that he maintained in all of his philosophical work after 1925. His later work presents novel ideas on the questions of time, but the novelty is mainly one of illustration, not of insight. Detailed implications of his theory of temporality are elaborated in *The Quest for Certainty* (delivered as the Gifford lectures in 1929), in *Art as Experience* (1934), and in his paper "Time and Individuality" (1938). Finally, in his joint work with Arthur Bentley, Dewey sought to bring a definitional accuracy to some of his main concepts about time that can only remind us of Kant's dictum that definitions belong at the end of philosophy, and not at the beginning as in mathematics.

In *The Quest for Certainty*, Dewey criticizes the traditional aesthetic and moral approaches to philosophy. The quest for certainty grows out of an emphasis upon past experience in our aesthetic and moral attitudes, and is fallacious. The aesthetic attitude is appropriate toward what is given to us as complete, but the experimental attitude, stressing control as it does, treats data as incomplete. Experiment is the most vital form of experience, and treats data proleptically, as signs for some future form of experience. Past meanings tend to become unimportant: "Everything in qualitative objects except their happening is ignored."[63] Only temporal qualities, the unnameable, indescribable qualities of existential process, are to be grasped. These temporal factors are referred back to the process in which they are seated as signs of happenings, and are not in the first place exploited as meanings for moral guidance in our world. Nevertheless, because a second phase of inquiry bears on the relations between events, the ordering devices of space and time are introduced. Although they include references to time, these ordering devices are themselves timeless. They are epiphenomena, and are dependent upon the histories, affairs, and moving complexes in nature for their effectiveness. What we might treat as an absolute matrix of space, time, and motion is really only secondary. The matrix, the set of ordering relations, provides us with a schema for translating our attention from one complex of events to another, but it is not itself an inherent feature of events.

Dewey introduced some implications of the then-new relativity theory into his interpretive framework. He thought that Einstein's work helped undercut the doctrines of Galileo and Newton that accepted the spatio-temporal order as an inherent feature of the world of nature. Einstein's work "signified that physical time designates a *relation* of events, not the inherent property of objects."[64] The objects of nature, Dewey thought, are themselves complexes of events. Temporal quality of an unnameable sort is a first mark of such event-complexes. Temporal order is simply super-added when an experiencing mind is present, whose own eventual nature is rhythmically ordered by what then become objects for that mind. In denying the subject-object dualism and in replacing it with a kind of inter-action between event-complexes marked with temporal quality, Dewey asserted:

> The new center is indefinite interactions taking place within a course of nature which is not fixed and complete, but which is capa-ble of direction to new and different results through the mediation of intentional operations. Neither self nor world, neither soul nor na-ture (in the sense of something isolated and finished in its isolation) is the center, any more than either earth or sun is the absolute center of a single universal and necessary frame of reference. There is a moving whole of interacting parts; a center emerges wherever there is effort to change them in a particular direction.[65]

The real world, Dewey is saying, is thoroughly caught up in relative non-being. It is a changing complex of strains of becoming in different phases. It is perhaps this kind of notion that leads some scholars to speak of a *new* Copernican revolution in Dewey's thought.

In setting out the distinction between temporal quality and temporal order, Dewey made some changes in terminology when he refracted his temporalist philosophy through the domain of aesthetic experience. One way to emphasize that form or structure is simply a more enduring kind of change is to speak of form as a rhythmic order inherent in change and variation.[66] The temporalizing device of speaking of form as rhythm was carried through by Dewey in *Art as Experience* (1934). A decade had inter-vened between the chief works setting out a theory of nature and those giv-ing an aesthetic philosophy. In *Experience and Nature*, the chapter on art does not use the idea of rhythm, whereas rhythm is a key term in *Art as Experience*, Dewey's main work on aesthetics. This latter volume allows us to see the full implications of the theory of reality scaled to a tempo-ralistic ground-plan.

Time and space as absolutes, in the Newtonian sense, do not exist. This

much is averred by all of the classical American philosophers, Dewey included. Absolute time and space are hypostatizations carried out by experiencing subjects who superimpose upon nature the fixities of a kind of moral experience exacted of us by religious interests. Temporality, Dewey counters in *Art as Experience*, is concrete endurance: "Time as empty does not exist; time as an entity does not exist. What exists are things acting and changing, and a constant quality of their behavior is temporal." The endurance that things and events display is reflective of the equilibrium that holds across temporalities, an equilibrium the experiencing subject construes as form: "Form is arrived at whenever a stable, even though moving, equilibrium is reached. Changes interlock and sustain one another. Wherever there is this coherence there is endurance."[67] Form is seen as coherent process, and coherent process is seen as rhythmic endurance.

Dewey expressed the notion of form as temporal rhythm, in opposition to some philosophers who held the substantialist view of time. Where they saw time as endless, uniform flow, or as sequences of point-instants, Dewey saw temporality as a feature of both nature and art, "as the organized and organizing medium of the rhythmic ebb and flow of expectant impulse, with fulfillment and consummation."[68] When perceived as rhythm, he elaborated, time is organized change, or growth, and "growth signifies that a varied series of changes enters upon intervals of pause and rest; of completions that become the initial points of new processes of development." In light of this view that form is temporal, a kind of rhythmic ebb and flow, Dewey developed his aesthetics so as to avoid that quondam classification which divided the arts into those of space and time. Such a division, he held, "denies rhythm to architectural structures, statues, and painting, and symmetry to song, poetry, and eloquence." Our actual world is temporal, enduring through its rhythms with their primordial temporal quality, and characterized by hazard and relative stability. In this burgeoning affair of affairs that reality is, "moments of fulfillment punctuate experience with rhythmically enjoyed intervals."[69] The world is an affair of affairs, a rhythm of rhythms, where the more enduring equilibriums can set the pitch for the less enduring.

Although Dewey's metaphysics of time achieved its most penetrating form in *Experience and Nature*, he attained full awareness of the significance of the problem of time in the lecture "Time and Individuality," which he contributed in 1938 to the James Arthur Foundation series at New York University. The series was published as *Time and Its Mysteries* in 1940. In his contribution to the series, Dewey held that time had become the central problem of philosophy. Indeed, he thought that the rela-

tion of the problem of time to the ideas of development or evolution is the most fundamental issue in philosophy at present.[70] He preferred, however, to move away from the liberal or progressive nuances associated with the idea of development, because the implication of that idea is that there is a change for the better, an unfolding of potentialities toward moral and rational preferences. Instead, he wanted to relate the idea of time to the idea of individuality. That denial and that affirmation, accordingly, is lodged in the title of his address. For individuals are concrete, plural, in various stages of process or passage, and thus are either evolving or devolving. They are caught up in the hazards of appearance and disappearance.

In the Arthur Foundation series on the mysteries of time, Dewey mainly reiterates views that he had worked out during his tenure at Columbia University. There is the familiar thrust that time and change are considered inferior aspects of experience because of moral rationalizations with their attendant quest for certainty. There is also the historical observation that Bergson and James had helped to dislodge change from the periphery of philosophical issues and install it at the center. Their ideas about flux and plurality presage his own stress upon time and individuality. He noted that Whitehead equated process and reality, and had introduced a new version of Heracliteanism. From such a rich gathering of historically based premises, Dewey drew up the thesis that genuine time is "all one with the existence of individuals, with the creature, with the occurrence of unpredictable novelties."[71] Such a thesis carries with it the implicit denial that essential aspects of human individuality, such as the self, could be in time without time being in them.

Individuals are events, Dewey held in this 1938 address. The events are not, however, like point-instants but have a temporal spread. They are life histories, so they are extensive events.[72] They overlap with what has gone before and they are vectors for transmitting the more rhythmic, enduring features into the future. Temporal sequence is the very essence of human individuals. Human individuals do not *have* histories while themselves remaining essentially unchanged; they *are* histories. But if such a view seems clear enough, it seems equally clear that individual physical entities are not very much like historical events. They seem fully ontic, finished and complete. This apparent dualism, Dewey thought, was part of the problem of time. But there could be movement from both sides toward resolving the differences between human individuals and individual physical entities. We have already seen how Dewey held that temporal order does not give a sufficient account of time in human affairs, for temporal order includes relations, and relations are timeless. Temporal quality—or "genuine time" as he called it in "Time and Individuality"—is

more basic than temporal order. So the primary movement to overcome the apparent dualism between human and physical individualities occurs on the other side, on the physical side. For Dewey showed that temporal quality and historicity are features that twentieth-century physics was increasingly attributing to physical entities.[73] The objects disclosed by physics were essentially relational, with time as a fourth dimension. This meant to Dewey that properties of "objects" are not attributes of substances, but are aspects of relations between natural, rhythmically enduring complexes. *Qualia* are expressions of the interdependence and compossibility of natural complexes. Dewey's use of the nonrealist doctrine of internal relations in this manner can only have been supported by two leading interpreters of modern physics, Arthur Eddington and Alfred N. Whitehead.

What saved Dewey—if there was a threat at all—from immersion in the Eddington/Whitehead approach was the probabilistic interpretation he brought to an understanding of physical qualities and the statistical laws summarizing them. This would redress any idealist tendencies by recourse to relations that are external in at least some respects. The subject matter of science is comprised of the tendencies to enduring relations between natural complexes, each of which has its own quality, its own urgency, for a while. For these natural individualities are extended events surrounded by a causal spread (statistically speaking). Dewey concluded that Heisenberg's principle of uncertainty or indeterminacy was a generalization upon the interpenetration of natural events, and the shifting cluster of properties that was supported by a web of rhythmic relations between events.

Thus, both human and physical individuals are events. Each individual is a history whose future condition cannot be deduced from its past conditions. There is real transformation, and not mere rearrangement. Time enters into the nature of all things and affairs, both human and physical. Time is inherent in them and comprises essential marks of their individuality. The principle of a developing career applies to all things in nature.[74] But the potentiality is, he added, a non-Aristotelian sense of potentiality, for there is no fixed end. Dewey's new category of potentiality includes an indeterminacy sense: what is potential is a consequence of interactions— the potency arises from external influences.[75] It is an ad hoc potentiality, and the question must be raised as to whether this so changes the meaning of potentiality that some other expression should be used, such as interaction or transaction. At any rate, Dewey concluded that time is a mystery, "the mystery of the existence of real individuals."[76] Their qualitative uniqueness includes the urgency of temporal quality that contributes to creative development but also enhances degenerative processes with all of

their accompanying fear and sorrow. We may recall that James's philosophy of time *ended* on a note of mystery.

6. SOME DEFINITIONS FOR A TEMPORALIST PHILOSOPHY

In the 1949 volume written with Arthur Bentley, *Knowing and the Known*, Dewey spoke of using the transactional approach, one that goes beyond the self-actional and interactional viewpoints. The self-actional approach holds "where things are viewed as acting under their own powers"; the interactional approach is "where thing is balanced against thing in causal interaction."[77] In the transactional mode of knowing, however, an investigator names and describes aspects and phases of action, and resists attributing properties to isolable entities or essences. Dewey applied this transactional approach to naming and describing temporality and space-time. The transactional viewpoint "demands that statements be made as descriptions of events in terms of durations in time and areas in space. It excludes assertions of fixity and attempts to impose them." The description requires a basic tetradic relation R (a, b, c, d). Lest their readers entirely miss their point, Dewey and Bentley provided a more explicit orientation in the body of their treatise. In discussing the word 'substance', they said "no word of this type has place in the present system of formulation." 'Entity', they went on, was a tricky word and serious inquirers would not use it.[78]

The definitions of terms in *Knowing and the Known* are typically quite complex. They are always at least triadic in structure, and often enough tetradic so as to conform to the ideal of a transactional approach. The relations in these definitions hold between 'aspects', not between 'terms' or 'relata'. One aspect in these relational definitions is always temporal, for Dewey and Bentley thought that time variables are essential aspects of knowing and what is known. Fact-Event-Designation is one system, not a dual or triple organization.[79] It is a single complex relation that is itself a natural fact. Dewey's reference here to 'event' was one that meant time-space complexes: " 'Event' involves in normal use the extensional and the durational." Affairs and happenings are somewhere and somewhen.

An interesting feature of this epistemological approach is the reciprocity and mutuality set up between the aspects in such relations. "Knowing and the known, event and designation—the full knowledge—go forward together. Eventuation is observed."[80] With such an approach, all aspects are aspectual and eventual. But this result has an unexpected implication. If all features or elements in these complexes of knowings-knowns are

eventual or aspectual—as the transactional approach required—then any aspect is specified into subsenses of itself through the medium of the others. Significantly, this introduces a degree of self-reference in all epistemological statements.

Dewey and Bentley did not eschew this unexpected result. Rather, they openly embraced it. "When we said above that designations are events and events designations, we adopted *circularity*—procedure in a circle—openly, explicitly, emphatically."[81] How little sympathy Dewey had for positivist approaches and how much residual empathy he had for idealism, can be seen in this truculent assertion that foundation statements in epistemology are circular. Temporal aspects, moreover, are always to be understood as registered in these complex, self-referential statements.

Aside from the importance of such formulations for Dewey's logic and epistemology, their implications for regularizing his metaphysical constructions concern us here. The philosophical dictionary-making by Dewey and Bentley introduced the following kinds of conventions:

> Events will be differentiated with respect to a certain range of plasticity that is comparable in a general way to the physical differentiations of gaseous, liquid and solid. For these we shall use the names Situation, Occurrence and Object. As for Designation, we shall organize it in an evolutionary scheme of behavioral sign processes of which it is one form, the names we apply being Sign, Signal, Name and Symbol.[82]

They are asserting here that 'event' is the generic term, and that situations, occurrences, and objects are species or subsets of the genus, event: "We may now proceed to distinguish Situation, Occurrence and Object as forms of Event. Event is durational-extensional; it is what 'takes place,' what is inspected as 'a taking place.' " Thus, an event is bipolar, a space-time complex. Event is most generic, and points at temporal quality. A situation is the way an event appears to us if we consider features of the surrounding environment of objects, or if we see objects transactionally as specifications within a complex. The differentia that the authors use to distinguish occurrence from object is exhibited with the help of a functional psychology: "When an event is of the type that is readily observable in transition within the ordinary spans of human discrimination of temporal and spatial changes, we shall call it an *occurrence*." Objects differ from occurrences in falling outside the scope of normal perceptual attention.[83]

The transactional approach to the understanding of events, Dewey believed, was related to developments in modern physics. Newtonian

physics had perfected the interactional approach with its absolute, space-time matrix. But Clerk Maxwell had already used 'transaction' in describing events in the physical world. Einstein had brought space-time itself into the realm of events that were to be studied. Space-time was a topical, empirical feature that changed with energy fields. Physics, Dewey and Bentley added in an expansive mood, is "the most potent of all existing sciences."[84]

One additional point about the joint work of these two authors must be made. In the later portions of *Knowing and the Known*, they broke away from a convention about the use of 'event' which had been reached in the volume's early sections. Dewey and Bentley now modify their early recommendations.[85] 'Existence' will replace 'event' as the generic term, and 'event' will be used as a specific form of existence. 'Event' will replace 'occurrence' in those contexts where 'occurrence' was to have been used. If followed rigorously in all of his work, this last terminological convention would require Dewey to restate some central positions he had reached in his metaphysics during the previous two decades.

The impetus for redoing 'event'—so that it is rather more humanized, more a feature of "ordinary spans of human discrimination"—probably came from Bentley, even though Dewey must have accepted it for inclusion in *Knowing and the Known*. For in a letter to Bentley in 1944, Dewey had said: "I think 'event' is a better basic word than 'existence'; 'e-vent' [is derived from, and conveys the sense of, its Latin root]: comes out of and goes into."[86] But 'existence', Dewey continues, was more static as a word. In addition, in a 1947 letter, Dewey told Bentley that "the transaction/interaction business" was an axis of his thought since he had gotten to know Bentley.[87] Thus, the transactional approach, with its attendant linguistic conventions, seems less organic to Dewey's views on time. The fact that the two authors had changed their designation for 'event' within the confines of a single book suggests that Dewey had not assimilated the implications of a full-blown transactional approach for a temporalist philosophy.

7. SOME CONCLUSIONS

The systematic character of Dewey's temporalist philosophy is exhibited in the manner in which he elaborated, in many different sectors of his thought, the fundamental conviction that temporal quality is a generic trait of all the world's constituents. Each existent, whether thing or person, partakes of the nature of an event. It gathers together in a rhythmic unity

a diversity of traits and activities so as to attain a relatively finished pattern as it interacts with its surroundings. Mobiles, those often elaborate artistic devices that enhance the decorative quality of well-designed rooms, are fitting images for suggesting the unique quality Dewey ascribed to things that endured in the natural world: each of them is a balanced tension of moving parts and changing features actively organized into a unified, harmonious ensemble. Living and enduring is an art, and living intelligently and compassionately is a consummate art. Augmenting this conception of a natural unity-in-diversity was an accompanying denial: there is no kind of transcendent or eternal realm that lies beyond nature and is only fitfully revealed in nature's moving images. Temporal quality, in the end, penetrates every aspect of existence. Existence is fully eventual.

An analogical argument in three stages traverses the entirety of Dewey's philosophical production. His point of departure for the argument was his skepticism of the eternal in either of its two forms: as an eternally changeless *now* that somehow comprises all reality within its scope, or as an eternally changing *then* that constitutes a perpetual, ordered fluxing of the material world. Instead, he attended to moving centers of temporal quality, each of them unique in its accomplished work. In its outcome, this was to be no philosophy *sub specie aeternitatis*.

In the first step of his argument, Dewey found such active, growing centers in the new psychology of his day. This psychology was progressively eroding one of the mainstays of Western psychology and metaphysics: the changeless self or transcendental ego. That more traditional self was replaced with a living, appetitive center having unique temporal quality and finitude. When the idealistic sources through which he had received his first philosophical nourishment could no longer empower the burgeoning empirical findings and experimental successes of the new psychology, Dewey supplanted these sources with naturalistic and realistic conceptions of the self as an integrating center of living activity. From Leibniz and James and Peirce did Dewey learn that there is life after absolute idealism.

In the second step of his temporalist argument, Dewey pursued the implications of his redrawn picture of the psyche by constructively aligning it with the new center of inquiry in biological science: the Darwinian theory of biological evolution. This theory provided an account of those once-successful species that disappeared because they progressively misread their experience; and of the appearance of the human species whose adaptive abilities were enhanced by the socializing functions of a shared language and the instrumentation of its generalizing concepts. The evolution within the psyche discerned by Leibniz and the functional psycholo-

gists was now seen by Dewey as part of a larger evolutionary development within the whole of nature. Physical evolution empowered biological evolution, which was patient of social evolution, which enhanced the development of the individual.

Based on this account, the human species can develop an experimentally grounded knowledge of the natural world, because nature has antecedently "created" humankind and has stamped its *imago* into humans through a series of natural modifications. The periodicities of nature find their echo in the rhythmic complexities of the human psyche. If the psyche, so understood, is fully naturalized in a world of changing states, so too could that world be sampled accurately through its most accessible product, human experience. This is no small part of the meaning of Dewey's view that psychology can provide us with an effective philosophical methodology. Such a methodological conclusion also underwrote what Dewey came to call *the* philosophical fallacy: confusing consequences with the causes of those consequences. The self for him is not a transcendent agency that *causes* us to have experiences. Rather, what we call self is an outgrowth of the transactions that arise amidst adaptive events within that experience. The eternal is not a primordial cause for Dewey but is pale consequence, an attenuated version of the rhythm of events. Temporal quality is a primordial feature in his scheme, and temporal order arises from it as the result of social conventions within linguistic activity. This temporal order, in its turn, is finally transfixed in the conception of the eternal. Thus would Dewey accept Leibniz's conviction that time is nearer to the eternal than to the temporal. He was not thereby ennobling the concept of time, but was calling attention to the problem of properly tracing time back to its basal perception—temporal quality. Dewey has followed James and, behind James, Hume in this empirical understanding of the origin of the concept of time as temporal order.

For Dewey, following the Darwinian clue, the "ego" knows the "world" because an earlier version of the natural order of things has actively brought about a living experience of which the natural psyche and the world of things are correlative products. The self is the issue of harmonious, adaptive transactions between different event gradients. With the substitution of the directives of the theory of biological evolution for the guidance of the Absolute Spirit or for a divinely ordained preestablished harmony, Dewey was able to project the directives of the newly naturalized psychology into his metaphysics of nature. Evolution provided him with a causeway between his accounts of psyche and of nature.

Hence the third step of Dewey's temporalism: the time-imbued configurations he assigns to nature are the functional patterns he first secured

in psychology. The concept of rhythm first detailed in his psychology be-comes the justification for his view that nature is indeed precarious, but is nevertheless stable. It is always a problem for a temporalist philosophy to include a suitable account of the stable or lasting traits of things. If some-thing changes, what is the seat of change? Dewey temporalized the sub-stance/attribute conception that lies behind our normal conviction that if there is change, there must be something that changes. For him, if there is a happening, then there is an event complex that is undergoing change. He substitutes differential rates of change for substance and attribute, with 'substance' referring to those events that change more slowly. Dewey sought to give definitional status to such a conception in his joint work with Bentley.

One outstanding difficulty in Dewey's temporalist philosophy can be noted. This difficulty is implied more neatly in his *New Republic* article of 1922, "Events and Meanings," than in any of his other writings on the na-ture of time. Briefly, the difficulty is that what he takes to be *most real* or most natural as a feature of all things—temporal quality—is *least impor-tant* as a feature of the temporal orders within which human value is achieved. To be human is to give events meaning, regardless of the fact that they might be meaningless in themselves. We give events meaning by thinking about them and conversing about them, thereby lifting ourselves above their remorseless, dumb passage. What we call time, or temporal order, arises as the result of these acts of thoughtful conversation. By their means, we can to some slight degree bend or rechannel events somewhat nearer to our heart's desire, and thereby achieve satisfactions and create values where none previously existed. By acting as a catalyst in a natural stream of happenings, humans create distinctively human lives. "Think-ing about events and celebrating them in tone and color and form might become more important than being an event."[88] If we abstain from experi-ences of temporal quality in order to moderate the powers of temporality, we create the human scene with its temporal orders and its consummatory values. In short, what is most remote from the generative powers of nature and is least real or least natural, becomes for Dewey most important for the achievement of value. Temporal quality is more natural than temporal order, and less valuable because it is so powerful, so overwhelming. We must escape it or abstain from it in order to achieve human value. In turn, what we call time or temporal order arises out of the foundational element, temporal quality, but is most important for humans. "Apart from conver-sation, from discourse and communication, there is no thought and no meaning, only just events, dumb, preposterous, destructive."[89]

Why—we must address the question to Dewey's view of the nature and

significance of time—is there this opposition between what is most real or natural and what is most valuable? Why must we be saved from mere events, buffeted to pieces in their midst? Why should we seek to save ourselves from that which is most primordial, most foundational? A philosophy which visits such a paradox upon us surely needs to be reworked in important ways.

Whitehead and
Temporal Extension

THE most disciplined view of time worked out by any major American philosopher during the classical period was exhibited in the work of Alfred North Whitehead. The greater discipline shown in his views is due in part to his investigations in physics and mathematics, which he carried out during a long professional career in England. His work was steadily influenced by relativity conceptions of the space-time continuum, and he is the only classical American philosopher to have carried out his speculations under the impress of an important non-Einsteinian interpretation of relativity theory which he developed himself. Although many of Whitehead's books and papers on the questions of time and space appeared during his years in England, where he taught mathematics and physics and was heavily invested in educational administration, the philosophical works for which he is best known were produced on North American shores. Certainly his stature as a philosopher is based upon the entirety of his teaching and literary activity in a career which reached its consummation in the United States. John Dewey alone can perhaps be said to have had more influence upon professional circles and the wider public in the United States than Whitehead.

During his extended professional career in England, Whitehead's philosophy of time was principally focused upon spatiotemporal continuity. Because diversities and discontinuities were taken for granted, the task he set himself was to explain the appearance of continuous extension and all its subalterns of smooth, abstract time and space. Had he written nothing after the 1919–23 materials which set out his philosophy of science, we

would have no important basis for distinguishing his emphasis upon continuous extension and the whole/part relations within it from, say, Peirce's emphasis upon time as the archetype of all continua. But it was Whitehead's very empiricism which led him to find in the *disjecta membra* of concrete experience the true germ and first root "of something far more deeply interfused" that was of a processual nature. After that, and during his American period, a certain processual connectivity was taken as primitive, and his new task was to explain the discontinuous and dispersive aspects of experience. Hence does he turn to setting out an epochal theory of time and passage. The approach he began to take after coming to North America emphasized discontinuity and perishing with about as much weight as, but probably no more than, the earlier approach had stressed continuity and becoming.

Our approach to Whitehead's philosophy of time is broadly divided to reflect this double beat in his work. In this chapter, with its emphasis upon his early investigations—which led to a new concept of nature stressing temporal and spatial extensity—we see him assembling one after another the elements that enter into his final constructions. In the following chapter, we see the senses in which he makes good his claim that his new concept of nature provides a vestibule for another kind of metaphysics. In this wider domain, a different view of time is sculpted, the epochal view. He vacated the first perspective and occupied the second as he came to see that continuity does not betoken actuality, but signifies potentiality in one of its guises. It is discontinuity that typifies the realm of the actual, a fact reflected in his epochal theory of time.

I. A MATHEMATICAL PROLOGUE

In the years between 1905 and 1917, Whitehead published some ten different studies which bear upon the notions of time and space, though often enough they treated such notions as asides in projects scaled to educational or mathematical tasks. Three of these studies were almost exclusively of a mathematical nature, four more comprised his presidential addresses to assorted educational assemblies, and the remainder were philosophical analyses of scientific conceptions. Taken as a group, these papers exhibit several salient characteristics: that otherwise straightforward ideas are presented as embedded in quite complex sets of relations; that space and time are presented as analogues, with the spatial characteristics most fully elaborated; that an initial dominance of spatial concepts is redressed into a clear dominance of temporal conceptions; and that the question of the relationship between the continuous structures of thought-time and the dis-

continuous modalities of the stream or flux of sense-time becomes ever more insistent. We shall organize our consideration of Whitehead's early studies around these characteristic themes.

In his *Dialogues of Alfred North Whitehead*, Lucien Price records Whitehead asserting that "I do not think in words. I begin with concepts, then try to put them into words, which is often very difficult."[1] By 'concepts' Whitehead apparently meant his way of grasping as a unified whole an entire configuration of entities and properties enclosed in relations of a fairly high order. He seemed to be able to visualize such patterns at a stroke in acts of nonverbal thinking, patterns which he then struggled to display under the limiting conditions of definitions, descriptions, and expository English. If we were to speak of the Ruy Lopez or the Queen's Gambit Declined, with all of their initial variations, as different concepts of chess openings, we would approximate upon Whitehead's use of 'concepts' in his remarks to Lucien Price. The term 'concepts' is used in this extended configurational sense in his 1905 memoir, "On Mathematical Concepts of the Material World." He is not so much combining concepts as abstract ideas into different pictures of the world, but rather is articulating into prominence features implicit in an intuited whole. Thus, his concepts arise as finished products of acts of analysis.

In his preface to the 1905 memoir, Whitehead clearly stated that the mathematical concepts of the material world must include references to time. Temporal features are essential because the physical world is undergoing change, and the new definitions of dimensions in space would control the more adequate theories of change presented in the concepts:

> The object of this memoir is to initiate the mathematical investigation of various possible ways of conceiving the nature of the physical world. In view of the existence of change in the physical world, the investigation has to be so conducted as to introduce, in its abstract form, the idea of time, and to provide for the definition of velocity and acceleration. . . . The main object of the memoir is the development of the theory of Interpoints, of the Theory of Dimensions, and of Concept V. The other parts are explanatory and preparatory to these.[2]

As Ivor LeClerc has noted, Whitehead's problems were cosmological during this period.[3]

In all, Whitehead discussed six concepts of the material world, displayed under five main headings. Common to all concepts is the fact that each is a cluster of categorial or entitative elements called 'ultimate existents'. These are set into patterns by certain relational or connective ele-

ments called 'fundamental relations'. The ultimate existents comprise the totality of elements present in the fields of the fundamental relations. Time—perceived in the abstract as made up of instants—occurs in each of these patterned wholes. It occurs once as a member of the class of ultimate existents—along with certain other entities or 'objective reals', like points or particles—and occurs also as a one-dimensional series with a dyadic order akin to that of the order of the real numbers. In either of these two guises, time is presented in a way that is commonplace in the science at the turn of the century. The idea that time is a series makes possible a mathematical treatment of the changes that occur in the physical world.

The first three categorial/relational complexes, or concepts I, II, and III, are called 'punctual concepts' by Whitehead, because the field of the essential relation in each concept contains points as simple entities. Concept I is the classical dualistic concept of Newtonian science where the objective reals are (1) points and (2) particles. The instants at which particles occupy points are ultimate existents but are not thereby objective reals. Concept II is a variant of concept I worked out by Bertrand Russell, where particles are discarded. Introducing particles was a concession to sense experience, giving the senses something to perceive. But if relations can be perceived, as Russell, James, and Peirce all believed, then a concept of the material world comprised of essential relations between points in space and instants of time would suffice. Concept III is a monistic variant of the classical Newtonian scheme where essential use of the notion of activity is introduced in a special way. That is, points are set in motion. They do not move *at* instants, but *through* instants. A more dynamic world concept is thereby obtained. Common to all three concepts is a spatial presupposition: points are objectively real for each. Hence the designation that they are 'punctual concepts'.

By way of contrast, the other three categorial/relational complexes, concepts IVa, IVb, and V, are referred to as 'linear concepts' by Whitehead, because the field of the essential relation in each concept contains lines as simple entities, following the fashion of projective geometry.[4] In these three concepts, the points are derivative, as classes of lines. The lines are lines of force or direction, and form the ether lying between corpuscles of matter. For the linear concepts, the problem of action at a distance would simply disappear. Continuity between regions is no problem at all, but how to account for separateness or atomicity of discrete states becomes a problem. Concept V, which Whitehead thought the most interesting of all the concepts, whether punctual or linear, had as its essential relation a five-term or pentadic relation.[5] The relation has as its field of ultimate existents both instants of time and linear objective reals, i.e., lines as directed

forces are taken as primitive. The formula for the essential relation of concept V, which Whitehead also considered to be a monistic Leibnizian concept, is expressed as R; $(abcdt)$. This expression is interpreted to mean that the linear element a intersects the linear elements b, c, and d, in the order bcd, at the instant t. Significantly, for this concept, the points in space are derivative, and relations between such points are extraneous, not essential. Moreover, the particles of matter are also derivative and the nature assigned them is inessential, not to be taken as a literal transcript of reality.

Geometrical propositions are to be defined anew when perceived in terms of these different concepts of the material world. Whitehead defines such propositions in terms of spatial *and temporal* properties: "A proposition of geometry is any proposition (1) concerning the essential relation; (2) involving one, and only one, instant of time; (3) true for any instant of time."[6] By means of such a definition, Whitehead set up an intersection between what he called the geometric and the chronometric sciences.

The following characteristics of concept V should be kept before us in all that follows, as buoys which helped mark the channels of his mature thought:[7] time is a necessary feature of a scientific concept of the physical world; space, in terms of an organized assemblage of linear objective reals, is a connected whole; and the minimum complexity required for an adequate description of the material world, signalized by the formula R; $(abcdt)$, is a spatiotemporal interplay of elements that runs somewhat beyond the normal descriptive power of the English language. Whitehead grew exceedingly cautious in his judgments about the effectiveness of natural languages for describing the world, because of their limited power to present factors in relations.

A distinction Whitehead made in *The Axioms of Projective Geometry* (1906) should be appended to these remarks about the 1905 memoir. The axioms of geometry are "statements about relations between points." These points, significantly, have no special kind of being:

> These points mentioned in the axioms are not a special determinate class of entities; but they are in fact any entities whatever, which happen to be interrelated in such a manner, that the axioms are true when they are considered as referring to those entities and their interrelations. Accordingly—since the class of points is indeterminate —the axioms are not propositions at all: they are propositional functions.[8]

But Whitehead's point can be generalized. *None* of the ultimate existents has metaphysical significance. Points, instants, particles, lines: all are variables that need existence theorems or metaphysical statements to em-

body them. Points and instants are deceptively simple because they have no real content. Something that has real content lies behind and tends toward them as a convergence to simplicity. By themselves, points and instants are high-level abstractions, and to take them as real is to hypostatize variables.

As it turned out, Whitehead believed that instants and points are instantiated through the human body, i.e., through experience, a belief set out in his classic survey, *An Introduction to Mathematics* (1911). In an argument reminiscent of Kant's deduction of some of the characteristics of space from the orientation of perceiving subjects,[9] Whitehead held that we organize the entirety of the world event or universe around our own personal space. The 'o' of arbitrary origin at the intersection of the geometrical axes of ordinate and abscissa is a highly abstract notion. "But in relation to the application of mathematics to the event of the Universe we are here symbolizing with direct simplicity the most fundamental fact respecting the outlook on the world afforded to us by our senses."[10] To our own "here," to the neighborhood of our own place, all of our anticipations are referred and related. To explore the universe is to group its topology around our own special *topos*.

Our place can be taken as a datum for orienting vectors and establishing periodicities.[11] Our bodily life includes a sophisticated array of periodicities—breathings, heartbeats, and so on. Although these periodicities reveal comparatively rapid variations when set alongside more stable recurrences such as tides, seasons, and the motions of the solar system, they nevertheless provide us with a ground of contrasts for noting that some recurrences and periodicities fall within the intervals of others. A sense of interlocking periodicities is the key to measuring time. Days, months, years: these intervals are marked off by different kinds of periodic change, and at the beginning of civilization provided distinct time measures. Whitehead believed that it was a first task of science in civilized nations "to fuse them into one coherent measure." Their internal consistency, and also their connectedness with the time of the observer, must be established. "The broad fact remains that the uniform flow of time on which so much is based is itself dependent on the observation of periodic events."[12]

If our understanding of the universe must somehow be referred to our own bodily experiences, then it is our sheer presence in a spatial sense that becomes fundamental. That we occupy a locus establishes the prime datum for relating ourselves to other occurrences and other places. The *spaciness* of space must be directly apprehended.[13] For Whitehead, this immediate purchase upon space is to be referred to a network of relatively stable bodily happenings. He thought that the practical importance of

space in setting up our scientific concepts of the material world was clear and evident:

> On the one hand, our space-perceptions are intertwined in our various sensations and connect them together. We normally judge that we touch an object in the same place as we see it; and even in abnormal cases we touch it in the same space as we see it, and this is the real fundamental fact which ties together our various sensations. Accordingly, the space perceptions are in a sense the common part of our sensations.[14]

Aside from the emphasis Whitehead put upon space as the fundament for grounding our knowledge of the physical world, his image recalls a theme of the Clarke-Leibniz correspondence having to do with Newton's metaphor that space is the sensorium of God. Space perception is the common, bonding feature of the sensorium of a perceiving subject, though in this case a human and not a divine subject. Space for Whitehead is something of a common sense, like Aristotle's sixth sense, that organizes the data of the particular senses, such as the data of sight and touch in his own example.

When perception affords us similar combinations of data bound together in a common space, we speak of a recurrence. If they occur together again and again, then we speak of a periodicity. Thus does the idea of time arise. "Our perception of the flow of time and of the succession of events is a chief example of the application of these ideas of quantity. We measure time (as has been said in considering periodicity) by the repetition of similar events. . . . Events of these types take the place of the footrule in relation to lengths." The prerequisite for arriving at a common social time is the formulation of rules for positioning some durations as parts of other durations. Such rules must agree with common sense, they must tend toward allowing an economical set of natural laws, and they must allow parallels between abstract mathematical time and the concrete episodic time that is a feature of our sensations and perceptions.[15] But importantly, to the degree that there is change, there apparently must be a seat of change. Recurrence in time, at this point in the development of Whitehead's philosophy, seems to require the compresence of properties in a space centered around a perceiving subject.

In *An Introduction to Mathematics,* space and time are dealt with in such a way that the notion of space is given the leading role in Whitehead's analogies, with conclusions drawn that exhibit similar properties for time. Moreover, the argument goes beyond the 1905 memoir, "Mathematical Concepts of the Material World." It includes perceptions by subjects among the entities that must be related by the essential relations. This pre-

figures a concern with epistemological questions manifest in the short essays of 1915–17. To move beyond the science of geometry to the science of dynamics, points, instants, and particles must be seen in relation to bodily sensations. Another study published about the same time, "The Mathematical Curriculum" (1913), expands upon two of the themes in *An Introduction to Mathematics*. Whitehead holds that mathematics cannot play its proper role in a liberal education if it is left in its recondite condition. In a liberal education, mathematics is to be demystified so as to remove its obscurities and to aid us in handling abstract ideas.[16] It must be related to our experiences. The educator in mathematics should set up those Baconian middle axioms that allow the mind to move easily from the concrete here and now to the abstractions of mathematics, without getting lost. Thus does Whitehead announce an educational strategy for mathematics that comes to fruition a few years later in the method of extensive abstraction, a method that is to allow sure passage from more immediate experiences of extension and duration to their limiting conceptions in points and instants.

A second theme that is developed further is the primacy of spatial experience in our perceptions. Mathematics deals fundamentally with the relations of number, quantity, and space. In dealing with space, geometry exhibits features that tie into experience more clearly than does algebra. The field of study in algebra is more abstract because of its treatment of discontinuous elements, whereas geometry handles space and the relations between spatial continuities. "Space is an obvious insistent thing to all."[17] It is evident to us because we constantly refer places in space to our own special here or "almost here." Whitehead, we speculate, had to overcome this predilection for spatial experience before he could see that continuity dealt with the realm of the possible and not the actual, and thus be prepared for developing an atomic or epochal theory of time.

2. SOME PRELIMINARIES ON SPACE AND TIME

Whitehead had argued in *An Introduction to Mathematics* that a first task of science in societies was to devise a uniform time scale or metric. But precisely how can the different approaches to time be blended into such a unified whole? In a paper entitled "La Théorie Relationniste de l'Espace," which he read at a 1914 Paris congress on mathematical philosophy, Whitehead identified the problem of time as one of creating a common time. It arises as the analogue of the question about the relation of distinct spaces to a single common space. Four kinds of space are specified in this paper. Two are versions of the apparent, phenomenal space that is related

to perceivers, and the other two are versions of physical space, the space of a hypothetical, abstract world. Regarding the former, we have (1) immediate apparent space comprised of the numerous fragmentary spaces of individual perceivers, and (2) complete apparent space, the total space of a social world, wherein distinct "heres" of individual spaces are adjusted to each other. Regarding the latter, we have (3) physical space proper, and (4) abstract space. In physical space are embedded all the objects in their temporal interrelations that "correspond to" the sensations of all known perceivers.[18] Thus, these objects are also correlated with the complete apparent space of the social world.

Time enters Whitehead's discussion in relation to the idea of perception: "Perceptions result from the changing relations among physical objects occurring in a given lapse of time."[19] The vagrant, changing things which appear to perceivers are processed into what we normally call permanent physical objects. The method is that apparent objects are first correlated with events in the physical world, and then these events are correlated with objects in the physical world. The entire thrust of Whitehead's argument here relies upon events as conduits between appearances and objects: "All progress in the analysis of the physical world consists in replacing unstable objects by permanent objects. . . . Each time that such a replacement takes place, the properties of relatively complex bodies are conceived as the properties of *events*, occurring in an ensemble of more simple component parts in interaction." Because there are endlessly large numbers of immediate apparent spaces and physical spaces, it will follow that endlessly large numbers of event types connect them. Time is at least as variegated as space, according to this conception.

Finally, with regard to (4) abstract space, we note that it has a harmonizing function. Just as the complete apparent space of a social group provides a common space for unifying the indefinite number of apparent spaces of individual perceivers, so too abstract space allows us a common space for harmonizing the large number of physical spaces. It is at the conclusion of this analysis of kinds of space and the relations between them that Whitehead shows how the entire drift of the discussion throws new light upon the significance of time. Time is presented as the medium in which relations that hold in one kind of space intertwine with relations that hold in another kind of space. Whitehead presents time as a kind of adhesive that adjoins the different kinds of space without any real slippage. That is, time is the ground of connectivity in space:

> The physical world exists in time and the time of the physical world is identical with the time of the complete apparent world and [with the time of] the various immediate apparent worlds of different per-

ceiving subjects. Common time is the place in which the parallelism of the different worlds is safeguarded and made possible. It is evident that, on this point, the real problem of time is the formation of a common time for the complete apparent world, outside [that of] the different times of the immediate apparent worlds of various perceiving subjects.[20]

A common time, once arrived at, makes a common space possible, so that parallels hold from next to next. A common time, once obtained, makes possible common perceptions of events, whose interrelations are then refined into common physical objects. Such is made plain in the 1914 Paris paper. The paper also makes evident that the idea of an event is just as important as the idea of an entity, and that any discussion of time and space must very quickly move into a discussion of the nature of relations between properties that are presented in spatial and temporal dress. The whole of Whitehead's approach will turn on his delineation of the problem of time and whether he solves that problem as presented: How is common time to be formulated? F.S.C. Northrop judged that Whitehead had not answered that question in a satisfactory manner even in some of his later, more careful treatments of time and space.[21]

In his 1915 paper, "Space, Time, and Relativity," read at a Manchester section meeting of the British Association for the Advancement of Science, Whitehead returned to the problem of a common time and space. The object of his paper was to interrelate the different standpoints on space and time as they are found in the various sciences. The sciences Whitehead mentions are mathematical physics, experimental psychology, metaphysics, and mathematics. Whitehead proposed to examine the senses in which the different approaches could be said to be dealing with different aspects of a single space and time. But experience gives us things in fits and starts. All we experience is a shifting scene. Wherever infinite space came from, it was not born of experience or direct observation.[22] Thus is the stage set for the body of the paper, for where did it come from if not from experience? Four main themes are deployed from that question: (1) the origin of time and space; (2) the nature of time and space; (3) the analogy of space with time; and (4) the relativity of space and time.

With respect to (1) the question of origins, inasmuch as time and space are not directly given in experience, they must arise indirectly. Space and time are either antecedent to experience and constitute the *a priori* conditions for all sensibility (Kant's position), or they are consequent upon experience, are *a posteriori*, and are built up somehow out of the materials of experience (Locke's view). Whitehead preferred the Lockean approach, not

because the *a priori* theory had no advantages—it does allow for the "absolute universality" of spatiotemporal laws—but because the *a posteriori* or experiential theory requires of us no conditions that are not also used in the construction of the other main concepts of science. Whitehead never second-guessed his choice on the basis of an economy of methodology, and would henceforth deliberately eschew the Kantian approach he had known so well in his earlier mathematical period.[23]

If space and time are to be considered as derived from the materials of experience, then (2) what is their nature? Whitehead reflected on two main alternatives. One is the absolutist view of Newton, where points and instants are taken as self-subsistent entities. The other is the relational view of Leibniz, where points and instants are features of relations between objects and successive configurations of objects. Whitehead's discussion reproduced in the main some of the contrasts of concepts I and III of his 1905 memoir. Most of the exposition of these central issues in his 1915 Manchester paper reflected that earlier emphasis upon space, and he simply noted that the same kind of explanations apply to time. A preference for the more dynamic Leibnizean concepts of the material world is evidenced, except now the need to probe more deeply into the nature of points and instants is shown: "Before the theories of space and time have been carried to a satisfactory conclusion on the relational basis, a long and careful scrutiny of the definitions of points of space and instants of time will have to be undertaken, and many ways of effecting these definitions will have to be tried and compared. This is an unwritten chapter of mathematics. . . ."[24] But what can be done is to regard points and instants as fully correlative, so as to prepare for those deeper definitional investigations. That is, the analogy between space and time must be spelled out in greater detail.

Another theme of the paper is (3) the analogy of space and time. Underlying the more abstract domain of points and instants is the concrete, originative domain of things and events. Point is to instant as thing is to event. Things are embedded in relations that hold between the spatial extension of things; and analogously, events are grounded in relations that hold between the temporal duration or extension of events. The properties of the extension of events in time are "largely analogous" to the properties of the extension of objects in space.[25] But what, now, is the relation between these two kinds of extension? The question about their relationship, Whitehead thought, had taken on greater significance because of the theory of relativity.[26] His suggested answer at this stage was that they both exhibit features of the more primitive relation of the externality of things and events: "Extension in space and extension in time both embody and

perhaps necessitate a judgment of externality. This suggestion is very
vague and I must leave it in this crude form."[27] Whitehead's suggestion
points back to his view in *An Introduction to Mathematics*, namely, that
all of the world event is positioned around our "here" or "almost here,"
and implies perhaps that our here and now, in contrast with a there and
then, gives a sense of apartness or separation basal in all experience. But he
also could not pursue this path very far without rethinking whether space
and time might in some non-Kantian sense exist prior to all human experience. Clearly, however, Whitehead wanted to probe behind the notion of
extension and, to do greater justice to the temporal side of his analogy, find
a concept more neutral than the concept of extension.

A fourth theme he pursued in his 1915 Manchester paper turned on the
fact that an "infinity of frameworks" is as effective in determining position and motion as is the absolute framework of axes and instants used by
Newton. Inasmuch as points and instants are not directly cognized in experience, the duration of events and the location of objects cannot be
simply given, either. The concepts of mathematical time and space, in
which duration and location are registered for scientific purposes, are the
smooth conceptions of the abstract world, not the fragmentary conceptions of the experienced world. These latter experiences within the apparent world are the only elements directly given. "All speculation must
start from these *disjecta membra* as its sole datum."[28] Whitehead concludes that if the data can indeed support the superstructure of a smooth-
running world, then there must be a certain uniformity of texture within
the fragmentary apparent worlds of individual subjects.

This notion of a "uniformity of texture" seems to play the same role in
Whitehead's speculations that "pure form of sensibility" plays in Kant's
philosophy. In the supplementary notes to his paper, Whitehead treated
the idea of the uniformity of texture with some direct references to the
transcendental aesthetic of Kant. He wanted to present a new slant on the
doctrines of the transcendental aesthetic. He proposed, accordingly, that
certain holistic features of experience be caught up in his notion of the uniformity of texture. Undergirding his interpretation would be the field concepts of the great English physicists, Faraday and Maxwell, concepts never
very far from his mind. The point of his discussion of the relativity of time
and space is that we perceive a whole of parts that stand in many different
relations, and space and time are simply some of the marks of these relations. Space and time serve to highlight the uniformity of the whole of
experience, and to diminish its most fragmentary differences.

Having committed himself to an empirical methodology, the question
about the origin of the uniformity of texture in experience becomes a

critical question. The uniformity is not part of the original condition of *disjecta membra*, but is somehow disclosed at subsequent levels when the experiential features are projected toward the abstract scientific tableaus of the world. Space and time seem to be projective properties that arise as we proceed away from the centers afforded by the "here" and "now" of the individual perceiver. At subsequent, higher levels where space and time are constantly present and are permanent features of a common world, a metric can be assigned to them. Quantitative concepts based on 'all' and 'some' are fully in order in treating space and time at this level. But at the lower levels, where we are closer to the *disjecta membra* of more immediate experience, 'whole' and 'part' are the important operational notions. They are more pertinent to the original texture of experience, where ideas of order and similarity first arise. They are more suitable for expressing the "middle axioms" of the idea of extension that lie behind our smoothly domesticated space-time structures. But of critical importance to Whitehead is this: the notions of whole and part associated with immediate experience are to be kept distinct from the notions of all and some associated with physical and mathematical science. Only where points and instants are accepted as the fundamental ultimate existents (as in the absolutist view of space and time) are whole/part relations the same as all/some relations. But if extension and their relations are more fundamental than points, this interpretation that whole/part is identical with all/some is excluded.[29] The linear concepts of the material world explicated in the 1905 memoir are once again shown to be more significant to Whitehead than the punctual concepts. Developments in nineteenth-century mathematics, by Poncelet and Steiner, had helped inform Whitehead that projective geometry is more basic than metric geometries, and that both Euclidean and non-Euclidean geometry can be derived from a projective base. This attitude of probing more deeply for projective and topological features is basic to Whitehead's approach to understanding the physical world.

Significant in these early papers is the way he gradually extends this geometric approach to chronometric considerations. It is fatal, he held, to confuse whole-part relations with all-some relations.[30] It is the same as reifying the abstract levels some sciences have achieved, and we are then prevented from attending to the fundamentals of experience from which those abstractions arise as so many different perspectives: "The physical world is in some general sense of the term a deduced concept. Our problem is, in fact, to fit the world to our perceptions, and not our perceptions to the world."[31] Space and time must be traced back through the middle axioms to the basal elements of things and events. Kant's error in the transcendental aesthetic would be that he accepted some structures as absolutely prim-

itive in experience, such as the pure forms of space and time, which were in fact to be traced back to part/whole relations between objects and events in experience.

3. THE PARITY OF TIME AND SPACE

In 1916, a new emphasis is revealed in Whitehead's investigations into the nature of time and space. In his presidential address that year to the mathematical association, entitled "The Aims of Education," he presented time quite on a par with space. No longer is the basis for an analogy laid in spatial features of experience and then inferentially extended to the temporal features. Perhaps an implication of the 1914 Paris address—that time is the ground for the parallelisms between different worlds—was beginning to surface in his speculations. No longer is 'event' being treated as a substitute in some contexts for the spatial expression, 'configuration'.[32] The notions of the stream of time and the processes of change receive more attention, perhaps under the urgent press of tragedies associated with the Great War. He addressed the educators about the discovery a child will make, that "general ideas give an understanding of the stream of events which passes through his life, which is his life."[33] This identification of the life of the dawning psyche with the stream of events is a distant echo of Plotinus's view that time is the life of the soul, and finds a closer parallel in the psychology of William James. For Whitehead, the present is no longer merely a complex configuration which exhibits the perspectives that radiate out from our spatial "here," but is an importunate center of value. The present is evinced as an "insistent present," and the aim of education is to relate the knowledge of the past to it: "No more deadly harm can be done to young minds than by depreciation of the present. The present contains all that there is. It is holy ground; for it is the past, and it is the future."[34] Royce, Santayana, and Mead also saw the present as the fount of past and future.

Whitehead's well-known polemic against inert ideas and their pernicious effects devolves from the line of argument where past and future are presented as intersecting in the present. They help energize the present, and lend it its special value. The value of the present has to do with respect and obligation: "The essence of education is that it be religious. . . . A religious education is an education which inculcates duty and reverence." Education is to do more than develop gifts. It is also to give character and continuity to the relations between those gifts, and thus will influence our social sense of time. It relates our duties to the passage of events: "Duty arises from our control over the course of events. . . . And the foundation

of reverence is this perception, that the present holds within itself the complete sum of existence, backwards and forewards, that whole amplitude of time, which is eternity."[35] This new note in Whitehead's thought, struck during the somber happenings of wartime, reflects those large-scale changes in human affairs and the upheavals of apparently stable institutions which closed Whitehead's first life.[36] That time has emerged as a more dominating presence in his thought, that change goes forward remorselessly during the intervals between "instants," is reflected in these images of time as holy ground and of eternity as time's amplitude. This is the first occurrence in Whitehead's published works of the association of the concept of time with the concept of eternity. The appearance of the idea of eternity is a significant clue that the problems connected with the idea of time are becoming paramount.

The salience that the problem of time has taken on for Whitehead is shown in another of his presidential addresses, delivered in 1916 to a section of the Mathematical and Physical Science Association, and entitled "The Organization of Thought." In this address, Whitehead defined a theorist as one who is investigating temporal relations, one "whose motive of thought is the desire to formulate correctly the rules according to which events occur."[37] Moreover, the theorist is especially concerned with immediate events. To the extent that he is successful in his formulations, the theorist is able to parallel the smooth set of abstract concepts with the actual, immediate events of experience. The immediate, apparent world of experience is a flux of sensations, emotions, and perceptions. It is rather like a continual chaos. Accepting the fact of this initial disorder is "the first step in wisdom."[38] How are our neat assemblages of concepts to be connected with the vague continua of the importunate present? The basic question that arises for the organization of thought is to formulate procedures for moving between the plurality of experiences and the unified world of scientific hypotheses. Whitehead's project, it turns out, was to show that there is a connection between the two levels, untidy experience and neat theory, in those cases where we can show that each has some potentiality for properties usually associated with the other. Process or change needs to be discerned, *in diminuendo,* in the realm of forms or essences, and ideality and relatedness need to be discerned in the apparent world. Indeed, an imaginative approach to experience finds some patterns already there. If we rule out such ideal experiences we will have insuperable difficulties in our theories of time and space.[39]

The patron saints of these two realms, the ideal and the practical, are identified by Whitehead as Plato and St. Benedict, respectively. The image of such symbolic leaders of organized thought worlds is set out in another

presidential address the following year, "Technical Education and Its Relation to Science and Literature." This 1917 address, delivered to the mathematical association, included the idea that just as Plato is the pathfinder for modern liberal education, so too is St. Benedict the guide for technical education. The one identifies an eros, the other a praxis. "Disinterested scientific curiosity is a passion for an ordered intellectual vision of the connection of events."[40] The logic of discovery and the logic of the discovered are related such that the one searches out the laws of nature "according to which events occur," and the other deduces the special instances which would be manifest in obedience to those laws. But the Benedictine praxis formulates procedures for energizing human experience by means of the antecedent theory. We owe our correct applications to "the Benedictines, who saved for mankind the vanishing civilisation of the ancient world by linking together knowledge, labour, and moral energy."[41] The Benedictines, with their concern for the present as the locus of value, reshape the smooth time of theory into the fullness of time: that seems to be Whitehead's conception.

Consistent with his emphasis upon an amplitude of time manifest within the present, Whitehead argued further that the present does not collapse into a passing moment but is a duration whose parts in some respects are a register of the larger vistas of time ("The Anatomy of Some Scientific Ideas," 1917). This durational present "includes directly perceived time-relations between events contained within it. In other words, we put the present on the same footing as the past and the future in respect to the inclusion within it of antecedent and succeeding events, so that past, present, and future are in this respect exactly analogous ideas." By a Principle of Aggregation, we extend the structure of the present outward into the past and future, and by the use of a complementary principle, the Principle of Convergence, we focus the structures of space and time into ever more simple units. By means of successive applications of the latter principle, we finally arrive at an approximately instantaneous world of particles, instants, intervals, and simple sense data.[42] These principles together give Whitehead's early version of how the world is elaborated and refined out of immediate perceptual content. The different world concepts he had set out in the 1905 memoir, "Mathematical Concepts of the Material World," are now shown to have arisen by an elaborate series of recensions.[43] The ultimate entities set out in the memoir—e.g., points, particles, and instants —and the fundamental relations are not themselves primitive, but are derived elements. "The material universe is largely a concept of the imagination which rests on a slender basis of direct sense-presentation. But none the less it is a fact; for it is a fact that we actually imagine it."[44]

The principal ideas Whitehead examined in "The Anatomy of Some Scientific Ideas" were facts, objects, time and space, and force fields. The most extensive treatment was allotted to time and space, a treatment that served as a bridge connecting his earliest ideas on time and space with the extended analysis he gave to those ideas in his mature philosophy of science appearing in the years from 1919 to 1923. That equal or greater priority is now given to time as compared with space can be seen in the fact that Whitehead held for the first time in this paper that spatial ideas rise out of temporal ideas and are functions of them. That is, thought objects in their different possible spatial relations depend upon the different durations involved.[45] We never perceive *things*, Whitehead now says, but only *events*.[46] The key idea from Whitehead's earlier work, which makes plausible the proposition that we perceive events, is the monistic interpretations of the material world which occur in some of the concepts explicated in the 1905 memoir. That is, if particles are introduced only to give the senses something to perceive, and if it is held that relations can be perceived, then a particulate ground for sensation is redundant. If events are, moreover, taken as complexes of relations, then obviously we may conclude that it is only events that we perceive, not things.

Now to understand the structures of time and space, Whitehead thought that we had to speak of time-parts and space-parts. These parts are given in the stream of perception. They are not thought objects initially, but are relations between sense objects.

> The fundmental fact is the sense-object, extended both in time and space, with the fundamental relation of whole-to-part to other such objects, and subject to the law of convergence to simplicity. . . . The relation of whole to part is a temporal or spacial relation, and is therefore primarily a relation holding between sense objects of perception, and is only derivatively ascribed to the thought-objects of perception of which they are components. More generally, space and time relations hold primarily between sense-objects of perception and derivatively between thought objects of perception.[47]

Sense-time and sense-space of the apparent world differ from thought-time and thought-space in that there are neither punctive elements nor ordered relations in the apparent world. Both time and space connect and disconnect objects found within them, but continuity is mainly a feature of thought-time and space. Both instants and points have their genesis in the movement from sense to thought, a movement superintended by the principle of convergence to simplicity. Point-objects are called fictions by "moderns," but they are still well-founded fictions, and correspond to a set

of facts. Rather than referring them to the idea of limits, Whitehead referred them to the topological idea of whole-part relations that are given in experience.[48] Fundamental to the ideas of whole and part is the notion of enclosure.

Whole and part relations are relations of enclosure. For example, aEb means that b is a part of a, or that b is enclosed in a. The pivotal relation of enclosure is further defined by Whitehead as a transitive, asymmetrical relation whose domain includes its converse domain. Importantly, aEb will always imply that a c can be found such that bEc. So extended objects in time and space are subject to indefinite divisibility. Given a set of enclosure objects, we would have a series that is a route of approximation.[49] Against this background, punctive elements of the thought world are used to give us more simplified abstractions. Points are ways of handling relations between enclosure objects in a series. In pursuing this line of argument, Whitehead's developing contrast between abstract space of the thought world and sequences of enclosures more typical of the sense world reenacts the contrast in classical Greek philosophy between space and place. In particular, John Philopon and Robert Grosseteste had held that the void is an abstract creature of reason and can never be actual as place is actual, preferring in this case the Aristotelian approach over the Stoic approach, which made space or the infinite void an actuality.[50] The modern thought has an ancient lineage in this instance: "The modern thought-object of science . . . has the complexity of the whole material universe. In physics, as elsewhere, the hopeless endeavor to derive complexity from simplicity, has been tacitly abandoned. What is aimed at is not simplicity, but persistence and regularity."[51] The idea of places within places, or Whitehead's enclosure objects, suggests precisely the persistence and regularity that is desired.

4. SPATIOTEMPORAL THEMES FOR THE PHYSICAL WORLD

Whitehead's systematic philosophy of nature is set out in a trio of books published between 1919 and 1922. The first two volumes, *An Enquiry concerning the Principles of Natural Knowledge* (1919) and *The Concept of Nature* (1920), broadly cover the same ground. Whereas the former reflects a greater concern with the mathematical and physical disciplines, the latter exhibits philosophical and historical interests. "The two works meet," Whitehead said, "in their discussion of some details of space and time." The purpose of the two books, he added, was to establish the premises for a new, more speculative physical synthesis. Besides providing for such a synthesis, he was also aware that his work pointed beyond that immediate

goal. It was also premonitory of a new metaphysical synthesis, for all of these books treat passage as an ultimate fact, and in passage, nature connects with ultimate metaphysical reality.[52] In the third book of this period, *The Principle of Relativity* (1922), Whitehead held that philosophy has the task of "determining the most general conceptions which apply to things observed by the senses."[53] The term he used for philosophy in this sense was 'panphysics'. The suggestion is that he will provide on another occasion a metaphysical account of time and space that is prepared on one of its sides by an account of time and space grounded in a reconstructed concept of the physical world.

Closely associated with these three books, which we treat in their bearing on time-space inquiries, is a group of short, exemplary papers which seem almost abstracts of the books, and which were prepared by Whitehead for more general audiences.[54] "Time, Space, and Material" (1919) is the very best route into the difficult doctrines of *Enquiry* and *Concept of Nature,* while "The Philosophical Aspects of the Principle of Relativity" (1922) presents an overview of *The Principle of Relativity.* Our analysis of Whitehead's panphysical concepts of time and space, then, is based upon the above-mentioned books and articles. In addition, some reference is made to several other articles of this period whose primary questions turn on distinguishing between the ideas of time, space, and matter as presented in the classical physical synthesis of Galileo and Newton, and upon those ideas as part of the new physical synthesis arising out of the work of Maxwell, Einstein, and Minkowski. This phase of Whitehead's inquiries into the nature of time-space will be somewhat clearer if we recall his preferences for (1) linear over punctual concepts of nature, (2) projective over metrical geometries, (3) force-fields and lines of force over atomic or discrete objects, (4) organic whole-part relations over quantitative all-some additive relations, (5) full, polyadic relational complexes over collapsed, dyadic subject-predicate expressions, (6) perception of relations over perception of material entities, and (7) *a posteriori* over *a priori* accounts of space and time. These preferences, we have shown, came into the forefront of his thinking as the result of his earlier investigations.

A. The Received, Classical Tradition

Whitehead believed that the ideas of time, space, and matter, as they are used in physical explanations of the world, had their origin in experience. Naïve common sense, as modified by Greek, Christian, Renaissance, and seventeenth-century thought, is the ground of these scientific notions.[55] The whole of his *Enquiry* is based on the supposition that the "scientific

concepts of space and time are the first outcome of the simplest generalisa-
tions from experience."[56] Perhaps as part of his disenchantment with Kant,
Whitehead had held that time and space are subsequent to experience, and
not *a priori* in any idealistic sense at all.[57] He much preferred the empirical
approaches of Locke and Mill. He held the inverse of Kant's view: rather
than space and time making experience possible by providing its formal
conditions, experience makes time and space possible by providing
grounds in such natural elements as relations and events. Especially does
relativity theory support the idea that space and time are not *a priori.*[58]

Inasmuch as space and time are the initial products of generalizations
from experience, it follows that any inductive account of nature would
be heavily invested in these concepts. A physical explanation, Whitehead held, is one that uses the idiom of time, space, and matter.[59] All the
treatises of science do, in fact, take time, space, and matter as ultimate.[60]
Indeed, to determine the meaning of nature is almost to be reduced to discussing just the characters of time and space.[61] But such a discussion, according to the received classical theory, is a discussion committed to emphasizing the disconnections or separations between independently real,
isolated bits of matter. For space and time are the means by which things
are spread out or dispersed. The absolute presupposition is that time and
space disconnect, and that space does more to disperse entities than does
time.[62] For the same thing cannot be in two places at the same time, but it
can be identically the same at two or more successive times. So it is clear
that matter/time relations differ from matter/space relations.[63]

If space and time act as disconnectors to disperse the material in it, then
matter as another ultimate element of nature must step forward as a prime
candidate for providing continuity and composition in nature. Whitehead
thought that the matter used by Descartes, Galileo, and Newton in the
seventeenth century was something of an anachronism. It was reverting to
"the Ionian effort to find in space and time some stuff which composes nature."[64] In general, Whitehead believed that the prospects of absolute matter were directly tied to the fortunes of absolute time and space.

The received tradition of classical physical science, then, held that at
a given instant in time there was a configuration or distribution in space
of some self-identical stuff, matter.[65] The basic facts were to be presented
in units of time/space/matter complexes, and a succession of such configurations comprises the series of states which makes up nature. Whitehead thought that such a view would, in strictness, commit us to composing an infinite number of chapters about nature's states, if nature is to be
described fully. Admittedly, such a view has some serviceability for physicalistic explanations. But even there, such notions as velocity and accel-

eration fare badly.[66] At an instant, there is no velocity, and nature is impaled.[67] But outside of physics, the explanatory power of the triumvirate of material bits occupying points in space at instants of time falls off rapidly. Iron, Whitehead reminds us, does not exist at an instant, but takes time to exist across a period or interval.[68] Any mode of functioning in nature takes a period of time for life forms to come to expression. But of even greater importance is the fact that there is no perception at an instant. Observation takes time. There is no such thing as an instantaneous observation. A suitable account of the principles of natural knowledge, one which allows for the condition of empirical observation, must be internally coherent and also adequate to the facts and processes of nature. The traditional classical account is to be questioned, not because of its lack of consistency, but because of its inadequacy. It is false to some obvious facts of biology and of the psychology of perception.

Taken on their own terms, the traditional versions of time, space, and matter are too simplistic. But inasmuch as science clearly works, those traditional conceptions are not merely fictional. The classical theory, especially as it uses the concepts of absolute time and space, is resting upon too slender a base. Indeed, Whitehead regards the ideas of absolute space and absolute position at an instant as metaphysical fairy tales. And absolute time is as monstrous as absolute space.[69] We do not experience instants, and yet one of the apparent strong points of the idea of absolute time is the belief that we experience this present instant. But where does the belief come from? There is no such bare time given in perception. The value of the idea of the specious present, he thought, is that it warns us against believing in instants as ultimate entities.[70] Our perceptions of the present contain both antecedent and subsequent features. Given perception across a duration, the ultimate data of experience upon which our science should be based are data disclosed as the content of the specious present. There is no knife-edge present, no instantaneous present.[71] Accordingly, as these abstractions are dismantled, a more adequate empirical synthesis of temporal and spatial elements can replace them.

A more satisfying account of the ultimate elements of nature will need to state, in its own way, the advantages that the absolute theory did provide. In a limited way, absolute space and time provided the field of the relations that would overcome the bifurcation in nature between scientific objects, like atoms and electrons, and perceptual states, like the heat presumably caused by the motions of electrons. For both the electrons and the perceived heat would be thought of as occupying the same time/space system. Moreover, a second advantage of the theory of absolute time is that time in some sense seems to extend beyond nature.[72] Insofar as time seems

to be more extensive than nature, it can hardly be derived from relations between elements in nature. A third advantage of the absolute theory of time is that it is difficult to derive the earlier/later relationship holding between members in a series, from other relational characters holding between members in the series. The recurrence of those relational characters, although quite improbable, does not seem impossible. But the recurrence of an instant of time is impossible. What Whitehead will show is that serial time is a high-level abstraction, not concretely given in experience, and that the irreversibility or irrevocability of time is based on the more concrete elements of nature, not upon the abstractive elements.

The order of business is thus established for Whitehead's constructive account of time and space by his reading of the liabilities and assets of the received classical account. First, he will illustrate that the bifurcation between natural fact and perceptual condition is overcome by the relation of extension holding between events. Inasmuch as that same relation of extension is also the root of time and space, it follows that time and space do give us the illusion of connecting molecules with perceptual states, as the classical view had held. Second, Whitehead will show that time seems to extend beyond nature because passage or process extends beyond nature. The time that derives from a more extended passage which is outside nature thus gives us the illusion of an absolute time. Finally, he will show that some events in a stream of passage do fall into overlapping sequences that converge toward the simplicity of instants in a series. In that the series derives from the sequences of events in the irrevocable passage or advance of nature, the illusion does arise that it is the series of instants that is irreversible. In being able to account for the residual strengths of the absolute space/time/matter triumvirate, Whitehead in dialectical fashion is able both to save the appearances of the first physical synthesis and to add to it the considerable explanatory power of the new physical synthesis that extends to the facts of biology and psychology. His new view points toward, indeed almost demands, a new metaphysics. Although he revealed that classical time and space were special cases of the time-space continuum of relativity theory, he also showed that alternative interpretations could be attached to relativity theory. He thus entered into a dialogue with the Einsteinian interpretations of time and space, as well as with the classical conceptions.

B. The Relational View of Time

At a 1922 symposium on ways to interpret Einstein's theory of relativity, H. Wildon Carr held that Einstein's approach was broadly consistent with the idealistic, relational view of time associated with the philosophy of

Leibniz: "The principle of relativity proposes in science precisely the methodological reform which Leibniz proposed in philosophy when he said, 'The monads are the real atoms of nature.' "[73] The principle of relativity reverses the methods of classical mechanics. It favors neoidealism, and rejects neorealism. Perceptive activity is salient. In his response to Carr, Whitehead held that the theory of relativity did not settle the basic issues between idealists and realists. In particular, idealists had no special claim on entities or relata that were force fields with spread and continuity. On the other hand, realists were not stuck with absolute space, time, and matter. They did not have to turn away from the eventual or developmental features that seemed to lie at the very core of things: "I cannot see why a realist should choke at having to swallow events."[74] Far from being unable to assimilate events in an adequate theory of nature, Whitehead thought that events were a large part of the staple diet and true sustenance of panphysics. Such a physics would give the formal characteristics of all existents, especially of organisms and psyches. Events for him were simply stock in trade for developing the regular features of all things in nature.

"The ultimate facts of nature, in terms of which all physical and biological explanation must be expressed, are events connected by their spatio-temporal relations."[75] In this assertion of his basic assumption, Whitehead presents a view that at first glance seems to make events a candidate for Aristotelian first substances. But in the light of what he says here and almost everywhere else, events *and* relations are equally primitive. They are not only duals that imply each other; both arise out of something even more primitive.[76] It is an Anaximander-type *apeiron* that is not yet articulated into relations and events. The ultimate facts of nature, when it is first characterized at all, are events-connected-by-relations. The ultimate facts are relational complexes.

Still, Whitehead did at times speak of events by themselves as ultimate, without the more careful qualification that they are also relata. His unguarded minority opinion can be found in assertions such as this: "Events, infinite and finite, are the primary type of physical fact."[77] This monistic version of the primary physical fact is not as fruitful as the dual version, events *and* relations. Nor is that monistic version a mere singularity. Whitehead was willing to speak conditionally of events as substances, and leave it to his co-inquirers to be cautious in distinguishing, as Aristotle had, between first and second substance: "If we are to look for substance anywhere, I should find it in events which are in some sense the ultimate substance of nature."[78] This incautious mode of expression would also seem to allow the view that space and time are attributes of these substantive events. But this is only an elliptical way of speaking of space and time

that Whitehead did use at times. For him, space and time are not relations between events; they are abstractions from the main relations between events, the relations of extension and cogredience.

One tends to take events as the ultimate facts or first substances when one refers to them in ways generally reserved for talking about substances. That is, events seem singular, because they cannot be compared.[79] But they also seem comparable because of the kinds of universals (called 'objects' by Whitehead) that are registered in them, exhibited in them as in a medium or field. Indeed, an event is a field.[80] Each event in addition has a character of its own. It is a contraction or a limitation of uniform relations between processes which conspire to make it contingent and unrepeatable.

Aside from regarding events as distinct fields that are open to the appearance of universals or essences in them, Whitehead further defined events in terms of certain spatiotemporal features that, strictly speaking, arise out of events. If such an approach seems somewhat circular, it does show that events are not subsistent but are relata, and that language is being pushed to the very limit in trying to make it a vehicle for exhibiting the fundamental facts in nature. "What we discern is the specific character of a place through a period of time. This is what I mean by an 'event'."[81] The event spoken of here is the percipient event, but we do find in percipience a model of what an event in general is like.[82] It is a tetradic ensemble—if not of even greater complexity—composed of relations between ingressing essences, short-term processes, long-term processes, and sideways or spatial deployments. Because events are unique, they cannot be recognized. However, universals or essences that are objective elements in events can be recognized. Just by themselves, events or happenings can only be endured or lived through, even though characters of one event pass on to become traits of successor events. Basically, events are the field of the essential relations. Events especially comprise the field of the relations of extension and cogredience. The relation of extension, in turn, is a version of whole-part relations: "If an event A extends over event B, then B is 'part of' A, and A is a 'whole' of which B is a part. Whole and part are invariably used in these lectures in this definite sense."[83]

Although Whitehead did speak in a derivative sense of events as connected by their relations in time and space, his general understanding was that the relation of extension, a relation between wholes and parts of wholes, was the ground of temporal and spatial relations. Stated more accurately, events in relations were the roots of time and space. But 'event' is an idea compromised by its abstractness, and propositions including 'event' are really propositional forms, as we saw earlier.'Event' is the most concrete of our abstractions, and can foster a correct understanding of time

and space.[84] But it was not as serviceable as other terms like 'passage' or 'process', which Whitehead introduced into his philosophy of nature so as to provide a basis for a new descriptive metaphysics. Yet the more deeply Whitehead moved into his analysis of the principles and concepts of nature, the more the metaphysical aim officiated over the lines of discussion. Nature is increasingly described as processual and not eventual.[85] The ideas of process, passage, and creative advance progressively dominate his constructions. Events themselves are "factors of fact," or elements of a more comprehensive organic whole. In turn, nature itself is a concept for describing different possible affiliations of factors in fact. The organic whole, from which all else emerges through a process of articulation, is itself processual.

Let us first examine how time and space are rooted in extension, and then consider how extension itself arises from whole/part relations.

C. Time, Space, and Significance

Whitehead had a special interest in the relationship between experience and significance. The idealist and empiricist traditions in modern philosophy had each in its own way included this question. In the later portions of *The Principles of Human Knowledge*, Berkeley especially held that perceptions signified other perceptions, and objects were pregnant with the referential presence of other objects. The entire book of God's creation, Berkeley thought, was written in significant symbols, and finite active spirits could read God's intent in the regularity and continuity of created objects. Kant, according to Whitehead, had simply inverted Berkeley's doctrine to hold that significance *is* experience.[86] Whereas Berkeley had maintained that experience is significant of a deeper Will, Kant had said that the transcendent is neither given in nor through experience, so significance is simply experience itself, especially on its relational or formal side. In his 1905 memoir, Whitehead had shown that, regarding some concepts of the material world, relations are held to be perceived. In *Enquiry*, he repeats that we can apprehend relations.[87] The theory of relativity, Whitehead decided, had given new weight to Berkeley's view of significance as present in the physical order, because the physical order was now cut loose from a material order. According to Whitehead, in undercutting absolute matter, the theory of relativity had avenged Berkeley. The immaterialist sides of Berkeley's doctrine are strengthened by relativity theory.[88] But because Berkeley had not touched absolute time and space in his arguments, the ghost of the old materialism still lurks there, disguised no doubt by Berkeley's voluntaristic theism. Whitehead meant to carry through Berkeley's argument so that the relation of significance is seen not as a relation be-

tween substance and attribute, but as a relation immanent in the structure of events which comprise nature. The entire topic of significance, in short, is basic to a full understanding of Whitehead's temporalism.[89]

A basic flaw of the absolutist view of nature—seen as an infinite series of chapters describing configurations of points and particles at instants of time—was that no one chapter has a plot connecting it to the next chapter. There was no physical relation between nature at one instant and nature at the next instant.[90] We cannot know of a uniformity that extends across parts of nature unless the relation of antecedence and subsequence is present from the beginning. However, the relations of extension between events can provide this uniform significance otherwise denied to them. The significance arises as the characters of some events are passed on to enter into the situation of other events. This fact of extensive relations between events is the very same thing as "the uniform significance of events."[91] The more we do by way of converting the attributes or adjectives of presumptively isolated events into relations between events, the more nature is seen as an interlocking field of events in organic whole/part relations. Indeed, the disclosure of an entity as a relatum is the very root of the concept of significance.[92]

One of the props of the absolutist view of time and space was that perceptions and scientific objects like molecules did fall within the same space/time framework. But a better way to answer the threat of bifurcation, Whitehead thought, was to show that perceptual objects (such as heat) and scientific objects (such as molecular motions) occupy different levels of abstraction than do the sequences of events that include each other as whole and part. So extension between events is the substitute for absolute space and time. According to Whitehead's reading of its history, philosophy has looked for a ground of relatedness ever since Hume.[93] The answer, Whitehead felt sure, was simply to begin with relatedness. If we begin with disjunction, we can acquire conjunction only by some "sleight of hand." So the principle to follow is the uniform significance of events in tableaux of whole/part relations. Events signify each other, and each event signifies the entire structure of which it is a part.[94] Like Leibniz's mirroring monads, each event includes a register of all of the others. It is on the basis of the mutual significance of events as parts registering some characteristics of the whole in which they are embedded that Whitehead came to the conclusion that any part of space/time mirrored *all* of space/time.[95] In light of this conclusion, Whitehead sought another interpretation of relativity besides Einstein's.[96] He thought that Einstein's view of the heterogeneity of kinds of space would undo the uniformity needed to justify the relationship of significance between whole and part. Although consciousness is clearly one form of significance, it is only one form.[97] Whitehead

believed that philosophy had made altogether too much of conscious significance as the seat of all significance, e.g., the general error of idealism. But if nature as a whole is taken as a field of significant relations between events in organic whole/part relations, then consciousness is appropriately humbled. Nature may indeed be closed to mind, in the evolutionary sense that much has gone on before mind ever appeared, but nature is certainly not closed to significance.

If we avoid the philosophical error of reifying abstract features of events into properties of isolated entities, we will come to notice the relations of events that betoken nature's passage. In general, the way to escape hypostatization would be to treat properties of things as their relatedness to things unspecified. Another reading would have it like this: put characters for causes.[98] The basic understanding of significance will then begin to stand out. Victor Lowe in particular has stressed the importance of this side of Whitehead's theory of nature.[99] As Whitehead puts it, "Significance is relatedness, but it is relatedness with the emphasis on one end only of the relation."[100] When we emphasize only one aspect of the relation, and allow the initial error to be multiplied by the deflecting powers of an errant language (Whitehead obviously learned Berkeley's and Locke's lessons on the tendency of language to deceive us), then we are accessories to the debasing of relations into entities indistinctly discerned, and to the final collapse of indistinct entities into substances with attributes. Temporal adjectives and spatial attributes; the serial properties of time: all should be traced instead to the relations of extension and cogredience between events.

D. The Diversification of Events within the Whole

The whole of all that is, the real ground of things, is directly given in perception. Such a whole is not yet given as nature, as a complex of entities external to us, for nature arises from that whole and is a special reading of its features. But the whole is directly sensed and is not yet diversified into parts.[101] Whitehead holds that we initially sense a totality from which we do not even distinguish ourselves; awareness and what there is awareness of are still submerged in an identity. The immediate sensing of the whole that separates nature from this unitary ground also separates the fact of our awareness out of that ground. Thus, nature and awareness are correlative notions, but neither is absolutely primitive: "The immediate fact for awareness is the whole occurrence of nature. It is nature as an event present for sense-awareness, and essentially passing."[102] Moreover, just as nature is differentiated from ground, so too are events differentiated within the whole of nature. The whole of nature and the parts into which that

whole is configured are simultaneous: "The unity of this general present fact is expressed by the concept of simultaneity. . . . Thus simultaneity is a definite natural relation."[103] To be sure, nature is eventual. A composition of events is all there is in nature. But relations and relata, as a unity of diverse articulations, are simultaneous. They are, Whitehead held, the ground of nature's continuity.[104] They are also the source of the more abstract relations of time and space. The whole is diversified into nature and an awareness of nature. Nature in its turn is diversified into events, relata, and the perception of events. Extensional relations of events are diversified into time and space, and cogitation about those extended forms of relatedness. Such is the hierarchic route laid out by Whitehead in his argument.

He denominates the breaking up of nature into these levels the diversification of nature. To sense that nature is "there" is already to separate out a part of nature that is "here," namely, ourselves. The sense of nature's being is accompanied by a diversification of the whole of nature into parts.[105] What we have is an emergent awareness, and in the divergence of this awareness from the whole, the awareness of a whole being discriminated into parts is well underway. Especially important is the event that is our bodily life. Whitehead had made the "here" of our bodily experience the prime datum in *An Introduction to Mathematics*, but it is now seen as an emergent, correlative aspect. Other preferred expressions he uses to describe this diversification of nature into whole/part relations at different levels of abstraction are pairs of terms like 'the discernible' and 'the discerned', or 'fact' and 'factors of fact'.[106] What Whitehead is referring to by means of these contrasts is the distinction between the background (of nature) and the foreground (of events and objects in nature).

Events are factors of fact, discerned elements against a background of all that is discernible. They are abstractions, i.e., elements that arise in the process of diversification. They are our most concrete abstractions. But their emergence as factors of fact does not really diminish the inexhaustible fund of all that is still present in the background of the discernible. A key mark of the whole fact of nature is its inexhaustible or unlimited scope.[107] The discernible, inexhaustible ground of all that is to which Whitehead refers is like the *apeiron* of Anaximander. It has not yet undergone limitation by reference to projections or canalizations that arise in connection with the emergence of our own here and now.

In his own theory of limitations, Whitehead was particularly taken by the concept of canalization used by Henri Bergson. Whitehead thought that the idea of canalization added content to the more negative idea of limitation.[108] He used the idea of limitation to show how nature is diversified into elements and factors. Fact, he could now say, is canalized into

events and extensive relations between events. Canalization also suggests how past characters of events can mold the appearances of future characters by streamlining those developments into a system of passage. Canalization neatly captures the uniformity of relations that reign throughout the whole system of nature. Uniform relations between events undergird the more highly abstract uniformities of space/time relations that hold between entities that are parts of the system of scientific objects. What Whitehead calls "the principle of the uniform significance of events" is another way of exhibiting that nature is patient of this item or that, for those items lie immanent within the whole formative system of nature. The most regular features of time and space, certainly those which lend themselves to a metric, are grounded in nature's canalizations of discernible fact into discerned factors.

We see that, for Whitehead, the concept of nature is immensely diversified. Entities are not isolated substances but are relational wholes. Although overlapping events in whole/part relations comprise the general structure of fact, these events vary in their nature according to perspective and to the degree of abstraction used. Different modes of diversifying nature terminate in different events. Accordingly, the entities that emerge as relata also differ. Moreover, the relations that depict the canalization of nature arise through different modes of diversification.[109] The analogy could be this: just as points and lines are duals in projective geometry, so too are entities and relations duals in the basic concepts of nature. Entities and relations are equibasic. Whitehead's general understanding about the level from which we prescind elements of nature is that the more the notion of flux is left behind, the higher the level of abstraction at which we are breaking out factors of fact. In particular, if we want a philosophy of nature that is close to the facts, we should *not* use mathematics as a model.[110] Whitehead's disclaimers about the serviceability of mathematical method as philosophical method echo Kant's strictures in part 2 of the first *Critique*. But Whitehead does go beyond Kant in holding that mathematical training sensitizes the investigator to a greater complexity of relations.[111]

Events embedded in extended routes of passage as contrasted with instants or points embedded in a series: that is the gamut run in Whitehead's account of the diversification of nature. He cites five main kinds of entities that make up the hierarchy of the articulated whole of nature: (1) events proper, (2) percipient objects, (3) sense objects, (4) perceptual objects, and (5) scientific objects. He then assigns these entities to two principal headings: events and objects.[112] That we are talking here about different kinds of objects given to us through different modes of intelligence is clear enough. The leitmotif of Whitehead's speculation is that different levels of

psyche prescind different elements from the undifferentiated whole of all that is.

A simplified version of the account of objects that are embedded in events is found in *The Concept of Nature*.[113] Sense objects are the most concrete, after which we have perceptual objects, and then scientific objects. This approach is broadly consistent with the account in *Enquiry*, except that it does not mention the most concrete elements of nature—events and extensions—but simply deals with the objects in those contexts. The most concrete of all events, to be sure, is the percipient event, the one associated with our own *locus standi*. This is the event of our being here, and 'here' is the most insistent of all our notions, the point of departure for all our projections.[114] Whitehead emphasized the insistence of the 'here' in *An Introduction to Mathematics*, and it is firmly reinforced in his philosophy of science. We especially should note the passage in "The Philosophical Aspects of the Principle of Relativity," where the status of the observer's body is taken as paramount.[115] Nature, Whitehead held, is closed to the observing mind, but nature is certainly not closed to the observer's body. The plurality of kinds of temporality and of different forms of space associated with each form of temporality is, in Whitehead's work, especially connected with the observer's present locus as the origin of a unique complex of projections.

E. Events, Extension, and Temporality

In Whitehead's view of nature, different levels of analysis detach different kinds of elements. The most fundamental elements of all—both entitative and relational—are events and extension. Events are the relata of the fundamental relation of extension;[116] every event or happening both encloses and is enclosed by some other event. The true relata behind all subsequent relata at the more abstract levels are events.[117] Whole/part relations have a special relevance in the case of the relation of extension. The fact that nature is external is due to the circumstance that whereas every other event is included in but also includes some other event—whereby each event enacts the role of both whole and part—every event is also outside and parallel to some other event.[118] There is no intersection between two such events at all. The being of some events differs from the being of others.

The relations of extension and cogredience are the basis of all of the connections and structures in nature, according to Whitehead.[119] Extension gives events as conjoined with or intersecting each other, whereas cogredience depicts events as disjoined or parallel to each other. The relation of extension, moreover, is the fundamental source of temporality: "Time and space both spring from the relation of extension." Clearly, time and space

are regarded as epiphenomenal. They arise from the empirical properties of extension.[120] They are high-level generalizations from experience, and not at all *a priori*. Time and space are relations between relations. They have to do with the way different relational complexes are oriented toward each other. They are derivative; it is extension that is fundamental. In Whitehead's 1905 memoir, extension and cogredience would be the sole fundamental relations holding between events as relata, whereas time and space would be extraneous relations. Time and space are not active, synthesizing conditions of events in passage; they are the passive conditions that accompany events.[121] They are the means, the abstract devices, for exhibiting and expressing the continuity and dependability of the natural passage of events. Events, together with extension and cogredience, are the elements that comprise the structure of happening. Time and space, on the other hand, are abstractions from this structure.[122] Although somewhat abstractive, events are still the most concrete elements. Whitehead is an eventualist in his accounts of nature, but only in some residual sense is he a temporalist. He does not accept time as basic, but he does take seriously time's fundaments.

The device of seating events closest to what is occurring, and of seating time and time's most abstractive elements farthest away from what is occurring, allowed Whitehead to account for the advantages offered by the absolute theories of time and space. These advantages were (1) accounting for some senses in which time extends beyond nature, and (2) showing that the time series is irreversible in the sense that no instants can recur. Now events are embedded in passage, and passage extends beyond nature. Nature arises out of the passage of all that is, but it does not strictly arise out of time, because time—especially serial time—arises as an abstractive feature from nature. We do, finally, construe as irreversible the earlier/later relation that holds between instants in the time series, because we directly experience the irreversibility of nature's passage. Aristotle had raised these questions about the way time extended beyond nature, and about the irreversibility of the temporal series. But those questions seem to defy any permanent resolution unless, Whitehead argues, there is recourse to more concrete levels of reality: to passage and to the elements of passage, like events and relations. Given Whitehead's relational view of time, these questions no longer in strictness arise.

It should be emphasized that, for Whitehead, time and space are not relations between events; they *express* the relations between events.. What they express is the double root of all natural relatedness: extension and cogredience. But some events are of such limited extent that they verge on being the particulate or instantaneous event. Of these events, it would

make some sense to say that they occur in time. But the preposition *in* in such contexts allows us to think either that space and time originate *from* the relations between events, or they originate *as* the relations between events. The former is the best version. Serial time is not the passage of nature itself.[123] Contrariwise, there is no passage or process at the level of serial time. Indeed, as Whitehead had argued, there is no connection between material configurations across successive instants. That was a drawback of the classical concept of nature.

F. The Modes and the Systems of Time

Nature has been spatialized at the abstractive level of serial time. That is, time sequences seem reversible in some sense, rather as positions of space can be occupied by an object which is moved, only to reoccupy the same position at a later time. The equations of physics work equally well whether time flows forward or backward, so direction is unimportant. At least this pertains where those equations would be expressed as the second power of the time variable, as t^2, because the same result is obtained whether a positive value (assigned to the forward motion of time) or a negative value (assigned to a regress in time) is squared. But past and future are fixed directions. The past is irrevocable, although temporal abstractions about the past may have a certain symmetry about them. Strictly speaking, the modes of time—past, present, and future—are modes of the passage of events. 'Past' and 'future' are used by Whitehead as features of passage.[124] Only through a circumlocution do they apply to time, for time arises from relations between events. The reality is events-in-passage, and past and future are modes of passage; only elliptically are they modes of time. Whitehead's distinction here can be taken as a correction of the other classical American philosophers who treated past, present, and future as direct modes of time.

Memory is an abstraction from passage or process. It is a percipient event that falls partly outside of other events. Memory is an escape from transience.[125] It allows a recognition of the way some aspects of passage recur; it reflects the past. By way of contrast, anticipation points toward what is coming into being, toward the future. It is the way we stake out and form the future as it is correlated with certain objects or characteristics embedded in the present. The duration of the specious present that comprises our extended locus here and now fades into memory, thus giving a past edge to this "slab" of duration. The duration of this temporal slab that is our specious present also rises toward its future edge, one marked by the limits of anticipation. Taken together, past and future comprise the zone of definition that evokes those extended events called durations. Our spe-

cious present, Whitehead held, "snaps" into a past and a present when the relation of the perceiving event to its associated natural duration changes its significance.[126] That is, the content and spread of the present is associated with the continuity and intensity of attention that relates a "here" to its associated "now." Aspects of the present become features of the past as the sweep of attention in a here-and-now is modified in its range.

For Whitehead, events are unchangeable elements of nature. They are actual and finished, even though they may become parts of more extended events. It is this unchangeability of events that is the source of the irrevocability of the past.[127] Analogies between time and space break down because of the different ways they are related to the passage of events. There is no irrevocability in spatial relations. Spatial positions can be reoccupied, but phases of passage cannot be taken up again. Temporal relations that exhibit the concrete passage of events are asymmetrical. The arrow of the passage of events, Whitehead would have it, flies in a single direction. Events, after all, are lived through or endured, sometimes in anticipation and sometimes with foreboding. But the sense of foreboding is predominant when our sense of events as unchangeable and fully actual is reflected forward toward the leading edge of the incipient event.

Besides being asymmetrical, processual time differs from space in another important way. Depending upon the mode of abstraction from a complex of events, there are different time systems.[128] But the three-dimensional space of Euclid, Whitehead felt, appears within any one of these different time systems. In this sense, he claimed that space is homogeneous, whereas Einstein, in treating space as "curved," conceived space as a heterogeneous medium. For Einstein, space is dependent in its structure upon the matter/force complex of which it is a function. Whitehead thought Einstein's view was a relapse into the idea of qualitatively different kinds of space associated with Aristotelian physics. Just as Galileo argued for a homogeneous space for all of nature in his discussion of the two competing world systems, so did Whitehead see himself as continuing the dialogue. Accordingly, he pressed for the uniformity of space against the heterogeneity ascribed to it by Einstein. The doctrine of uniformity, if upheld in this instance, would be one way Whitehead accepted a fundamental monistic assumption of the classical world view of Galileo and Newton.

Still, Whitehead did allow for a heterogeneity in nature, but he associated it with different complexes of durations (with their concomitant serial time systems), and not with space.[129] The different time systems, in turn, arise from different modes of projection from a percipient here-and-now. He also accepted the concept of a uniform connectedness of things that is called simultaneity. Simultaneity is taken as primitive by White-

head, and is taken as derived by Einstein, defined in terms of light signals and equidistance between points. For Whitehead, simultaneity is to be described in terms of an immediate association between the "here" of a percipient and a contiguous duration that comprises the "now" of all the rest of nature seen as present. A duration is the whole of nature that is simultaneous with a percipient event.[130] If this triadic relation is stated in a way that emphasizes simultaneity, then we would say that simultaneity is an extensional whole/part relation between a set of characters of all of nature, with a subset of characters disclosed in the percipient that is here. Thus, simultaneity is an elemental relational factor in the whole fact of nature, in the same way that events are elemental. Experiential simultaneity is quite simply foundational for Whitehead.[131] There is no clearer way of distinguishing the Whiteheadian and the Einsteinian interpretations of relativity than considering the different ways of handling simultaneity.

Whitehead, of course, had long been accustomed to looking behind the differences between Euclidean and non-Euclidean geometries to the nonmetrical constructions of projective geometry. Having—almost from the first of his work in mathematics—never taken Euclidean geometry as basal, he also felt no reason for stating a new physical synthesis in the quondam non-Euclidean geometries. Indeed, he came to feel that Euclidean geometry enjoyed all of the tactical advantages of stating the obvious spatial relations of immediate experience within a format of three dimensions, and at the same time avoided the disadvantages of treating nature in terms of qualitatively different kinds of space.

Given sets of four variables to be associated with a space-time continuum, p_1, p_2, p_3, and p_4, and q_1, q_2, q_3, and q_4, one perspective will have p_4 as a temporal variable that shows up as q_1 or q_2 or q_3 in another perspective. That is, what is a track across a time series in one system will be a point element within another system. Or, what is exhibited as a spatial variable in one system, at q_1 or q_2 or q_3, will occur as a temporal variable p_4 elsewhere. But despite this difference between time systems, where a kind of convertibility between spatial and temporal characters is shown, it is still the case that within each time system there exist three spatial characters that can be assigned to the structures of the classical Euclidean geometry. Thus does Euclidean geometry cut across different time systems.[132]

Finally, we should note that, taken as high-level abstractions, space seems to arise after time. That is, time arises in the diversification of nature before space puts in its appearance. Perhaps such a result is to be expected, with the heterogeneity of time systems finally giving rise to uniform Euclidean space, once the time factor has been selected because of its association with an individual percipient.[133] Whitehead is careful to point

out that spatial order is an expression of order in time. Spatial routes in nature are subsequent to and depend upon historical routes in nature.[134] Those routes are fundamental expressions of significance. Elsewhere, space is said to differentiate from time, but time is not said to differentiate from space. Still, there can be no time apart from space and no space apart from time.[135] This seems to make space and time duals of each other. Perhaps one way to show that the one has priority over the other but cannot exist without it is to relate time to the way events have priority over objects because they are the medium in which objects appear. Events and objects are dual notions for Whitehead, and so too are time and space. Time and space mirror at their level of abstraction the form of the relations between events and things at the more concrete level.

Perhaps the ultimate priority of the processual over the entitative is the priority associated with certain fundamental question-types over other question-types. Within Whitehead's erotetic emphases, fundamental questions of the when, where, and whither types are more important in giving rise to certain constants of externality than questions of the which, what, and how types.[136] The human perceiver begins to diversify nature in terms of the questions addressed to nature. Routes of significance are set up through the channeling effects of the questions. The answers we give in terms of events or objects or relations are presupposed in the framing of certain kinds of questions. A metaphysics, then, might simply be an elaboration of responses to acceptable question-types. In any case, for Whitehead, those six question-types initiate our sifting and probing of nature. If it is true that events are situations for objects, and time systems provide an order for spatial order, it is because in the first place, 'when' and 'whither' legislate for our human modes of perception over 'which' and 'what'. Plato and Aristotle had asked 'what' and 'which' questions, and their answers had successfully cast a subject/predicate pall over nature. But framing questions that lean toward process instead of those that lean toward entities and substances would give a new orientation to scientific concepts. Even refusing to ask why-type questions[137] is to commit oneself to what is immanent in the present. Not to ask why, but to ask when and whither is to emphasize the functional and phenomenological aspects of the present as it undergoes passage into a future. We should not, Whitehead thought, raise why-type questions because they too easily imply a reason or mind lying behind things. Be behavioral in forming concepts of nature. Describe the sensible in terms of the sensible.[138] These are the advisories Whitehead gives for uncovering the constants of externality.

Whitehead and the Epochs
of Time

IN 1924, Alfred North Whitehead was extended an invitation to join the philosophy faculty at Harvard University. His acceptance of the invitation and his arrival upon the American academic scene were external events accompanying a considerable expansion of his philosophical interests, and provided a stimulus for recasting many of his earlier views in the light of his deepening metaphysical interests. Beginning with the Lowell Institute lectures in 1925, which with certain additions were published as *Science and the Modern World*, nature is no longer seen as closed to mind, but is to be probed with mentalistic and experiential categories.[1] The categories of life and organism are promoted from their earlier rank of simple frontier guards located at points where the domain of the older mechanism broke down, into a new role of superintending powers that could assign to mechanism its limited province of validity. Intimated in some notes appended to the second edition of *An Enquiry Concerning the Principles of Natural Knowledge* (1925), where a new priority is given to the idea of process over extension, more fully developed views of time and space-time are set out in the Lowell lectures. Those views differ enough from Whitehead's earlier conceptions that commentators on his work seem divided into those who merely suggest that he has extended the scope of his investigations, and others who more severely state that he has changed directions by taking on new problems.[2]

Whether these emphases are to be appraised as changes of scope or as results of a change in direction is of less importance than identifying the cen-

tral question of Whitehead's philosophy of time at the stage to which he had brought his investigations. That question can be stated in terms of the interplay between his experiential methodology and the somewhat marginal status he had assigned to instants and points. He believed that instants and points were never directly experienced. Although an abstractive process of convergence to simplicity gives us these elements, they still arise indirectly, as creatures of an idealizing process. Though well-founded enough to be serviceable in and contributors to the success of the natural sciences, they are also products of a divergence from concreteness. Lacking the extensity or duration associated with concrete events, the problem was that instants were still resorted to in order to show how some events are strictly prior to other events.

The whole/part relations that hold within an extended sweep of events give us overlapping events. Within the overlapping processes, there is a partial antecedence of some one event to another, partially subsequent, event. But we still, in the same piece of analysis, resort to instants to show where *all* of some part of an event is wholly prior to *all* of some part of a subsequent event. Instants, which by the abstractive process are emergent from the overlapping passage of events, are being taken as grounds for separating parts of concrete events from each other. But this would make distinct events emerge by reference to the continuum of instants. The upshot is that to describe fully the concrete realm of overlapping yet disjunctive events, we swing back and forth between using the most concrete and the most abstract features of their passage. But this is opportunistic, and has us illegitimately identifying significant features of concrete passage, i.e., that some part of one event is antecedent to some part of another, in terms of quite abstract features.

In his appended notes to the 1925 edition of *Enquiry*, Whitehead states that he had not given sufficient attention to process. By so stating, I believe Whitehead is implying that relations of inclusion and exclusion between overlapping and yet distinct events must be defined in terms that are concrete and immanent within the passage of these overlapping events. The rule goes that we are to define the sensible in terms of the sensible.[3] In this case, it means we are *not* to distinguish between separate events by having recourse to those prescinded entities we call 'instants'. In substance, Whitehead has begun attending closely to a when-type question. He has substituted a when question for a how question: When has an event gone so far that it is really separate from an earlier event with which it nevertheless still overlaps in significant respects? Addressing different questions to nature, he argued in *Enquiry* (1919), gives us different constants of ex-

ternality. When and whither questions are more germaine to our immediate experience of passage than where and how questions, which are germaine to measuring aspects of passage.

If when and whither questions about events can be answered successfully, we can then account for the *total* precedence of some parts of some events over some parts of subsequent events—with which they overlap or in which they are partially included. What sets events apart from others, and thus makes passage real, must be something immanent in the event: that is the result of answering the question, "When does an event come to be?" Whitehead's epochal theory of time in part arises out of the displacement of the concept of the instant from our experience of the passage of the world. Instants are the fruit of how and where questions. Epochs are the fruit of when and whither questions. The question is one of defining the actual apartness of events in the midst of the extensive connection of events *without* appealing to those abstractive features, instants, whose existence presupposes the apartness of events in the first place. This is the issue that was coming to the fore in Whitehead's investigations by 1925.

The apartness of events, and hence the actuality of the passage of events, is to be explained by concrete features within events. For a full decade, such an approach channeled a good deal of Whitehead's speculations on the nature of time. That general strategy is realized by means of concepts available through some of his preferred philosophical sources. Several concepts make up the controlling milieu of Whitehead's more developed philosophy of time: the concept of mirroring (which he takes quite beyond Leibniz);[4] the concepts of internal and external relations (which he develops out of versions set forth by Bradley and Russell, and out of the squabbles between idealists, the New Realists, and the critical realists concerning the nature of relations); and the concepts of limitation and conformation (which he takes quite beyond Aristotle and Bergson). These notions have more work to do than most others in his views about processes in the world and the passage of the world.

I. RECASTING THE SCIENTIFIC SCHEME

Whitehead held that the received tradition of mechanistic science was not rich enough in its applications to account for such leading ideas as life, organism, and functional interaction. He felt that such concepts "collectively form the Achilles heel of the whole system." A more adequate system of scientific thought would appeal to these notions in a coherent way, and not just as ad hoc scaffolding. The scientific scheme must be recast, and the concept of organism is to be foundational in it. Of critical im-

portance is his belief that such a recasting is to begin with the notions of time and space: "In outline, my procedure is to start from the analysis of the status of space and time, or in modern phraseology, the status of space-time."[5] A correct understanding of space-time would afford both a way out of the mechanistic system of natural philosophy and proper access to the philosophy of organism. The philosophy of Leibniz influenced Whitehead's move in this direction in the same way that it had influenced Dewey's change of emphases.

The concept of event that controlled the mechanistic concept of nature was that of a congeries of fundamental existents, of instants, points and particles, fixed in a single tableau. In order to recast such a scheme, Whitehead attacked the idea of the event as a composite or aggregative whole. He emphasized instead the organic aspects of a happening. Taken this way, an event is in the first place a fused whole where linear features of continuity supplant the punctual features of discontinuity, and a confluence of durations is substituted for the spatiotemporal particulate features of the classical concept. The old system presented events under the format of external relations, whereas Whitehead's preferred system of organic mechanism exhibits events under the format of internal relations.[6] So his new-model event is more like an estuary (a water passage comprised of a river current meeting an ocean tide) than an escapement (where the motion of a physical object is discharged in one direction in equal steps, as in a clock). The technical term Whitehead uses to capture the idea of an inward confluence proper to the unifying event is 'prehensive occasion'. Space and time, it develops, are to be perceived as aspects of the interrelations of prehensive occasions. But the salient conception that controls many sides of the discussion in *Science and the Modern World*—the concept of internal relations—is present from the first as an element in Whitehead's concept of the prehensive occasion. The concept of internal relations contributes to a concrete understanding of 'event' by referring to experienced features of events. According to Whitehead, the prehensive occasions are the fundamental elements of actuality. They are realizations of special patterns of forces and relations in a region. They are the unit of things real. In turn, space and time arise out of the situations of these occasions.[7]

We begin with the immediate occasion as the locus for understanding all the other more remote occasions. A particular future and a particular past are already present in the immediate occasion.[8] The initial actual occasion has routes leading into and away from it, routes that are also graded into other occasions. The immediate occasions mirror the more remote occasions, in senses yet to be described, and thus each occasion is a repre-

sentative of the others. Let this figure represent an immediate prehensive occasion, A.

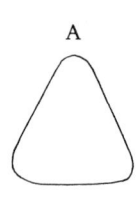

FIGURE 1

Given with A, by means of mirroring or mutual determination, is an entire community of occasions, with B and C as contiguous events.

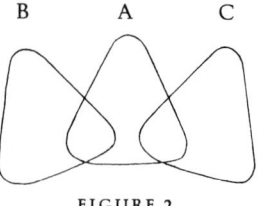

FIGURE 2

B and C, as surrogates for the remote occasions in the community of occasions, would be understood inductively from grounds immediately given in A. Reciprocally, the community of occasions provides the basis for understanding the particular relations holding for A, B, and C as relata. The overlapping regions of B and A, and A and C, provide a context for exhibiting sets of relations between those regions. Those relations, in turn, set the groundwork for a common space and time.

Space and time have three characteristic marks that arise out of the space-time continuum of actual occasions. These marks are the separative, the prehensive, and the modal aspects of space-time.[9] The separative aspect would be the ways in which B and A and C are apart or irrelated, as indicated by the arrows between the events B and A, and A and C.

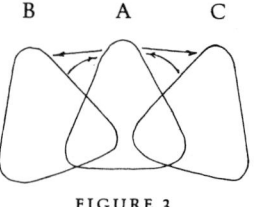

FIGURE 3

The regions of overlap between B, A, and C provide the grounds for the prehensive aspects of occasions. They indicate that the actual occasions within a community are fused together in such a way that each of B and A, and A and C, are essentially modified by responding to characteristics of the other. The spirals within the intersections of our figures suggest this sense of inward intensification through the mediation of the other.

B   A   C

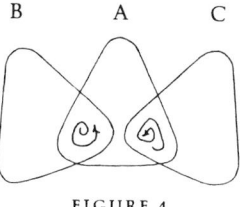

FIGURE 4

The third mark of the space-time continuum holding within a community of occasions is the modal aspect. Each occasion has peculiar or unique features, a different look, vis-à-vis other occasions. This is suggested by giving to each of B, A, and C a shape that is proper unto itself.

B   A   C

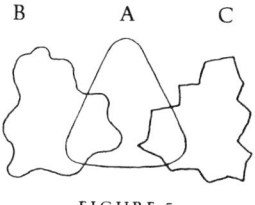

FIGURE 5

If separative, prehensive, and modal characteristics of space-time, which we symbolized consecutively in figures 3, 4, and 5, were selectively mapped onto a single diagram, we would have the following:

B   A   C

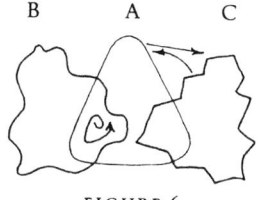

FIGURE 6

If figure 6 is compared with figure 2, it is suggested that the minimum complexity needed for understanding Whitehead's philosophy of time—as compared with a philosophy that allows for events as bare happenings in

a sequence—is associated with the additional features given in figure 6, but not in figure 2.

Taken by itself, and understood apart from the prehensive and separative marks that are features of its special community of occasions, event A seems perfectly fixed and definite, self-identical, and unique. Thus, there may arise from a foreshortened understanding of the modal characteristic of space-time the idea of the simple location or obvious fixity of an event.[10] Simple location is the modal character taken as a sufficient condition for describing the structures of space and time. So taken, the uniqueness of an occasion is highlighted, but its uniqueness is not perceived as a trait that arises out of the organic relations holding within a community of occasions. Thus, events are seen as items in an aggregate, not as nascent elements of a holistic configuration or gestalt. We would then fail to discern how the organic wholeness of the event enters into, and then limits, the characters of the parts of that organic whole.[11] It is precisely this inward intensification and limitation of events that distinguishes the prehensive occasions of Whitehead's organic mechanism from the unit events of classical mechanism.

In order both to avoid the more separative nuances of "volumes" of space and the merely prehensive nuances of "durations" in time, Whitehead apparently preferred to speak of "regions" of space-time. Speaking thusly would also have the considerable advantage of animating a whole host of understandings associated with the field theories of Faraday and Maxwell, theories which were *au début* nonmechanistic. A region of space-time is "a volume of space through a duration of time." All three of the characters of space-time detailed above are dependent upon the interior relations of events, and upon the manner in which events or occasions mirror each other: "Space-time is the specification of certain general characters of events and of their mutual ordering." An important rider to this claim is the sense in which the time that is associated with the succession of cosmic epochs is antecedent to and implicated in the kind of space-time displayed within the community of occasions in this particular cosmic epoch. For space-time is also a creature of a wider evolution beyond nature out of which space-time arises as a limited mode. As discussed previously, Peirce, Santayana, and Royce argued their own versions of this doctrine.[12]

For Whitehead, the community of occasions which constitutes nature as we know it is a register of that broader cosmic context where the succession of epochs interpenetrate each other. Processes within nature as we know it are reflective of the cosmic processes that generated nature's emergence in the first place. That is, our more restricted world with its

attendant natural laws is modal in character, and mirrors inwardly in those laws some of the traits of the community of cosmic epochs. A cosmic epoch for Whitehead is a prehensive occasion or event writ large: "Each volume of space, or each lapse of time, includes in its essence aspects of all volumes of space, or of all lapses of time."[13] Each natural occurrence is a register—in a way that is limited and actual for itself—of the scope of all that has been and is now taking place.

The very concreteness of an occasion is in part due to the special way it limits its appropriation of features of other occasions and epochs into its own constitution. As opposed to Aristotle's use of matter as the principle of individuation, Whitehead uses the operation of mirroring. Space and time arise out of this mirroring: "Space and time exhibit the general scheme of interlocked relations of these prehensions."[14] Mirroring is analogous to the activity of valuing, where strands from other complexes of experience are selectively introduced into a new ensemble.

2. DISTINCTIONS IN SPACE-TIME AND TIME AS EPOCHAL

The modes of time, e.g., past, present, and future, reveal different aspects of the community of occasions, depending on the manner in which some occasions mirror others. Some events are contemporaries of others in the sense that their phases do not overlap. This is the sense in which contemporary events are causally independent of each other. An event in this posture "mirrors within itself the modes of its contemporaries as a display of immediate achievement."[15] There is no mediating influence of cogredience one upon the other. Alternatively, some events fall within the causal influence of others. Such an event "mirrors within itself the modes of its predecessors, as memories which are fused with its own content." Events may also be tilted, through anticipation, toward events that are still coming into being. In this case, the event "mirrors within itself such aspects as the future throws back onto the present." In sum, depending on whether the mirroring of some events into others is in the mode of direct memory, the mode of immediate achievement, or the mode of premonitory anticipation, past, present, and future arise as distinct modes of time. Past, present, and future as modes of time are further exhibitions of the structure of space-time, as dependent upon the way events or prehensive occasions are postured toward and within each other. A fundamental posture displayed in the passage of events is that some events arise earlier than others, and the others are subsequent to them. That is, past, present, and future as modes of time arise out of the more fundamental relations of 'earlier than' and 'later than' between occasions embedded within the passing world.

Clearly, the concepts of mirroring and of internal relatedness are important for the whole of Whitehead's account of events as prehensive occasions, and for his explication of space and time as manifestations of the community of events. Earlier, we saw him arguing that a first task of a society was to create a unified time-sense out of the manifold of private times and diverse natural periodicities. If we take both natural objects and persons as extended events or occasions, we would be satisfying that earlier task by holding that space-time arises out of a community or society of actual occasions. The later doctrine answers the earlier question after the earlier question has been restated in its most cogent form. The cogent form of such questions for Whitehead is one that is aligned with the question of internal and external relations. Internal relations deal with the actuality of occasions. They account for an event being *where* and *how* it is.[16] External relations, contrariwise, deal with possibilities and not actualities, bearing as they do on the connections between events and eternal objects.

Space and time give us, in a sense, the morality of a community of events in their stance toward each other and in their ingredience in each other. The whole of the world is mirrored into our bodily life, and throws inward the nature of that functioning bodily life into each of its parts. Functioning organisms, through anticipation, are able to cast their settled states of achievement forward into the emergence of subsequent or future events. The mirroring of the whole into each of its parts transmits the value of that whole forward into an historical route of events.[17] Thus, the mirroring of whole into part has a replicative or multiplier effect. The effects of wholes are magnified through their imprinted parts. The efficacy of occasions turns on this multiplicative, internalizing relation of a whole being reflected into parts:

> An event is the grasping into unity of a pattern of aspects. The effectiveness of an event beyond itself arises from the aspects of itself which go to form the prehended unities of other events. Except for the systematic aspects of geometrical shape, this effectiveness is trivial, if the mirrored pattern attaches merely to the event as one whole. If the pattern endures throughout the successive parts of the event, and also exhibits itself in the whole, so that the event is the life history of the pattern, then in virtue of that enduring pattern the event gains in external effectiveness. For its own effectiveness is reenforced by the analogous aspects of all its successive parts. The event constitutes a patterned value with a permanence inherent throughout its own parts; and by reason of this inherent endurance the event is important for the modification of its environment.[18]

The effects achieved internally through a unification of aspects into a whole become powers whereby the event mirrors its achievement into other events.

Of critical importance for Whitehead's recast organismic approach to space and time is the manner in which space and time distinctly emerge from the society of events, and in the way time is differentiated from space. Space and time do comprise the unity, space-time. They are fused with special "intimacy" in relativity theory. But there is diversity in their unity. Space is disclosed more in the separative aspects of space-time, and time is disclosed more in the prehensive aspects of space-time: "We must not proceed to conceive time as another form of extensiveness."[19] Fundamentally, though, space is differentiated from time through certain references to the organic nature of the world. Events are individuated by internal relations. In turn, time differentiates itself from space, i.e., is a diverse aspect of unitive space-time, through the further effects of mirroring. Time arises through the realization of intensity and value in the field of extension.[20] Contrariwise, space as a diversifying aspect of space-time is the extension of the potential of a complex of occasions, but does not in the first place contribute to the further actualization of that complex. Time is a contributor to actualization because it can act as the medium for a unified quantum of value. Fusion—through the interpenetration of aspects into each other as prehensions in time—is another way of stating the principle of individuation in Whitehead's philosophy of organism. This view seems to be based upon accepting some of the implications of the fact that one of the most obvious disanalogies between space and time is that thought—which plays an obvious role in the realization of value—can be said to take place in time or across time, but thought cannot sensibly be said to be in space at all.

The pattern that arises through an internal fusing of aspects is then multiplied into the parts of the whole that emerged. The pattern is to be understood functionally. It provides us with a route of limitation toward a fully actual, singular being: "It is in this endurance of pattern that time differentiates itself from space."[21] The space-time continuum is a context for possibilities. As some selections are finally made by the inward mirroring that abruptly closes off any ingression from outside, an actual entity has been realized.[22] There has been both restriction and achievement. At this moment, time becomes real as a finished unit or epoch which reflects the complementary aspects of realization and restriction. The new unit flings the world process onward.

The separation of time as actual from the potentiation still associated with the space-time continuum has one additional mirroring effect. Time

by itself ceased to partake of the continuous nature it had in space-time, and takes on discontinuity. It now reflects the singularity of each actual occasion. Time becomes epochal.[23] It is now to be seen as a succession of epochal durations. This epochal nature is the mirror image of what the internal relatedness of actual occasion was for the emerging occasion. Time as epoch is the fitting alter ego of emergent occasions as modes of value and realization. But even taken epochally, time is still a dependent thing, arising as it does from characteristics of events or occasions. Two things should be noted about the epochal view of time. In the first place, it allows Whitehead to answer the question about accounting for the separateness of events without appealing to instants. Instants, in their turn, can be said to arise from epochs by extensive abstraction from events that are already separate. That is, the epochal theory of time removes a deeply buried circularity of thought in Whitehead's earlier view. So it is correct to say that the epochal theory arises as a logical result of Whitehead's processual account of nature. Second, Whitehead has clearly corrected traditional English empiricism. In sum, where Hume had taken the separateness or apartness of discrete impressions as primitive, Whitehead showed that the separateness of events arises out of a kind of valuing activity. Such a finding is, of course, intimately associated with a different approach to the problem of value in Whitehead's work.

3. THE EPOCHAL AND THE ETERNAL

The 1925 version of the epochal theory of time that appeared in Whitehead's first Lowell lectures, *Science and the Modern World*, was refined in 1926, in his second series of lectures, *Religion in the Making*. 'Epochal occasion' is substituted for 'event' or for 'prehensive occasion' in his discussions of religious experience, with the result that additional implications of speaking of time as epochal or quantumlike are disclosed. Moreover, if time is related to a succession of epochal occasions, then what is to be made of the lapses or intervals between occasions? Whitehead's answer clearly calls attention to the relationships between the temporal and the eternal. Furthermore, and perhaps most important, the aesthetic aspects of experience are presented in the 1926 Lowell lectures as the primordial aspects; aesthetic order and aesthetic value are set up as basal.[24] Other kinds of order, including temporal order, would then be satellite to aesthetic order.

An epochal occasion is a unity of opposites. The oppositional features of being and becoming, and mind and body, are included within it. Every epochal occasion has two sides: created and creative.[25] It is in part its own

product. But to enact limitations for itself, it must also transcend itself dynamically. It enacts its relationships to all other epochal occasions in a mirroring system of cross-references.[26] Each epochal occasion is thus seen by Whitehead as a microcosm that represents to itself the universe. As created, epochal occasions are concretions. They are modes of unifying many different elements into a single, fused entity. As a complex of internal relations, each epochal occasion is specified into a hierarchy of different senses of itself through limitations by other epochal occasions which it mirrors into its own nature.

Epochal occasions are alike in being a unity of opposites, but they differ in their degree of individuality: "The most individual actual entity is a definite act of perceptivity." Less individualized occasions would be ones where the mental and physical poles are unified in such a way that the physical pole, where memory and causal action are primarily reflected, is dominant. But where the mental pole with its associated perceptive and anticipatory features dominate, a more fully individualized entity is exhibited. Indeed, it is the realm of feeling and perception that is fundamental. The foundation of the world, Whitehead avers, is in aesthetic experience. It is upon that metaphysical claim that his other concepts are now to pivot. Moral experience is dependent upon a prior aesthetic experience. All order is aesthetic order.[27] But inasmuch as all aesthetic order is a display of God's immanence, it follows that all order and relation—aesthetic, moral, conceptual, and temporal—are declinations of the divine ground. Time as epochal is an epiphenomenon of God's nature under the aspect of diversity. Intentionally or otherwise, Whitehead's argument at this point debouches into the older neo-Platonic accounts of the nature of time, especially that of Plotinus.

Third, what of the lapses or intervals between the epochal occasions? Whitehead believed that the lapses of time are places where the world is still flung forward through the ingredience of additional eternal objects: "In the most literal sense the lapse of time is the renovation of the world with ideas."[28] As occasions in their creative mode take on additional eternal elements in the form of ideas that enter into the zone of activity, those occasions reach a kind of repletion associated with a consummatory act of feeling or perceptivity. In reference to that final fusion into a unity, in virtue of which the integrative nature of the whole is then mirrored into its parts, sealing those parts off from involvement with additional eternal objects, a sense of completion is experienced as an act of negation. There is refusal, and the creative occasion has created itself through its internal mirroring of whole into part. An epochal occasion has been created that sets that occasion off from other occasions.

4. THE NEW CONCEPTION OF TIME

The results of the two series of Lowell Institute lectures, *Science and the Modern World* and *Religion in the Making*, were confirmed by Whitehead in his address to the Sixth International Congress of Philosophy that convened at Harvard University. The address was entitled "Time" and was published in the 1927 congress proceedings. That he chose this topic for that forum illustrates the significance he attached to the problems associated with the questions about time and passage. His address shows that he had reworked the ideas about time that were presented in *The Concept of Nature* in the light of both Lowell series. Indeed, no better way can be found to meter the distance covered in passing from his philosophy of science to his metaphysics than a side-by-side reading of chapter 3, "Time," in *The Concept of Nature*, and the new model of that topic in his congress address, "Time," composed a few years after his arrival in the United States. Let us analyze the 1927 "Time," and then compare and contrast it with the 1919 "Time."

In *Science and the Modern World*, time was exhibited as rooted in the ordering of events. In *Religion in the Making*, it is held that all order is in the first place aesthetic order, turning on predication associated with perceptivity. The aspects of this fundamental aesthetic order, set out in the 1927 "Time," are supersession, prehension, and incompletion. The modes of time, as time present and past, are treated in relation to the concepts of objectivity, immortality, simultaneity, and the concretely epochal.[29] The traditional marks of time's irreversibility and seriality are shown to arise out of certain abstractive and quantizing procedures working on the underlying matrix of events.

As opposed to Descartes, occasions or events replace substances, and supersession as passage of occasions into other occasions replaces the changelessness of substances. Supersession means that each occasion supersedes some occasions, and is superseded by other occasions. What Whitehead had called the separative aspects of time in *Science and the Modern World* are betokened here in the concept of supersession, with more of a sense of passage added in the later version. Each epochal occasion also reflects these relations of antecedence and subsequence internally in its own nature. Through mirroring internally its causal antecedents in memory and its anticipated consequences in expectation, each actual occasion reveals its communal, nonisolated character. Thus, each occasion is internally a supersession.

For Spinoza, body and mind are modes of substance. For Whitehead, however, they are modes of occasions. The abstractive opposites of mind

and body are concretely united in occasions. But opposed to Spinoza and more in accord with Leibniz—who held that appetition within monads gives rise to an inner articulation of states—Whitehead holds that the mental features of the occasion supersede the physical as the occasion develops internally. This is important because time is more closely related to the physical than to the mental pole of the occasion. In both physical and mental senses, temporal relations are internal to a society of occasions, but time "only derivatively" is concerned with the mental pole of the occasion. Where Plotinus had held that time is the life of the soul, Whitehead holds that time is related to the bodily life of the soul that mirrors its surrounding region, and displays internally the gradience of energy transfers in that region. This inward display within a single organism is the prehensive aspect of time. Continuity with other occasions is shown. The occasion is also vivified through its prehension of eternal objects through its mental pole, and converts that external relationship of new possibilities into an internal relation of concrete completion. Many vectors are drawn into an organic unity within each actual occasion. The eternality of objects entering at the mental pole are fused with the temporality of antecedent and subsequent occasions at the physical pole to make of each occasion an interplay of the eternal and the temporal.[30]

Such a system of interrelated prehensive occasions is not, however, sufficient to account for temporality. For a system of mutually related occasions can itself be a timeless system simply by allowing different combinations of memories and anticipations to recur in a never-ending cycle. In order to throw such systems off-balance in a way that would rule out the completeness of the cyclic system, it is necessary to say that the component occasions in the system must themselves be lacking in concreteness with respect to their constituent elements. Thus follows Whitehead's definition of incompleteness, one of the necessary predicates of time. An occasion is incomplete to the degree that it prehends the coming objectification of occasions which will follow it.[31] That is, to the degree that an occasion mirrors features of what will supersede it, but indistinctly in that those future occasions are not actual, that occasion is incomplete and meontic. There is nonbeing in it. Here, in the 1927 publication, "Time," Whitehead makes clear that some prehending activity is a deutero-prehending: Some prehension is of the prehensions within occasions coming to be. Occasions are responding to their own openness.

An occasion has objective immortality through its supersession. That is, there is an inclusion of antecedent occasions in subsequent occasions. Whitehead's metaphor is that an occasion "enshrines the memory" of the precedent event it supersedes. This memory is a physical memory and is

the basis of both causation and the irreversibility of passage. But the inclusion in an occasion of the consequent states that will supersede it is more like an "implanting of hope." There is an anticipation of those future concretions that lie beyond this present occasion. This is the future that makes of the world system an open, incomplete system. But there is also a sideways openness in the world, for not all occasions are antecedent or subsequent to a given occasion. Some are prehended as immediately present, but in neither a causal nor anticipatory sense. Such occasions, Whitehead says, are prehended in the mode of presentational immediacy. This mode of prehension is, in his judgment, one of the roots of simultaneity.[32]

Finally, in the 1927 address to the international congress, Whitehead relates the epochal nature of temporal order (first set out in *Science and the Modern World*) to the aesthetic ground of all order (disclosed in *Religion in the Making*). Continuity has to do with the realm of the possible and the abstract, whereas supersession concerns the realm of the actual and the concrete.[33] This opening out of some distance between the notions of continuity and supersession signals his attainment of another level in his philosophy of time: the continuous deals with the potential and not with the actual. Time, his new understanding allows him, is epochal and not perpetual. Perpetuity and continuity are closely related concepts, related as species to genus, with perpetuity being the temporal form of continuity. But epochs and actual occasions are not instances of these concepts. Rather, they are associated with actual organisms and with consummatory phases of aesthetic experience. Temporal reality comes in quanta, just as energy comes in quanta.

5. COMPARISONS OF TWO TIME CONCEPTS

The most important differences between the 1919 discussion of time in *The Concept of Nature* and the 1927 discussion in the international congress proceedings turn on Whitehead's elimination of vestiges of the classical mechanistic world view that still clung to his reconstruction of the concept of nature. Several of those remnants can be traced to his implicit acceptance of the importance of external relations in his more scientifically oriented work. His patience with external relations is highlighted in the methodological dictum that mind is external to nature.[34] When the doctrine of internal relations becomes dominant in both Lowell lecture series, a revised concept of nature is called for. Internal and external relations have undergone a reversal of emphasis in his thought in the years between 1919 and 1927. Mechanism did not take time seriously because it worked with a single time series spanning the whole of existence, and because it al-

lowed for a multiplicity of validly isolated events with no more than external, extensive relations between them.[35] Whitehead's 1927 view takes events as enduring occasions with prehensive, unifying marks that reflect internal relations within and between events. For his later view, even contemporary, simultaneous events are mirrored internally in their independent associates.

The concept of supersession in the later paper displaces to a secondary position the 1919 concept of extension.[36] In the early version, extension was a root of both space and time. Especially important is the internal supersession (1927) over the durational extension within events (1919). This internal supersession gives greater weight to causal ideas in depicting the process of going from present to past to future. The internal supersession places passage, not duration, at the heart of each incipient occasion, for duration typifies the older view, with an emphasis upon contemporaneous events, and overlooks the causal change associated with physical and bodily states.[37] Time, in the 1927 view, is said primarily to relate to the physical pole of occasions, and only secondarily to the mental pole. This emphasis helps clarify the notion in *The Concept of Nature* that mind and body are in time in different senses. The later view thus places mind and body in complementary, not separative, opposition.

A second significant development between the two treatments deals with the displacement from a central position of the concept of cogredience. The idea of prehension supplants the role assigned to cogredience in 1919, in explaining the nature of time. Prehension is like cogredience in including the marks of immediacy and compresence of elements in a complex event. But the notions importantly differ in the degree to which the marks of fusion, organism, and perceptivity control the meaning of the concept of prehension. If nature is perceived as closed to mind, as in the earlier view, cogredience is with extension a root of space and time. But if nature is opened to mind, so that states of awareness are included in the class of ultimate existents which fall within a concept of nature, then prehension becomes one of the new roots of time.

The idea of incompleteness (1927)—which betokens the fact of a constant openness to the future with a concomitant unsettling response to openness in the present—quite undercuts the centrality of the idea of continuity (1919) at the base of temporality. Each occasion captures certain aspects of its future within its present activity through anticipation or expectation. Without this incompleteness, we could simply have an overall acosmic system. Just as Leibniz had held that there is in monads an internal principle of change, a principle of appetition that also supplies an individuating detail of change, so Whitehead holds that the anticipation or ex-

pectation of a possible future brings about an internal supersession within each prehensive occasion. Time is incomplete and thus discontinuous because the real occasions it reflects do continue the sway of the objective past over the possible future. Continuity in the old sense is not primitive for Whitehead, but comes into being: "There is no continuity of becoming, but there is a becoming of continuity."[38]

A fourth mark of temporality in "Time" (1927) is objective immortality, an idea derived from treating memory anew, and presuming that causality is the condition of objective immortality that holds primarily between the physical poles of events. Giving the role of memory such emphasis and reinterpretation is significant in showing how nature is open to mind, and mind to nature, through the mediation of our bodily conditions. To understand something about memory is to understand something about the nature of causal efficacy between past and present. This stress upon immortality as a mark of the concrete world from which we abstract our space and time relations is an outgrowth of the distinctly heightened role that aesthetic and phenomenological categories play in Whitehead's developing cosmology. That role is set out dramatically in a conclusion drawn in the 1927 paper, which is directed at showing that "individual perceptivity is the ultimate physical fact."[39] The drama, however, resides less in that thesis itself than in an implication that follows from crossing that thesis with the concept of whole-part relations.

The concept of whole-part relations, which controlled all lines of discussion in *The Concept of Nature,* is modified in his later work. Whitehead said in the Tarner lectures that the extensive whole-part relation is transitive and asymmetrical.[40] This characterization, however, is compromised by its alliance with the substance-attribute relation, a relation that is also transitive (an attribute of an attribute is an attribute of the thing itself) and asymmetrical (if P is a predicate or attribute of a substance X, then X can never be a predicate or attribute of P). The absolutely salient point is that substances can *have* properties but cannot *be* properties. This is the reason that whole-part relations in the received metaphysics, including the metaphysics underlying mechanistic concepts of the world, are intransitive. But from *Science and the Modern World* on, Whitehead has in effect overturned this leading directive of substance metaphysics. The notion of mirroring, as understood within a format of internal relations, overturns the substance concept: the part has aspects of the whole, and the whole has aspects of the part; the unified whole is internally composite; contemporaneous epochal occasions mirror each other, and thus are predicates of each other. From this point forward, the whole-part relation of extension in

Whitehead's philosophy of organism is transitive and symmetrical, not transitive and asymmetrical.

In one important respect, a leading idea from "Time" (1919) is brought forward and synthesized with a notion in "Time" (1927). The idea of the incompleteness of time, e.g., the reflection into time of the underlying separateness of actual events, is central to the epochal theory of time. That theory is a most singular feature of Whitehead's movement *beyond* the reconstructed concept of nature he gave in the Tarner lectures, and his statement of the philosophy of organism in the Lowell lectures. As disclosed in the Lowell series, the key features of his epochal theory of time were: (1) its independence of the main version of relativity theory; (2) its dependence upon the notion of an extended background energy field in all of nature; and (3) its dependence upon the twinned doctrines of mirroring and internal relations. In "Time" (1927), Whitehead added an additional essential mark to the epochal theory, the view that (4) there is a continuity to time that also betokens its involvement in external relations.

Inasmuch as the idea of supersession displaces the earlier idea of the extensive field, it is clear that quantum concepts can be given greater weight in framing a concept of nature. The philosophy of organic mechanism, given the discreteness of the primal organic events, could equally well be called a philosophy of quantum mechanism. Obviously, Whitehead drew upon relativity theory, with some reinterpretations, in his first version of a reconstructed concept of nature. A first-generation quantum theory was just taking shape as Whitehead wrote *Science and the Modern World* in 1925. To hold that supersession is not continuous is to emphasize its quantum features. Supersession deals with contoured actualities, and continuity deals with potentiality. "Supersession," he said, "cannot be regarded as the continuous unfolding of a continuum."[41] This emphasis upon the actual cell-like or droplike character of actuality would mean that a concept of time which reflected its real roots in nature would be an epochal concept. Each occasion has a time quantum associated with it: "The occasion B which acquires concretion so as to supersede A embodies a definite quantum of time which I call the 'epochal character' of the concrescence. The epochal theory of time is the foundation of the theory of atomic organisms, and of the modern physical quantum-theory." The times associated with each occasion, Whitehead also sets out in this context, are comparable with respect to their unit parts.

From this possibility of comparison, it follows that time is continuous when associated with the realm of the potential, and discontinuous when associated with the realm of actual events or occasions. There is no conti-

nuity of becoming at the level of actual occasions, but there is a becoming of continuity at the abstractive level where other possibilities may be envisaged. At that abstractive level, time quanta are divisible and countable according to ideally limited unit parts that fall across a continuum. Thus, synthesized into his 1927 theory of time is a view about time as a continuum, a view brought forward from the 1919 Tarner lectures. Put another way, if the proper qualifications are introduced, some parts of that earlier theory can be seen as special cases of his more mature theory.

A complete account of the developmental state, reached in Whitehead's philosophy of time during 1927, must include an analysis of two or three notions that appeared in another study published in that year, *Symbolism: Its Meaning and Effect*. Obviously, to the degree that we claim to have knowledge about time, especially as that knowledge deals with things not immediately present, we are relating statements about mental phenomena *now* present to experiences we remember as coming *before* this present experience, or to experiences we anticipate will come *after* this present experience. Questions about time, then, raise logical issues about the nature and validity of certain kinds of inferences, and about the concreteness or abstractedness of the temporal expressions that occur in those inferences. In dealing with some of these issues in *Symbolism* (1927), Whitehead throws additional light on time in relation to passage.

Whitehead had held from the very first that the ideally limited parts of time are not concrete. Instants are not to be thought of as time units in which bare happenings occurred. Such a belief in mere happenings or bare occurrences would be a variant of the fallacy of misplaced concreteness. The variant would apply principally to time and would take us from a belief in durationless happenings to the acceptance of time as a pure succession. "I directly deny this doctrine of simple occurrence. There is nothing which 'simply happens.' Such a belief is the baseless doctrine of time as 'pure succession.' "[42] Whitehead believed that the tradition of English empiricism, especially as shown in Hume's treatment of impressions, had erred precisely through its treatment of individual sense impressions as valid isolates which are bare, durationless occurrences. Moreover, in that there is no perceived relation between the data arising in discrete occurrences, it would follow that an active mind or spirit must be postulated to constitute the relational fabric of experience. Those who accepted the Humean analysis of experience, including Kant, have simply misread the facts.[43]

Whitehead was convinced that we know more about the passing, perishing world than we notice. Through a sort of protoknowledge, we prehend more than we apprehend. Much of this deep, background knowing is

intricately intertwined with our bodily states, and we fail to register it in our abstract accounts of time and succession. Such accounts neglect the most dominant but least noticed aspect of perceptual occasions. The fundamental mark of time from which we prescind is the succession of occasions of perceptivity, with a concomitant derivation of state from state: "Time in the concrete is the conformation of state to state, the later to the earlier."[44] Pure succession, as an uninterrupted continuity of instants or moments, is the product of a graded series of abstractions from this fact of concrete conformation. This is how continuity becomes.

The concept of conformation, where the past lays its hands upon the present and in part molds the present in its own image, is a new device in Whitehead's expanded understanding of time. It is a more positive notion than the idea of channeling or canalization which he had used in his earlier work. The present essentially conforms to the past, though there is of course more to the present than mere conformation to the past. The freedom that is also an essential mark of the present is dependent upon other features of Whitehead's scheme. But the past is the destiny of the present, and exacts of the present a fateful conformity: "The immediate present has to conform to what the past is for it."[45] Importantly, conformity of the present to the past provides the ground for denying that the present simply happens, or that there are mere occurrences lodged in isolable moments in a strict succession. Every occurrence has entangling alliances with factors from its past, and so cannot simply happen. According to Whitehead's analysis, Hume overlooked the relation of conformation, and then found that the concept of cause was groundless. Hume and his followers overlooked the derivation of state from state. They had constructed upon a doctrine of isolable impressions an account of time as a series of successive, disconnected moments.[46] In the accounts of both Hume and Whitehead, the problems of time and causation are treated together. Whitehead's use of a direct kind of perception associated with bodily states to illustrate the concept of conformation provides *pari passu* a way around the destructive Humean account of causation.

The Principle of Conformation, as Whitehead came to call it, provides his answer to Hume and to Kant.[47] Mind is not the basic synthesizer of experience. Rather, our bodily states and our reactions to the external world mediated through those states are the creators of the tissue of experience. Santayana had emphasized shock experiences in accounting for our conviction of a really existent external world in *Scepticism and Animal Faith.* In a similarly realistic vein, Whitehead believed that anger and terror, although inhibiting certain data, nevertheless "wholly depend upon a vivid apprehension of the relevance of immediate past to the present, and

of the present to the future." Almost against our will, we are driven to notice the constraints that previous events in our lives place upon immediately subsequent events. "The perception of conformation to realities in the environment is the primitive element in our external experience."[48] This basal element of conformation, almost unnoticed because it is a condition of all of our noticing anything whatever, is the concrete element in our time experience and our experience of causality. Whitehead names this conformation of state to state the experience of "causal efficacy." Causal efficacy is detected by us in its two main conative modes, aversion and appetition, with aversion being the basis of the experience of anger and terror mentioned earlier. In short, causation is rooted in valuing experiences, and both time and causation are features of the achieving and avoiding of certain kinds of positive and negative value. From the valuational point of view, the epochal theory of time calls for a correspondingly reworked theory of extension or continuity, namely, the theory of conformation. Thus, in Whitehead's revised views about time, the epochal and the conformal senses of time are correlative notions.

According to Whitehead, the conformation of the present to the past, with an associated independence of the present from the past, is the most primitive of our complex experiences.[49] In the interaction of present and past, a settling of accounts occurs, as value is realized in emergent occasions and as some of the conditions for those values are passed on to mold the present. Whitehead summarizes this aspect of his views in a motto he first used in *Symbolism: pereunt et imputantur.*[50] The phrase—taken from the sundials that religious houses used as clocks—means, "the hours perish and are laid to account." Whitehead interpreted the inscription to mean that "our experience arises out of the past: —it bequeaths its character to the future, —for good or for evil." The 'pereunt' of *pereunt et imputantur* is the basis of immediate presentations from experience, of shifting sounds and sights both scattered and close by. The 'pereunt' reflects the facts of presentational immediacy, and is less important in localizing and organizing experience than is the causal efficacy reflected in the 'imputantur' of *pereunt et imputantur*. Data given to us in the mode of presentational immediacy are projected or deployed to provide the basis of spatial relations.[51] But the sense data in the mode of causal efficacy show us the adjustments of bodily organs so that characteristic marks are laid across experience reflecting the conformation of state to state. Temporal relations find their basis in this conformation, and the conformation of state to state in earlier-later relations is more significant for the organization of experience than is the deployment of state beside state in spatial relations of coexistence. Hume, Whitehead concluded, had completely inverted the true situation. In displacing sense data based on conformal

states, Hume had also unraveled the true significance of time and causation as basal features of experience.

Both modes of perception—presentational immediacy and causal efficacy—are at the root of our space-time system. The percipient body is nested in a system of conformations and restraints on the basis of causal efficacy. Sense data in different projections are referred to the percipient body as the basis of a more social projection into an organized world.[52] All of these projections away from the percipient body as the locus for projection are related to an antecedent conformation of bodily state to external happenings, a conformation which thus reflects the values attached to experience. *Pereunt et imputantur*: our reactions to things pass away and are no more, but preemptively those reactions lay certain restraints upon the present to which the present must conform. This conformation is the concrete presence of time, of past time as a source of power over the present. It is also reflected in Peirce's metaphor of the past as the sheriff's hand upon one's shoulder.

6. TIME, PROCESS, AND EXTENSIVE CONNECTION

The notions of the passage of events as a process involving both perishing and conformation, of time as both epochal and continuous, and of the interplay of internal relatedness with external relatedness are integral to Whitehead's descriptions of reality found in his major metaphysical statement, *Process and Reality*. The principle of relativity in his philosophy is now explicitly said to overturn Aristotle's substance approach to philosophy, because for Whitehead a "substance" or actual entity *is* present in another subject.[53] Indeed, he said that the explication of being present in another actual entity is a main task of his philosophy of organism. In later years, Whitehead again compared his thought to that of Aristotle in holding that "almost all of *Process and Reality* can be read as an attempt to analyze perishing on the same level as Aristotle's analysis of becoming."[54] The flux of things must be treated in a double sense if it is to be treated adequately: as becoming and as perishing.

The theory of time set out in his Gifford lectures, 1927–28 (published as *Process and Reality* in 1929) arises within the framework of the theory of the extensive continuum. The extensive relations within this continuum include temporal and spatial extensiveness. But extensive relatedness is more than spatiotemporal extension, and also goes beyond whole-part relations. In displacing whole-part relations from the center of his theory of extensive relatedness, Whitehead's account of time and space seems to introduce an emphasis that redresses certain claims he had made in the years immediately preceding. He is obviously aware of securing the

advance he had made since his writings in the philosophy of science, 1919–23. That earlier account, he held, was too one-sided, and in being one-sided was in error.[55] The root of the difficulty was in placing too much emphasis upon the overlapping relations that typify whole-part complexes, and in not attending sufficiently to the significance of relations that set events apart due to eternal objects that are ingredient in them.[56] That is, real continuity was stressed over real discontinuity, and the potentiality associated with the extensive continuum was mistakenly confused with actuality. The actuality of spatiotemporal quanta was depreciated, and the potentiality of relating extension to *serial* extension was made too dominant.

But both kinds of extensive relation are fundamental. The extensive relations *in* things are, in his corrected version in the Gifford lectures, no more important than the extensive relations *between* things. The criticism of his earlier theory of extension by Theodore De Laguna was in part responsible for Whitehead's development of a theory of the continuum that underlies the epochal aspects of time.[57] Whitehead accepted De Laguna's view that the idea of extensive connection is the more primitive, more general idea and that the extensive relations of whole and part can be defined in terms of it. Briefly, the point is that the extensive connections of inclusion and exclusion are equibasic. All relations of spatial and temporal connectedness as set out in *Process and Reality* are to be seen as ultimately grounded in the undefined essential relation of extensive connection: it is *sui generis*. Time as potential and continuous must be balanced by time as actual and discontinuous.[58] Time must be taken as epochal in the locus of the actual entity.

One way to rework spatiotemporal extensiveness so that it plays its proper role is to develop a distinction between *abstract* and *real* potentiality. A general, abstract potentiality is especially related to those pure potentials that are eternal objects. Real potentiality is a medium of potentiality comprised of spatial and temporal extensiveness. It is the extensive field for incipient actuality, and the shadowy conformation that the plenitude of actual events cast across the pure realm of general potentiality. Real potentiality is a complex, relational matrix of whole-part relations that underlies all of the past, present, and future.[59] Past, present, and future are modes of time that presuppose a more general, nonmetrical spatiotemporal continuum. It is this continuum (that Whitehead associates with Plato's Receptacle in later writings) that makes up real potentiality. It provides the field in which extensiveness is atomized into epochs under the press of actual occasions and of God as principles of individualization and limitation.[60] It is only on attaining this view of the nature of time as both

a continuum (of real potentiality) and as a plenitude (of discrete actual epochs) that Whitehead is able to set out his most developed account of the modes of time, past, present, and future, which is found in *Adventures of Ideas*. The Gifford lectures secure what is then detailed in the later work.

Real potentiality, as a complex relational continuum, is a nonmetrical continuum. But this complex extensive continuum is indefinitely divisible, and is unbounded in its spatiotemporal extensiveness. Again, the extensive continuum seems to play a role in Whitehead's cosmology like that of the *apeiron* in Anaximander's cosmology. In both cases, the extended unbroken field is undifferentiated (*apeiron*) but is capable of taking on character or limitation (*peron*). In itself nonmetrical and topological, it is capable of taking on metrical characters. Actual entities, Whitehead holds, are related to each other according to the determinations of this extensive continuum. It provides certain kinds of canalization or conformation that constrain the subsequent relations between actual occasions.[61] All world order reflects the conformal features laid upon actual occasions by the temporal and spatial order that arises in the background continuum. The reality of the present conforming to the past and of the future conforming to the present is in part secured through the real potentiality of the continuum as extensively connected. The continuum is also the basis of the mirroring effect which channels the structure of the whole into each of its parts. Each actual entity, moreover, mirrors every other because all partake of a deeper continuum that is implicated in each processual event.[62]

The resultant time theory has it that the atomization of temporal extension is shown in the epochal actuality of each occasion. This theory of time would be closer to one of Whitehead's linear theories of the world as set out in the 1905 Memoir. The ultimate existents in this theory would not be Leibnizean in cast, for Leibniz's ultimate existents change, whereas Whitehead's become but do not change.[63] Each of Whitehead's actual entities is a society of elements that grow together or concresce in a zone of actualization. The quantum aspects of each concrescence have certain associated, temporal features and certain features of a spatial volume. But these spatiotemporal features do not arise in a common, serial time. Rather, each actual entity becomes the locus of the world that is centered for it, and no two actual entities would demarcate the same world.

Actualization, according to Whitehead, is a genetic process of growth, not a process of coordination. It has to do with the concrescence of actual entities as they arise out of the extensive continuum. These occasions of emergence into actuality are not in physical time and are not subject to the physical relations detailed in spatial and temporal coordinates. Epochs are

not in physical time, but make possible certain of the determinations of time that we call physical. We say "certain of" because "physical time expresses some features of the growth, but *not* the growth of the features."[64] Physical time is epiphenomenal, and arises through the coordination of some features of temporal successiveness. In turn, temporal succession is based upon the genetic, causal process. Temporal succession has to do with change, whereas the genetic process—which is more basic—has to do with growth. It reflects the creative emergence of epochs. In sum, according to Whitehead's theory, time as epochal takes precedence over the relations of successiveness in physical time.

Both physical time and physical space presuppose the relation of extension. Extension in turn, as we see in De Laguna's correction of Whitehead's starting point, is to be taken as extensive connection: "The extensiveness of space is really the spatialization of extension; and the extensiveness of time is really the temporalization of extension. Physical time expresses the reflection of genetic divisibility into coordinate divisibility."[65] There are extensive relations *in* things and extensive relations *between* things. This dyad of extensive connections provides the fundaments for internal and external relations. The organic philosophy, in short, is equally beholden to each mode of relatedness. Moreover, inasmuch as nature is an extensive field, nature will never be a completed, single whole, but will always be in the process of a creative advance. Nature is fundamentally active, always enacting new combinations and connections. It is this creative advance of nature that gives rise to the very problem of time itself.[66] That problem is doubly rooted in the genetic processes of growth and in the processes of perishing. To round out the analysis of Whitehead's additions to his theory of time in *Process and Reality*, we have to examine both of these processes.

An adequate metaphysics must exhibit both Heracleitean and Parmenidean motifs among its several features. It must include the refrains of process and of permanence. Whitehead believed that these two antithetical notions reflected some of the very deepest features of human experience.[67] Elucidating this experience shows how primitive is the vague belief that "all things flow." But the passage of things is reflected against a background of permanence, or, if permanence were stressed, it is reflected against a background of passage. The dialectic between process and permanence comprises one of the fundamental polarities of thought, and each pole is disclosed with equal urgency in our characterizations of experience. Thus, the main problems of time are seated in the questions associated with process and permanence, and their interrelations.

The two emphases can be found in liturgical aspects of religious experience. Whitehead thought that they were tellingly exhibited in the hymn by

Henry Lyte and William Monk, "Abide with Me; Fast Falls the Eventide."
The two clauses give us "a full expression of the union of the two notions
in one integral experience."[68] The first line, "abide with me," sets out the
quest for permanence; and the second, "fast falls the eventide," places the
permanent within the all-encompassing flux. Taken together, the two
lines have "formulated the complete problem of metaphysics." A metaphysics of substance proceeds from the notions reflected in the first clause,
whereas a metaphysics of flux captures the ideas registered in the second.
An adequate metaphysics, however, will treat both together in their integral unity.[69] A sound philosophy of time, in turn, will be tied to both those
salient conceptions, allowing for continuity and conformation through
time and for discontinuity and uniqueness of achievement as between different times.

A discovery of modern Western thought, Whitehead believed, was that
there are two species of process or fluency. These kinds are concrescence
and transition, and they can be tellingly illustrated in language drawn from
Locke's philosophy.[70] Concrescence for Locke is "the real internal constitution of a particular existent." It has to do with the growing together of
a group of conditions into a single, determinate actuality. It is clearly an
affair of internal relatedness. Transition, on the other hand, is the "transition from particular existent to particular existent." It has to do with the
extension of a sequence into new items in a series. It is clearly an affair of
external relatedness. The one, concrescence, moves to actualize its final
cause, whereas the other, transition, is the basis of the operations of efficient cause. We thus find in Whitehead's account of the two kinds of
process an additional basis for his account of a philosophy of organic
mechanism, which he said, in *Science and the Modern World*, was a synthesis of classical modern mechanistic philosophy and the organic philosophy of internal relatedness. Moreover, just as De Laguna's correction of
the theory of extension led Whitehead to take the notion of extensive connection as the primitive, undefined relation in his philosophy, so too the
corrected version of extension allowed him to formulate an exact statement of the two kinds of process. Extensive connection, as we saw, is both
connection *in* things and connection *between* things. In discussing the
two kinds of process, the first mode of extension is what we would call the
concrescent mode, whereas the second mode of extension, that holding
between things, is what we would call the transition mode of process. The
former is a teleological process; the latter is an efficient or instrumental
process. Taken together, they are alternating phases or currents through
which reality passes in becoming actual.

The two sides of process, then, are transition and concrescence. Concrescence is an idea that exhibits the inward gathering of things, a many

growing into a one. Concrescence shows that centripetal forces are present in process. Conversely, transition points at the relation between one thing and the next. It deals with externalizing relations, with forces not centripetal but centrifugal. The contrast between concrescence and transition evokes some images from the cosmology of Empedocles. Especially pertinent here would be the Empedoclean relational forces, Eros and Polemos, which drive the cosmos through its appointed rounds. Polemos, the deity of strife, lies behind the perpetual perishing in Empedocles's cosmos, and transition as the power of dispersion lies behind the perpetual perishing in Whitehead's cosmos. "The ultimate evil in the temporal world," Whitehead avows, "lies in the fact that the past fades, that time is a 'perpetual perishing'."[71] This perishing is said to lead into processes of growth. This is analogous to the way the dispersion of Polemos fades into the integrative activity of Eros in the cosmos described by Empedocles. Whitehead's view does not, of course, present a cyclical cosmic process, as does the view of Empedocles.

Whitehead hoped that permanence and flux are ultimately to achieve a synthesis or reconciliation. Creation would then have attained that final term, the condition of everlastingness.[72] In some of Whitehead's valedictory remarks, found in his final interpretation in part 5 of *Process and Reality*, he seems to be trying to close the gap between two of the basic Greek conceptions of time, *chronos* and *kairos*. Kairos is the ripe time, the time of value and decision, the time of things that have grown together into a single whole. Kairos is that telic time where the power of action is most distinctly revealed. The other kind of time, however, is not that organic concrescent movement toward a single whole. It is the measured time of one interval or moment following upon another. The titanic power and separating effect of this kind of perishing time is caught up in the myths about Chronos. Kairos and Chronos, living concrescent time and transitory time, have represented a fundamental duality in the Western philosophy of time since the pre-Socratic philosophers, dramatists, and poets. Whitehead seeks to combine the notions by receiving them into the nature of God: "Each actuality in the temporal world has its reception into God's nature. The corresponding element in God's nature is not temporal actuality, but is the transmutation of that temporal activity into a living, ever-present fact."[73] Time undergoes an apotheosis of sorts in entering into God's nature. Time's future, Whitehead believes, is to take on everlastingness. In short, there will be a consummation in which transition and perishing no longer exist, for the divine nature itself is not temporal.[74] Concrescence, as the ingathering of all the scattered past and presents, will find its final kairos in God's nature.

7. THE RECEPTACLE AND THE MODES OF TIME

In his Gifford lectures, Whitehead showed that spatiotemporal relations are dependent upon the primitive, essential relation called 'extensive connection'. In *Adventures of Ideas*, published in 1933, Whitehead held that space and time are dependent upon the Receptacle, an idea introduced in Greek philosophy. Whitehead wanted to show that his revised concept of nature could be used to retrodict some of the fundamental notions of Greek cosmology. In effect, we find him mapping the key ideas in his philosophy of time and space across the vague continents of thought that had been espied in Greek myth and philosophy. Extensive connection, conformation, real potentiality, passage: all are used to probe and revivify the idea of the Receptacle. Our space-time, he says, is a compromise between the Platonic Receptacle and the Actual World.[75]

In *Adventures of Ideas*, three main themes dominate Whitehead's development of the ideas of the Receptacle and space-time. The first is the idea of the Receptacle as a kind of *place*, with spatial aspects then being differentiated within this locus. The second is the idea that elements or factors are related to each other by internal and external relations, so that there exists a real diversity-in-unity within the Receptacle. But at this point Whitehead introduces an essential modification of the Greek Receptacle, for the Receptacle he discusses is both a mode of relation *and* a relatum. The Receptacle, in short, is internally related to its contents, and Greek science went astray in ignoring that fact. So, thirdly and predictably, this matrix of all becoming itself has a processual nature. For if it is internally related to its contents, and if those contents exhibit traits of temporality, it follows that the matrix of all becoming is itself involved in growth.

As a kind of place, the Receptacle is an enduring locus whose function in Plato's thought was to unify the events in nature. So taken, it provides emplacement in a single medium for the exhibition of occasions. Itself bereft of all form, its power is the power of receptivity or ingression of form within it. But its successive acts of reception are constrained by previous acts, so that a kind of destined effect also arises in the matrix of becoming. The exact character of the Receptacle varies with the passage of events, for paths are laid out which bear upon future occasions. So the space-time Receptacle is not the mother of becoming, but is, as Plato had held, the foster-mother. That is, it does not have procreative powers. (Eros, the struggle to exist, provides that agency.)[76] But as foster-mother, it has a nurturant, caretaker function, working to bring a measure of character to the otherwise inexhaustible diversity of the actual entities that arise within it.

A second theme in Whitehead's account of the Receptacle is that the various actual occasions are beholden to each other because they are antecedently embedded in it. Occasions are actualized partly by reason of their emplacement in the community of occasions. It is of the essence of an actual occasion to be an element qualifying the Receptacle, and these qualifications of the Receptacle enter into its proper nature. This qualified Receptacle is then graded into new emergent occasions. Through the medium of this potentiating matrix, past occasions lay constraints upon occasions yet to come. Whitehead held that this was also Plato's doctrine of the Receptacle: "The Receptacle, as discussed in the *Timaeus*, is the way in which Plato conceived the many actualities of the physical world as components in each other's natures." Not only are the actual occasions taken as powers qualifying each others' natures through their emplacement in a world field, but this locus is also the field of human actions. The entire course of history is set within it. So human acts and what we call natural events jointly inhabit the same domain.[77]

This total world is a unity-in-diversity.[78] It is an abidingness-in-transitoriness. Everything that comes to be does so through the process of being specified internally by the presence of other elements projected into its own process of growth. Whitehead holds that space-time relativity makes the totality of all things a Receptacle that unites all events. The classical modern concept of nature saw space and time unifying the world by imposing a constitution upon it from outside. This would be consistent with the approach given in the punctual concepts of nature Whitehead described in his 1905 memoir. But the Receptacle unites immanently, not just transuently. It is the way each actual event adjusts the rest of the world event.

The last of the main conceptions that controls Whitehead's view of the space-time Receptacle is the processual nature of this matrix of becoming. In responding to what already was, it engenders a development beyond its present condition. Qualifications of the Receptacle enter into the Receptacle's own nature. Both Plato and Epicurus, Whitehead thought, endeavored to express the idea that there is a "real communication" between things and events in their doctrines of the world locus and the void. There are continuing transactions between all eventualities. These transactions make of the world a world process. The essential mark of this developing world fact is that it is "process with the retention of connectedness." It is the idea of a flux within and across a unified field, the idea that there is essential connectedness or relativity of features within the field.[79] Whitehead thought that this character of the cosmos was depicted both in the relativity physics of his day and in the theory of the world locus of Plato. Space-time relativity makes of the totality of things something like the Re-

ceptacle that unites all things. The Receptacle Whitehead describes is a matrix for transition and is, accordingly, a matrix in transition. Because it is a medium in transition, it imposes its own component of transitoriness upon occurrences within it. It afflicts occurrences in the world with a past, present, and future as necessary modes of actualization.

Whitehead did not think that a consideration of time led directly to classifications about things in the world.[80] But indirectly, time does lend itself to the differentiations we call past, present, and future. That is, transcendental ideas like being, one, time, and so on, do allow of modal qualification. It does make sense to speak of the modes of being or the modes of unity. Likewise, it makes sense to speak of the modes of time, of time as present or past or future. Temporality is in all things, but not in the same manner. It is in some things as time past, but in other things as time present or time future. Important to all of what Whitehead says about the different modes of time in *Adventures in Ideas* is the thoroughgoing interdependence of these modes; they are immanent in each other. If Whitehead's use of the Receptacle is consistent with Plato's ideas, his use of the interdependence of time's modes is consistent with Stoic ideas.[81] Both Whitehead and the Stoics held that past and future are conformal features of the present.

Whitehead used metaphors to show the immanence of the future in the present: the future is "something for" the present, "lives in" the present, is "in the crannies of the present." The future is a gadfly for the present by provoking it. It stings the present into renewed struggles for the realization of alternate possibilities. In substance, these metaphors mean that the future is in the present as a mirror image of what an idealized present could become if the actual present perishes in becoming a phase of that more ideal condition. Both intuition and common sense, Whitehead felt, confirm that the future and the present are interacting in the experiences we are now having, as reduced to second or half-second durations of the specious present.[82] To identify the structure of these short-range, immediate bursts of present experience is to call attention to certain relational properties.

The future is immanent in the present through the process of self-completion. Each actual occasion works upon its relative nonbeing so as to bring forth a more finished nature. Each occasion seeks to embody or emplace itself. In constituting itself, it both reenacts what it has been and anticipates what it is yet to be. It both acquires a diverse content through its reenactments and takes on propositional features as it transfers its posture from the multiple to the unitive phases of what it grows toward. The reality of the occasion is the transition between the two states. "The whole

doctrine of the future is to be understood in terms of the account of the process of self-completion of each individual actual occasion."[83] This statement of the meaning of the future is especially relevant to Stephen Pepper's judgment that the root-metaphor of Whitehead's metaphysics is the idea of the purposive act, and that the structure of the metaphysics is in major respects a transcript of the structure of the purposive act.[84] This interpretation is keyed to the interplay between the anticipatory and consummatory phases of the *positive* purposive act, or appetition: the present anticipates its connections with the future. Anticipation of a kinship with the future assures that "the present bears in its own essence the relationships which it will have to the future."[85] In vaguely prehending the character of the universe as passage, each occasion also imbibes its own share of that character.

In its turn, the past is immanent—through channeling effects—in the incipient, virtual present that is its immediate future. The past lays a necessity upon the future. Whitehead's main term here is 'constitution'. The constitution of the present ensures that the future will embody it, because that constitution is comprised of relations and patterns of activities that bespeak the more general features of the space-time Receptacle. The essence of the present includes the extensive connections the present will have with the future. The present is the medium for parlaying the conformal aspects from the past into the future. Those conformal aspects, however, mingle with the open or incomplete aspects of present time to bring about a future that is both free and necessitated. There is openness or freedom in the present because contemporary events are independent of each other. The relation of causation from past to present is transitive, whereas the relation of contemporaneity is nontransitive. That is, contemporaries of the same occasion may or may not be each other's contemporaries.[86] Although relations between past and present events are causal, the relations between contemporary events are more spatial, for "space expresses the halt for attainment," and time more directly has its roots in causal efficacy.[87] These contemporary events, according to Whitehead's descriptions, are more like Leibniz's monads that do not have (causal) windows open to each other, yet still mirror each other's nature (through shared antecedent conditions). As opposed to the Leibniz's "closed windows" image, Whitehead says that contemporary events are "shrouded from" each other.[88] So there are compossible types of order in the present, where each occasion can enjoy its unique value experiences. As with Leibniz, however, there is a shared presence, if not a shared present, among contemporary occasions because of their emergence from a common past: "The whole antecedent world conspires to produce a new occasion," so

there is some commonality between contemporaries that are otherwise "shrouded from" each other.[89] That shared nature, moreover, is due to the common future they are jointly channeling, and which is also antecedently reflected in them. There is still a dispersiveness among contemporaries in their direct separateness of achievement and appreciation. Indeed, spatial experience is the expression of this joint association of valuing centers.

Whitehead views past-future relations as the main form of temporal relations, and relations between contemporaries as the main source of spatial relations. The past prehends the form of the future that shall conform to it.[90] The future shapes the present in providing a possible route to self-completion, but contemporaries are independent from each other and are differentiated in an exterior mode. Events or occasions that stand in anticipatory causal relations with each other make up the field of a special kind of relation that Whitehead calls a 'nexus'.[91] A nexus is a more local version of the overall, extensive, transitive character of the world process. This continuous, transitory world process is itself an event composed of events, a multipli-ordered occasion that provides emplacement, and exacts perishing, of all that exists. The mutual immanence of the modes of time and space is called by Whitehead the Genus of Patterned Nexūs. This genus is the extensively connected, dispersive, and incomplete space-time field. It is the Receptacle or matrix that hastens along all things while also providing them grounds for the realization and enjoyment achieved by each actual occasion. *Pereunt et imputantur.* "Time and space express the universe as including the essence of transition and the success of achievement. The transition is real and the achievement is real."[92] The cosmos is continually perishing, and in perishing provides routes to future satisfactions.

8. CONCLUSION

There are four turning points in the development of Whitehead's philosophy of time. The first is his preference for the linear concepts of the material world, developed in his 1905 memoir. The memoir embodies his first sustained criticism of the classical concept of the physical world which was set forth in the work of Galileo and Newton. In Whitehead's view, the continuous features of time and space are as important as, and certainly more economical than, the discontinuous aspects. For example, the problem of action at a distance simply dissolves if events are regarded as embedded in continuous lines of force in the physical world. This preference for the continuous features within the world of experience dominated Whitehead's work until his writings of 1925 and 1926. Those of his commentators who see a mathematical pretension working in Whitehead until

the last (despite Whitehead's own disclaimers about the scope of mathematical method) must feel that, with the appearance of the epochal theory of time from 1925 on, he has broken the faith expressed in his writings about the importance of the linear extensive concepts of nature. Whitehead's belief throughout most of his *scientific career*, that continuity expressed actuality, was supported by his interest in the linear concept V in the 1905 memoir.

Another turning point was that of upgrading time so that it was as important, and then more important, than space. This change was revealed about a decade after the 1905 "Mathematical Concepts of the Material World," in the writings from 1914 to 1917. During this period Whitehead was involved in university administration in London, and with planning for adult education, and along with other members of the upper administrative levels of English society, he was shocked at the moral devastation and human costs of the Great War. It was also during this period of time's receiving its majority alongside space that Whitehead explicitly adopted the British empiricists' approach to foundational questions. Experience was to be explained on its own terms, without any recourse to a Kantian *a priori* in treating the questions associated with spatiotemporal experience. So time must be approached on temporal grounds. The emphases Whitehead disclosed in his fully appointed writings of 1919–23 were adumbrated when he told an audience of the British Association in 1916 (and then reread his paper for the Aristotelian Society) that a theorist is one who investigates temporal relations. In 1917, he added that spatial relations come from temporal relations. Such an approach amounts to a Magna Carta for an alternate set of concepts that explain the physical world. Whitehead's non-Einsteinian interpretation of relativity theory precisely reflects this ascendancy of the temporal over the spatial aspects of experience. For Whitehead emphasizes time and its heterogeneity, and regards the structure of space as constant or homogeneous across different time systems. Conversely, Einstein's interpretation of relativity makes space heterogeneous in its structure.

The third turning point came into prominence about a decade after the second, in the 1925–27 writings, when an epochal theory of time is set out. As we reconstructed this change, the argument was this: If experience is to be explained on its own terms; and if spatiotemporal features of experience are foundational in the sense of suffusing all of experience; and if time has priority over space so that space is derived from it; then time and the events from which it is abstracted must be explained in temporal terms. In particular, events must be demarcated by concrete features of passage, and not by instants. So Whitehead's main question came to be this: When has

an event grown to be individuated or limited enough to be set off from happenings which are subsequent to it? His answer to this when-type question was composed in terms of circumstances *internal* to each concrete event, and not by appealing to abstract, *external* features such as instants. The result of his answer is the epochal theory of time.

A final turning point came into prominence about the same time as the third, and arose when Whitehead traced all types of order back to aesthetic order. Behind the kinds of order associated with growth or concrescence, and with transition and perishing, are acts of peceptivity and valuation which are the foundation of all ordering and relating whatsoever. Temporal order is to be associated with the psychical aspects of experience, and with the vectors of value revealed in the perceiver's positive response toward or aversive departure from satisfactions, consummations, and acts of perishing. Considerations of this kind begin to swing wide of a philosophy of time and take us into the upland terrain of Whitehead's descriptive metaphysics. As it turns out, his philosophy of time is an episode in that metaphysics, albeit an important episode. Time is only penultimate. It derives from the factors of process and permanence, which are co-ultimate.

Common to the six major American philosophers is the conviction, stated often enough in about so many words, that the main problems of philosophy center around the nature of time and time's ways. But because time is so problematic, special emphasis is then thrown upon the uncertainty of the human condition. For man is the being whose nature is rooted and riven in time, and whose fundamental myths about himself bring a temporal perplexity into his highest aspirations.

Due to the wide public appeal of many of the writings of our canonical six, and to the special attention that continues to be given to the appropriation and evaluation of their works, a multiplier effect has projected their occupation with questions about temporality into a preoccupation of North American culture. To be sure, philosophical questions about time have not singlehandedly fueled the North American version of late twentieth-century Western culture, with its almost obsessive interest in living for the moment and, paradoxically, its anxious flight from the merely momentary. But the exacting investigations into the nature of time and its relation to reality—which are found in the works of Peirce, James, Santayana, Royce, Dewey, and Whitehead—do confirm and help channel the interpretations we give to the flux of events and to our quest for permanence amidst change. The tides of change run so deeply, at such increasing rates, and with such profoundly unsettling effects that the problems associated with the temporal features of experience have supercharged our quest for meaning with a moral urgency and personal desperation to act as humane-

ly and to think as incisively as possible. In a period when achieving equilibrium at one's spiritual and rational center is almost impossible, philosophical questions that bear on the nature of change and permanence cannot help but be projected into every aspect of late-modern Western culture.

The tangle of themes our six authors sought to tease apart is, thus, a tangle associated with the demise of modernity. That they sought to reconstruct a format for understanding a changeful self and a changing physical world within a fluxing configuration that possessed features of permanence was their common project. The powerful interplay of cosmological and moral questions, which is found in their probes into the nature of time, has added an almost unaccountable heft to their deliberations, as well as an aura of foreboding that makes them appear to be prophesying in the midst of their cool and clean analyses.

One of the routes along which these temporalist emphases have been extended in philosophy, and beyond philosophy into sociology and social psychology, is in the work of George Herbert Mead (1863–1931). His views of time were also conditioned by the interplay between passage and permanence in the experience of the human organism. Although his original formulations of many of the problems concerning the nature and modes of time were known mainly to a select circle of colleagues and students at the University of Chicago, by the late 1930s his thoughts had become widely available through the posthumous publication of four separate volumes comprised of his lectures, his papers, and student lecture notes.[1] There is now a substantial corpus of Mead's work that is drawing increased attention in several areas of American thought. His presence is more dominating now than during his lifetime, and he is being recognized as a pivotal figure in American thought, perhaps especially because of his influence on the early work of John Dewey.

A deeply methodological impulse in Mead's thought is shown in his treatment of time.[2] His approach to the nature of man is thoroughly naturalistic and social. Humans are fundamentally actors in the world and on the world, and are not observers who have somehow been inserted into it from outside. Our views about time and its modes of present, past, and future are extensions of the structuring of our biosocial acts. The act at the human level is depicted by Mead in terms of the relations between the anticipatory and consummatory phases of a common social experience, especially as that experience is modulated by the presence of symbolic and interpretative elements of a shared language. If processes of ideation as stabilized by a shared language were not entrained in our social experience, we would have no time sense either. We might experience aversive and appetitive moments in a changing world, but we would not construe those

negative or positive impulses in terms of what is past or what is future.[3] Other forms of sentient life, unavailed of symbolic mediation, have no past or future at all, nor, strictly speaking, have they a present. So it is really in the complex character of human social experience, as laced through and through with ideation, that time becomes a distinctive and prevalent mark of the human condition. Moreover, a determinate kind of society will have as its correlate an enjoined sense of special relations binding, without serious interruptions, its present into a succession of presents. That is, our view of the present or, more accurately, of this nest of circumambient presents, is a function of our existing mode of social organization.[4]

For Mead, the perspectives of both space and time are implicit in the way an organism perceives and responds to troubling or inhibiting features that arise in its world. It is within the organism's dynamic response, as conditioned by its attention to maintaining its own vital interests, that certain features or qualities stand out. Attention abstracts those features; they are steadied in action, and are then said to exist. There is no independently existing moment in which qualities are simply given: "The unit of existence is the act, not the moment. And the act stretches beyond the stimulus to the response."[5] Moreover, because there is a symbolic prevision of the consummatory phases of the response, one is afforded a sense of standing outside the actual passage to the completed response. The time sense and the space sense arise together. The distance experience, mediated through the sense of sight, is the pledge of a contact experience. "We find here the fundamental relation between the future and the past in the present." Space, in turn, is dependent upon our recall of contact experiences, of our manipulation of objects in our surroundings. Royce had emphasized the faculty of willing at the root of the time experience, and Mead stresses that time and space derive from the dynamic activity of the organism as it responds to certain features of its environs that are selected as the organism moves toward the consummatory phases of the act. This reconstruction of the field of action, as correlated with an adjustment on the part of the organism, is what Mead refers to as cognition. The higher levels of cognition, where interpretation plays a major role, include logic. The logic would be a temporalist logic of the interim concept and the emergent judgment. The entire cognitive process at this level would essentially recapitulate the methodological approaches of the experimental scientist.[6]

Probably too much attention has been given to the opening sentence of Mead's *Philosophy of the Present*: "The subject of this lecture is found in the proposition that reality exists in a present." The danger is that the present in which reality is said to exist may be taken in a substantive sense as

something that can stand alone as a unitary here and now, or as a meta-physically transfixed present transcending the passage of time, or as a scientifically objective space-time continuum in which events will fall, with full transposition between the perspectives these events occupy. Mead specifically argues against these interpretations as he gradually unfolds the proper meaning of the assertion that "reality exists in a present." A correct view of the present captures the idea of passage, the idea of the irrevocability of some aspects of the past in the present, and the idea of something emergent which leads this present into another present.

Mead distinguishes between the content of events and the structure of events. *That* something is taking place is obvious enough, especially as given in contact experiences. But *what* is happening is much less clear.[7] For *what* has happened and is happening depends upon the intent and the prospects of the organism as it adjusts to the world that is coming into being out of the world that is there. *What* an object or event is, is dependent upon the way we use it for its contribution to our adapting to our physical and social surroundings.

Each present is characterized by passage, by a falling away of the manipulatory and ideational aspects of this present as we approach the high ground of consummatory values. Each present is also characterized by channeling, by the presence of necessary conditions, although these conditions are not sufficient to extend an identity to the emergent. The emergent aspect of the present thrusts the existing present into a new alignment around *that which* takes place. As we construe through ideation *what* takes place, we realign the content—the *that*—of the past under new headings so it becomes a new past for this novel present. With regard to the content of the past, the *that*, the past is irrevocable. But with regard to the new covering structure for that past, the past is tentative and hypothetical. *What* an event is depends upon the interest and attention disclosed in the act.

Mead's theory of time and the modes of time is not very remarkable if simply taken as a theory about the ways present, past, and future interpenetrate. Santayana also asserts that the past and the future are projects that extend away from this limited present. Royce emphasizes the role of the will and attention in laying out the vectors of the past (that which is intensive in the present) and the future (that which is protensive in the present).[8] Peirce's distinction between near and remote futures and pasts, where the near future and the close past comprise this present and endow it both with irrevocability and with conditions for change, is broadly consistent with Mead's view. Peirce's "dead hand of the past" is the *that which is* that makes the content aspect of the past irrevocable for Mead.

But there is methodological novelty in Mead's view. He bases his view of past, present, and future upon the structuring found in the act as it develops from impulse and perception to manipulation and consummation. The act reflects the adjustment of the biosocial human organism to the changing environment. That is, research in sociology, social psychology, and historiography can be carried out in a manner that would test the senses in which the past is operational in our present social behavior. Such research would allow us to appraise the manner in which our present schemes of ideology require of us a new past and a new future. Mead, then does give us a kind of process philosophy that leads away from the thought of the major figures we have discussed. His work illustrates how several of their temporalist themes have entered into the broader currents of American thought. Beyond philosophy, sociology, and social psychology, this would also hold true of theology, as evidenced in the work of Henry Nelson Wieman.[9]

Aside from the nuances associated with raising most of the fundamental questions of philosophy in the context of the temporal passage that infects all things, the analyses of these major American philosophers are so diverse that it would be specious to try to gather all of their main arguments into a single framework. The decades in which they were active were propitious for specialist analyses. That they gave us versions of philosophy that can be described fairly as realism, pragmatism, panpsychism, idealism, or experimentalism is clear enough. Still, the wide-ranging versatility expressed in a book like Wilbur Urban's *Beyond Realism and Idealism* (1949) does suggest the possibility of a rapprochement among these different views about the nature of time and its relation to reality. The enormous volume of specialized investigations that have been given over to the examination of temporality in many fields, along with the founding of the International Society for the Study of Time—all within the last two or three decades that separate us from Dewey and Whitehead —suggest that the work of analysis has proceeded apace, and that a synthesis of fundamental views may not be far off. Although the recent synthesis set out by J. T. Fraser in *The Genesis and Evolution of Time* (1982) may not carry the day, it does have the advantage of being consistent with suggestions about the reality of temporal levels set forth by both Royce and Santayana. Moreover, the image that William James used, concerning a banquet where many elements of reality meet at a common table of time and space, may be serviceable in an extended way. For man is a temporal being, and to be invited by these philosophers to partake of a rich metaphysical repast is to be invited back to oneself for renewed meditations on becoming and perishing in essentially human ways.

INTRODUCTION

1. Henry Steele Commager, *The American Mind: An Interpretation of American Thought and Character since the 1880s* (New Haven: Yale University Press, 1950), p. 53.

2. Merle Curti, *The Growth of American Thought*, 3d ed. (New York: Harper & Row, 1964), p. 517. The words occur in the opening sentence of chapter 21, "The Delimitation of Supernaturalism."

3. Perry Miller, ed., *American Thought: Civil War to World War I* (1954; reprint ed., New York: Holt, Rinehart and Winston, 1965), p. ix. Miller believes that this American ideology had disappeared by 1890; see p. xi.

4. Hugh Hawkins, *Between Harvard and America: The Educational Leadership of Charles W. Eliot* (New York: Oxford University Press, 1972), p. 42.

5. George Santayana, "The Spirit and Ideals of Harvard University," *Educational Review* (April 1884), reprinted in *George Santayana's America*, ed. James Ballowe (Urbana: University of Illinois Press, 1967).

6. Max Fisch, "Justice Holmes, the Prediction Theory of Law, and Pragmatism," *Journal of Philosophy* 39 (1942): 94. Fisch traces the prediction theory of law developed by Holmes back to the early 1870s and the Metaphysical Club, p. 87.

7. Morton White, *Social Thought in America: The Revolt against Formalism* (1947; reprint ed., Boston: Beacon Press, 1957), p. 13.

8. Ibid., p. 11.

9. Stow Persons, *American Minds: A History of Ideas* (New York: Holt, Rinehart and Winston: 1958), pp. 266–67.

10. White, *Social Thought in America*, pp. 71–72.

11. Commager, *American Mind*, p. 17.

12. Samuel P. Hayes, *The Response to Industrialism: 1885–1914* (Chicago: University of Chicago Press, 1957), p. 43.

13. Leo Marx, *The Machine in the Garden* (New York: Oxford University Press,

1964). Marx judges that "by 1844 the machine had captured the public imagination" (p. 191). He also holds that "to see a powerful, efficient machine in the landscape is to know the superiority of the present to the past" (p. 192).

14. A rather complex scientific finding in the 1890s concerning entropy, i.e., the Second Law of Thermodynamics, helped rivet the attention of both philosophers and theologians upon the problem of time. According to Jammer, "Ever since Boltzman (1895), in his rebuttal of Zermelo's recurrence objection, reduced (local) anisotropy of time (the "arrow of time") to statistical irreversibility, the entropy concept has played an important role in philosophical discussions on the nature of time. . . . The concept became also a battleground between idealism (Jeans, 1930) and materialism (Kannegiesser, 1961)." See Max Jammer, "Entropy," in *Dictionary of the History of Ideas*, ed. Philip P. Wiener (New York: Charles Scribner's Sons, 1973), 2:118. The concept of entropy has to do with the possible impending heat death of the universe.

15. Jacques Maritain, *Reflections on America* (1958; reprint ed., New York: Gordian Press, 1975), pp. 25–26.

16. Ibid., p. 94.

17. Max Lerner, *America As a Civilization* (New York: Simon and Schuster, 1957), p. 718.

18. Michael Kammen, *People of Paradox* (New York: Alfred A. Knopf, 1972), chap. 4, p. 107.

19. Edward H. Madden, *Chauncey Wright and the Foundations of Pragmatism* (Seattle: University of Washington Press, 1963), p. 25.

20. Edward H. Madden, ed., *Philosophical Writings of Chauncey Wright* (New York: Liberal Arts Press, 1958), p. xvii.

21. Madden, *Chauncey Wright*, p. v.

22. Fisch, "Justice Holmes," p. 88.

23. Robert C. Whittemore, *Makers of the American Mind* (New York: William Morrow & Co., 1964), p. 352.

24. Francis Ellingwood Abbot, "The Philosophy of Space and Time," *North American Review* 99 (July 1864): 64.

25. Ibid., p. 65.

26. See Chauncey Wright, *Letters of Chauncey Wright*, ed. James Bradley Thayer (1878; reprint ed., New York: Burt Franklin, 1971), and Wright's letter to F. E. Abbot, December 20, 1864. See also Charles S. Peirce, *Writings of Charles S. Peirce*, vol. 1, *1857–1866*, ed. Max H. Fisch (Bloomington: Indiana University Press, 1982), pp. 242–43.

27. Whittemore, *Makers of the American Mind*, pp. 353, 357.

28. Madden, *Philosophical Writings of Chauncey Wright*, p. xii.

29. Curti, *Growth of American Thought*, p. 546. Curti adds that "Peirce forecast James's conception of the 'open universe.'"

30. A chronological edition, *Writings of Charles S. Peirce*, is being prepared under the auspices of the Peirce Edition Project at Indiana University-Purdue University at Indianapolis. The first volume appeared in 1982 (see note 26, above). Upon the completion of this critical edition, a fully developmental approach to the genesis of Peirce's philosophical system will be possible. For some fairly complete information on the dates of the composition of Peirce's writings, included in the original six volumes of the Harvard edition of Peirce's *Collected Papers*, see Justus Buchler, *Charles Peirce's Empiricism*, app. 2 (New York: Octagon Books, Inc., 1966).

31. Lerner, *America As a Civilization*, p. 719.

32. Bertrand Russell, *A History of Western Philosophy* (1945; reprint ed., New York: Simon and Schuster, 1967), p. 811. Russell made this judgment about James's later life.

33. Lewis Mumford, *The Golden Day* (New York: Boni and Liveright, 1926), chap. 4. See especially section 5 of the chapter.

34. Ibid., p. 182.

35. Arthur C. Lovejoy, "The Thirteen Pragmatisms, II," *Journal of Philosophy* 5 (1908): 29.

36. Ibid., p. 39.

37. See the introduction by Richard J. Bernstein to William James, *A Pluralistic Universe* (Cambridge: Harvard University Press, 1977), p. xiii. This is volume 3 in the Harvard Critical Edition of *The Works of William James*.

38. Jacques Barzun, *A Stroll with William James* (New York: Harper & Row, 1983), p. 124. Barzun cites the phrase James used for his thought, "my *flux*-philosophy," p. 265.

39. Ibid., p. 263.

CHAPTER I. PEIRCE AND THE PREVALENCE OF TIME

1. *Critique of Pure Reason*, A:33, the Müller translation. Kantian distinctions help set the framework for Peirce's analysis of time. Murphey judges that Peirce's distinction between time and space arises out of Kant's contrast between inner and outer sense, in Murray G. Murphey, *The Development of Peirce's Philosophy* (Cambridge: Harvard University Press, 1961), p. 89. See also where Murphey says that Peirce's "theory of space and time is heavily indebted to Kant," p. 380.

2. Morris R. Cohen's introductory essay to the early collection of some of Peirce's important essays, *Chance, Love and Logic* (New York: Harcourt, Brace and World, 1923), still deserves close attention because of its emphasis upon how Peirce's work as an experimental scientist helps to form some of Peirce's main philosophical doctrines. For a more recent restatement of this emphasis, see Edward C. Moore and Richard S. Robin, eds., *Studies in the Philosophy of Charles Sanders Peirce* (Amherst: University of Massachusetts Press, 1964), p. 486, where the editors note that Peirce's career was a scientist's career, and judge that this fact should be "the standing premise of Peirce studies."

3. Charles Hartshorne, "Continuity, the Form of Forms, in Charles Peirce," *Monist* 39 (1956): 521–34. The treatment of time is on pp. 530–31.

4. Čapek holds that Peirce defended the theory of eternal recurrence, i.e., the cyclical theory of time. He also notes that Peirce's tychism is incompatible with the cyclical, recurrent view. See Milič Čapek, "The Theory of Eternal Recurrence in Modern Philosophy of Science, with Special Reference to C. S. Peirce," *Journal of Philosophy* 57 (1960): 289–96. But Peirce does not hold this doctrine. Indeed, he criticizes it and asserts that real recurrence *cannot* hold for time. See Carolyn Eisele, ed., *The New Elements of Mathematics* (The Hague: Mouton Publishers, 1976), 2:249–50, where Peirce says "observation leads us to suppose that changing things tend toward a state in the immeasurably distant future different from the state of things in the immeasurably distant past," and that "it is an important, though intrinsic, property of time that no such reckoning brings us around to the

same time again." Peirce may contradict himself on the point. See Murphey, *Development of Peirce's Philosophy*, p. 388.

5. In the Condemnation of A.D. 1277, the medieval Christian church rejected the Averroist doctrine of the eternity of the world for about the same reasons that Peirce rejected the eternality of time. Such doctrines are too necessitarian and fatalistic.

6. We use the standard convention for referring to Charles Sanders Peirce, *Collected Papers*, vols. 1–6, ed. Charles Hartshorne and Paul Weiss (Cambridge: Harvard University Press, Belknap Press, 1960), and vols. 7–8, ed. Arthur W. Burks (1958). Thus, 4.67 means volume 4, paragraph 67 in those papers.

7. The contrast between Peirce's naturalistic and supernaturalistic accounts would be consistent with the judgment of Thomas A. Goudge that there are two incompatible sets of premises exhibited in the thought of Peirce. See Thomas A. Goudge, *The Thought of C. S. Peirce* (New York: Dover Publications, 1969), p. 5.

8. In Indian philosophy, there are also categories for things that come before time, such as *prusa* and *praktri*. Sanat Kumar Sen, "Time in Sankhya-Yoga," *International Philosophical Quarterly* 8 (1968): 414–15.

9. The view that the Forms are not eternal but came to be was on occasion Plato's own view. See *Republic*, Book 6, p. 508, where he says of the objects of knowledge that "these derive from the Good not only their power of being known, but their very being and reality" (in the Cornford translation).

10. In an early fragment from 1860, where Peirce set out a brief proof of God's nature as infinite, it is argued that causal sequences and time arose at the same "moment" through God's creative activity, so time itself could not be caused. See Charles S. Peirce, *Writings of Charles S. Peirce*, vol. 1, *1857–1866*, ed. Max H. Fisch (Bloomington: Indiana University Press, 1982), p. 44. For a discussion of Peirce's answer to Kant's Fourth Antinomy on the relation of a necessary being to a world ordered in time and space, see Murphey, *Development of Peirce's Philosophy*, pp. 45–46.

11. Carolyn Eisele, "Peirce's Philosophy of Education in His Unpublished Mathematics Textbooks," p. 55, in Moore and Robin, *Studies*, where Eisele judges that "the principle of continuity is the foundation of his mathematical structures just as it is the cement that holds his philosophical principles together"; W. B. Gallie, *Peirce and Pragmatism* (Harmondsworth: Penguin Books, 1952), pp. 198–203, for a discussion of the methodological value of the principle of continuity in organizing scientific inquiry.

12. Charles Hartshorne concludes that Peirce was quite overpowered by the idea of continuity, and that his overemphasis upon synechism was a serious flaw in his philosophy that kept him from using the language of events. "His immense enthusiasm for continuity, concerning which he grew more eloquent perhaps than on any other topic, was an insuperable obstacle." See "Charles Peirce's 'One Contribution to Philosophy' and His Most Serious Mistake," p. 470, in Moore and Robin, *Studies*.

13. Synechism is a regulative principle of logic, and not constitutive in metaphysics. Still, for Peirce, logic itself arose in the course of time. See 8.153.

14. See Paul Weiss, "Biography of Charles S. Peirce," in *Perspectives on Peirce*, ed. Richard J. Bernstein (New Haven: Yale University Press, 1965), p. 8. "Though Peirce's tychism, or theory of absolute chance, received more consideration and favorable attention, it was his synechism, or doctrine of continuity, which he considered his real contribution to philosophy, holding it to be, however, a regulative

principle rather than an absolute metaphysical doctrine." Parmenides gave the concept of synecheia a special role in his philosophy. He uses 'syneches' in his *Hymn* to deny that being changes in time. "[Being] was not in the past, nor shall it be, since it is now, all at once, syneches" (line 6). But Parmenides' next use in line 25 is close to Peirce's meaning; "[Being] is all syneches, for what is clings close to what is." See G. S. Kirk and J. E. Haven, *The Presocratic Philosophers* (Cambridge: The University Press, 1957), pp. 273, 275.

In the *Enneads*, III. 1.4, Plotinus uses synecheia to deal with the continuous flowing of causes out of other causes, a notion that for Plotinus works *against* the idea of a fixed, universal system. This use is also one that Peirce brings to his synechistic universe. See Stephen Mackenna, trans., *Enneads* (New York: Pantheon Books, 1957).

The doctrine of fallibilism in Peirce is most likely not extended to cover his commitment to synechism. According to Kemp-Pritchard, Peirce's belief in synechism is a case of an hypothesis that has no negative consequences. See Ilong Kemp-Pritchard, "Peirce on Philosophical Hope and Logical Sentiment," *Philosophy and Phenomenological Research* 42 (Sept. 1981): 88.

15. There is no implication here that space and time are to be treated together as a kind of space-time. Although Peirce thought that space was four-dimensional and not three-dimensional, he did not consider time as the candidate for that fourth dimension. "Nowhere does he suggest that it is time or that space and time should be treated in the same geometrical structure, such as the four-dimensional space-time manifold of the Special Theory of Relativity." See Randall R. Dipert, "Peirce's Theory of the Dimensionality of Physical Space," *Journal of the History of Philosophy* 16 (1978): 61–70. See also Murphey, *Development of Peirce's Philosophy*, p. 384, to the effect that time was not the fourth dimension.

16. Francis E. Reilly, *Charles Peirce's Theory of Scientific Method* (New York: Fordham University Press, 1970), pp. 109–10, has some discussion of the way Peirce dealt with continuity as a kind of generality or closely related to generality. Generality seems to be a species of continuity in its turn, perhaps an early or vague moment in its development. But we must not go much beyond conjecture on this matter because Peirce seems not to have explored the relation between continuity and generality, except as manifestations of Thirdness. "While he insisted throughout his later writings that true generality is but a rudimentary form of continuity, his failure [in 6.31] to associate the two conceptions in any way indicates clearly he had yet to make a careful analysis of thirdness," as Thompson summarizes the matter. See Manley Thompson, *The Pragmatic Philosophy of C. S. Peirce* (Chicago: University of Chicago Press, Phoenix Books, 1963), p. 113.

17. The priority of time over space is also instanced by Peirce in his mathematics. He held that the simplest and most fundamental division of geometry was topical geometry or topology, and it had precedence over the other two divisions, graphics and metrics. But "topics presupposes the doctrine of time." See Eisele, *New Elements*, 2:514, 521, 530, for this idea of Peirce and some of its variants.

18. At best, Peirce may have intimated such a language of events for such contexts. Mostly, Hartshorne is correct that Peirce did not use the language of events. See note 12, above. But Peirce *did* include a discussion of events as part of his prologue to a topical geometry in Eisele, *New Elements*, vol. 2, pp. 249, 250, articles 7 and 8. See also part 5 of chapter 1, "The Constituents of Time," where Peirce's view of events is discussed.

19. See also Ibid., p. 249, Definition 28, no. 4, where Peirce is defining the connec-

tion of the parts of time, and says "given any two instants, *I* the earlier, *J* the later, there are always instants later than *I* but earlier than *J*.

20. Such an idea of a discontinuous continuum or continual continuum would then fall under the criterion suggested by Manley Thompson that the proof of pragmatism "would essentially involve the establishment of the truth of synechism." In Thompson, *Pragmatic Philosophy*, p. xiii.

21. The additional possibilities from outside the continuum would make it a growing continuum. In his review of the first six volumes of Peirce's *Collected Papers*, John Dewey said that the insistence upon growing continuity, or generality of ways of action and disposition, differentiates the pragmatism of Peirce from that of James. See Dewey's review, "Charles Sanders Peirce," *The New Republic* 89 (Feb. 1937): 416.

22. My interpretation here is tentative, and some of what Peirce says runs against it. If time is a true continuum of a single dimension, and if for any two instants one is earlier and the other is later, and if time is unidirectional, then time would *not* have many tracks with some running toward and some branching away from each other. Peirce does say things that suggest time is not multiply tracked. See Eisele, *New Elements*, vol. 2; 481, 249. But Peirce also distinguishes between pure hypothetical time and physical time, and these abstract characters of time arise when he is talking of pure hypothetical time or mathematical time.

23. Sir James Jeans, *Physics and Philosophy* (New York: Macmillan Company, 1945), pp. 59–60. See also Goudge, *Thought of C. S. Peirce*, p. 242: "We have to remember that Peirce was thinking within the framework of classical mechanics as commonly interpreted at the end of the nineteenth century."

24. Peirce is working in the context of levels or degrees of being, ranging from the more abstract to the more concrete. Part of the unity exhibited in such a hierarchy for Peirce is the idea of law as permeating every level. See the thesis of William Paul Haas, *The Conception of Law and the Continuity of Peirce's Philosophy* (Fribourg: The University Press, 1964), p. 2, to the effect that "there is indeed a unity in the thought of Peirce, precisely with respect to the conception of law which runs through his thought at every stage of its development and in every branch of his philosophy, revealing the uniqueness of his insight." See also p. 22, for a similar statement of Haas's thesis.

25. This would be an example of Ernest Nagel's judgment, as he explored the theory of categories that Peirce set out, that the triad of categories is "a persistent melody running through most of Peirce's writings." Nagel's early review of Peirce's *Collected Papers* dealt with his theory of signs and his theory of logic as well as his categoreal theory. See Ernest Nagel, "Charles Peirce's Guesses at the Riddle," *Journal of Philosophy* 30 (1933): 372.

26. The ideas of present and past, the ideas of tense, begin to arise in Peirce's philosophy at this point. The distinction is important to Peirce, according to A. N. Prior, "his thought being at this point reminiscent of, and indeed, consciously indebted to, that of Aristotle and the scholastic logicians." A. N. Prior, *Time and Modality* (Oxford: Clarendon Press, 1957), p. 112.

27. We distinguish between dates and between present, past, and future by reference to volitional acts. For Peirce, the past is the zone of memory and the future is the zone of volition. Past and future, time and space: These are distinguished by volition, by reaction, and resistance. "They are distinguished only by a brute sense of reaction which, unlike a Kantian intuition, is strictly noncognitive." See Manley Thompson, "Peirce's Concept of an Individual," in *Pragmatism and Purpose*, ed.

L. W. Sumner, John G. Slater, and Fred Wilson (Toronto: University of Toronto Press, 1981), p. 145. See also Gallie, *Peirce and Pragmatism*, p. 195, where Peirce is interpreted to mean that facts gain reality by action against other realities. "It is not time and space which produce this character. It is rather this character which for its realization calls for something like time and space."

28. Reese argues that Peirce identifies "the basic philosophic categories with modes of being which are—though Peirce was not always consistent—also modes of time." See his analysis in William Reese, "Philosophic Realism: A Study in the Modality of Being in Peirce and Whitehead," p. 237, in *Studies in the Philosophy of Charles Sanders Peirce*, ed. Phillip P. Weiner and Frederic H. Youngblood (Cambridge: Harvard University Press, 1952).

29. William H. Davis traces some of the implications of this denial in his examination of the theory of knowledge of Peirce. See William H. Davis, *Peirce's Epistemology* (The Hague: Martinus Nijhoff, 1972), p. 10. He judges that for Peirce, "all knowing is inferring, and inferring requires comparison throughout a span of time," and that experience cannot be an "instantaneous affair, but is an event occupying time, and coming to pass by a continuous process."

30. Time, actuality, haecceity: the ideas are treated as overlapping ideas by Peirce and they importantly bear on the interplay of tychism and synechism. His way of treating them has not yet been sufficiently analyzed, according to Prior. See Prior, *Time and Modality*, p. 116, where he says that "by and large, [Peirce's] insights into the relation between actuality, possibility, time and individual identity are still waiting to be adequately formalized."

31. Peirce's distinction between these two sides of the future, the near, and the remote, serves to highlight what is sometimes called his futurism. This emphasis upon the future is made plain in John F. Boler, *Charles Peirce and Scholastic Realism* (Seattle: University of Washington Press, 1963), pp. 105, 115–16. What Boler calls Peirce's "special theory of real potentiality" can be seen to require the near future/remote future distinction.

32. Dewey, "Charles Sanders Peirce," p. 416, where he says of Peirce's notion of experience that "each experience contains an element of expectation, of virtual prediction. Every brute experience has consequences that are anticipated as part of the experience. This element constitutes the phase of continuity; . . . It is the business of inquiry to develop this element of foreshadowing the future." Again, the notion that the future is somehow reflected into the present so that the present can foreshadow the future can be seen to rely on the distinction of the near and remote future. Farther on, we will examine the way Whitehead treats a similar distinction in his account of the future's operation upon the present.

33. "Pragmatism's restriction of the actual to the reaction-event, coupled with its insistence that a law be stated in terms of what would be, requires the type of causality in which the future acts upon the present. This is not quite the same as saying the future is real now; rather, it implies that, whenever the causal law is real, it operates by final and not efficient causality." Boler, *Charles Peirce*, p. 126.

34. The notions of antecedence and consequence are serviceable both in logic and in dealing with time. Dipert implies that considerations of tense or of a tense logic underlie Peirce's efforts to harmonize the main logical relations. "For Peirce's logic, there are deep similarities—and minor psychological differences—which Peirce sees among the copula, the conditional and the notion of logical consequences, all of which he represented by the common symbol, ———▶. In 1883 Peirce attempted to state this similarity by asserting that they are temporally related;

when we contemplate this first idea (general term, proposition, or series of propositions) *then* we are led to contemplate the second idea." See Randall Dipert, "Peirce's Propositional Logic," *Review of Metaphysics* 34 (1981): 591.

35. In Eisele, *New Elements*, 2:248, Definition 20, where Peirce says that "an instant is a state of time in which there is no room for an alteration." The definition is consistent with instants being where Firsts appear, but *not* Seconds. For in his Definition 18, Peirce defines "alteration" as "an otherness in the characters of an individual thing."

36. Perhaps I go too far in smoothing out a contradiction by suggesting that it is only a "surface contradiction" when Peirce *does* appear to say that all instants *can* be placed in a single continuum. See Ibid., p. 249, Definition 28.1, where he says that "of any two instants, one is later, the other earlier." But I think that where Firsts are exhibited, the mathematical instant is not the same as the temporal instant.

37. Ibid., p. 248, Definition 21, where "a moment is a time in which no change which can in any way be made sensible can take place." In that "a change is a gradual alteration in time," according to Definition 19, it seems clear that a moment is a unit of time where there is mystery and power. I would hazard that for him, actualities or *haecceities* come to be in moments.

38. See Murphey, *Development of Peirce's Philosophy*, chap. 18, for a general discussion of Peirce's philosophy of time and of the role of the concept of event in that philosophy. See also James K. Feibleman, *An Introduction to the Philosophy of Charles S. Peirce* (Cambridge: M.I.T. Press, 1970), pp. 358–59, where Feibleman judges that "it would be impossible to examine time without also introducing events, since one cannot be understood without the other." Clearly, Peirce does speak in the language of events, though not in a way that the event becomes controlling in his philosophy. See also note 12, above.

39. Victor Lowe judges that Peirce meant his metaphysics to conform to his logical ideas, that, as we said, logical opposition plays a role in happenings. Lowe believes that Peirce's discussion of time shows how metaphysics conforms to logic. See "Peirce and Whitehead As Metaphysicians," p. 433 in Moore and Robin, *Studies*. For a discussion of an "extraordinarily modern ring" that can be discerned in Peirce's analysis of the nature of the event, see R. M. Martin, *Primordiality, Science, and Value* (Albany: State University of New York Press, 1980), pp. 276–78.

40. Objective time seems to exhibit the historical arrow of time, and is partly a case of man's striving or willing to develop or create new meaning. So this law of the mind would grow out of the striving aspects of mental activity, where the mind is seen as a unity of feeling, striving, and meaning. See also Charles Hartshorne, *Beyond Humanism* (Lincoln: University of Nebraska Press, Bison Books, 1968), p. 185.

41. Much Peirce material has still not been published, and this judgment like so many other judgments concerning his work is subject to being set aside in the light of the publication of additional manuscripts.

CHAPTER II. JAMES ON THE PLURALITY OF TIMES

1. William James, *Pragmatism* (Cambridge: Harvard University Press, 1975), p. 64. With regard to the centrality of the problem of the one and the many for James,

see the introduction by Richard J. Bernstein to William James, *A Pluralistic Universe* (Cambridge: Harvard University Press, 1977), pp. xix–xxi. In commenting upon the special emphasis James gives to the problem of the one and the many, Levinson observes that James turned the question of Parmenides on its head: "James asks how things maintain their coherence and continuity despite all the real changes they undergo." See Henry S. Levinson, *Science, Metaphysics and the Chance of Salvation* (Missoula: Scholars Press, 1978), p. 119.

2. Henri Bergson, *An Introduction to Metaphysics: The Creative Mind*, trans. Mabelle L. Andison (Totowa: Little, Adams & Co., 1965), p. 211. For James, reality is not finite or infinite: it is indefinite. "It flows without our being able to say whether it is in a single direction, or even whether it is always and throughout the same river flowing."

3. William James, *Some Problems of Philosophy* (New York: Greenwood Press, 1968), p. 99.

4. Bernard P. Brennan, *William James* (New York: Twayne Publishers, 1968), p. 126.

5. William James, *Pluralistic Universe*, p. 103. The emphasis is added.

6. Ibid., p. 232.

7. Bergson, *Introduction to Metaphysics*, p. 210. "Reality, as James sees it, is redundant and superabundant."

8. James, *Problems*, p. 144.

9. Ibid., pp. 148–49. See also Levinson, *Science*, p. 134, and his judgment that "James' indeterminism is a *temporal* indeterminism; it is an indeterminism relative to *prediction*, not to conditions *per se*."

10. James, *Pluralistic Universe*, pp. 103–5; and James, *Problems*, p. 157.

11. William James, *The Will To Believe* (Cambridge: Harvard University Press, 1979), p. 199. That space and time are set off against the self as autonomous continua reveals that James is criticizing Hegelian idealism. In his introduction to this volume, Edward H. Madden shows that it is James's purpose "to point out theoretical difficulties with absolute idealism" (p. xxxv).

12. Apparently James was not completely single-minded in maintaining the independence of space and psyche. See Brenda Jubin, "The Spatial Quale": A Corrective to James' Radical Empiricism," *Journal of the History of Philosophy* 15 (1977): 212–16. Jubin shows that the 1879 article, "The Spatial Quale," contains a Kantian element of the constructive activity of the intellect in our experience of space not found in *Principles*, chap. 20, on space.

13. James, *Will To Believe*, pp. 199–200.

14. Ralph Barton Perry, *The Thought and Character of William James* (Boston: Little, Brown and Co., 1935), 1:674, 698.

15. James, *Will To Believe*, p. 201.

16. Ibid., p. 270.

17. Ibid., p. 290.

18. William James, *The Principles of Psychology* (New York: Henry Holt & Co., 1908), 2:35.

19. James, *Will To Believe*, p. 197.

20. Ibid., p. 198, n. 3.

21. Donald H. Bishop, "The Carus-James Controversy," *Journal of the History of Ideas* 35 (1974): 509–20.

22. William James, *Essays in Radical Empiricism* (Cambridge: Harvard Univer-

sity Press, 1976), p. 46. See also Charlene Haddock Seigfried, *Chaos and Context: A Study in William James* (Athens: Ohio University Press, 1978), p. 32, for the view that this primal stuff is something of a chaos. "In *Essays in Radical Empiricism* James realizes that spatial and temporal relations are not immune to the judgment that the universe is to a large extent chaotic. These relations have no privileged position in respect to the arbitrariness of the world as it appears." Seigfried goes on to say that features both of order and of chaos are originally given (p. 33).

23. James, *Pragmatism*, p. 87.

24. James, *Will To Believe*, p. 192.

25. Craig R. Eisendrath, *The Unifying Moment: The Psychological Philosophy of William James and Alfred North Whitehead* (Cambridge: Harvard University Press, 1971), p. xi.

26. James, *Will To Believe*, p. 193.

27. Ibid., p. 194.

28. James, *Pragmatism*, p. 84.

29. Perry, *Thought and Character*, p. 479.

30. James, *Pragmatism*, p. 83. See also William James, *The Meaning of Truth* (Cambridge: Harvard University Press, 1975), p. 42.

31. Bruce Wilshire, *William James and Phenomenology* (Bloomington: Indiana University Press, 1968), p. 169, where it is shown that James hypothesizes a connection between durations and brain processes. "This feature of the brain process, whatever it be, must be the cause of our perceiving the fact of time at all." But given James's view of the social origin of the category of time, Wilshire tends to saddle James with a reductionist view.

32. James, *Pragmatism*, p. 116.

33. Ibid., p. 118.

34. Some writers have sought to make this side of James's philosophy explicit. See Cushing Strout, "The Unfinished Arch: William James and the Idea of History," *American Quarterly* 13 (1961): 505–15.

35. Andrew J. Reck, *Introduction to William James* (Bloomington: Indiana University Press, 1967), p. 69. James desired to do the same thing for philosophy that he had done for psychology in his *Principles*, but "he never succeeded in composing an authoritative, systematic treatise in philosophy."

36. Existentialists and James both stress time, but James is optimistic in his conclusions. See Julius S. Bixler, "The Existentialists and William James," *American Scholar* 28 (Winter 1958–59): 80–90.

37. See Hans Linschoten, *On the Way toward a Phenomenological Psychology* (Pittsburgh: Duquesne University Press, 1968), chap. 9, sec. 16, "Experience and Time." In this account of James's psychology, it is argued that James is "a forerunner of Husserl in his formulations of his view." There is both retention and protension in the flux, and these orientations provide the fundamental elements in self-consciousness and reflection.

38. Perry, *Thought and Character*, p. 84. For a strong criticism that time is a sensation, see Gerald Myers, "William James on Time Perception," *Philosophy of Science* 38 (1971): 353–60.

39. William James, "The Perception of Time," *Journal of Speculative Philosophy* (Oct. 1886), p. 375. This paper appears as the famous chapter on time in *The Principles of Psychology*.

40. James, *Pluralistic Universe*, p. 104.

41. James, *Problems*, p. 125.

42. D. C. Malthur, "The Historical Buddha (Gotama), Hume and James on the Self: Comparisons and Evaluations," *Philosophy East and West* 28 (1978): 254, where James is shown to share with Gotama and Hume "the methodological primacy of immediate experience over concepts." Malthur goes on to add that although the atomistic empiricism of Hume is postreflective, the empiricism of James and the Buddha is prereflective (p. 260).

43. James, *Problems*, p. 70.

44. William James, *Psychology: The Briefer Course*, ed. Gordon Allport (New York: Harper Brothers, 1961), p. 333.

45. James, "Perception of Time," p. 377; idem, *Psychology*, p. 33; idem, *Problems*, p. 155.

46. James, "Perception of Time," p. 378.

47. Ibid., p. 397. To say that the specious present is retrospective is to say that it is fading into the past, and to say that it is prospective or protensive is to say that it is leading away into its future. John Wild judges that James has the entire field of experience devolve from our own personal center. See John Wild, *The Radical Empiricism of William James* (Garden City: Doubleday & Co., 1969), p. 173, where he says that James "is referring here, I believe, to the passage of the whole world-field that is centered in our own existence."

48. James, "Perception of Time," p. 388.

49. Ibid., pp. 388, 402.

50. William Barrett, "Our Contemporary, William James," *Commentary* 60 (1975): 55. Barrett judges that we are now in the midst of a James revival (p. 56).

CHAPTER III. ROYCE, ETERNITY, AND TIME

1. J. E. Creighton, ed., *Papers in Honor of Josiah Royce on His Sixtieth Birthday* (New York: Longmans, Green, 1916), p. 282. Royce studied with Rudolf Lötze at Göttingen, spoke of being influenced strongly by Schopenhauer while in Germany, and said that he was "a good deal under the influence of the Romantic School, whose philosophy of poetry I read and expounded with a good deal of diligence." The papers in this volume were delivered at a meeting of the American Philosophical Association at the University of Pennsylvania in December 1915. Hereafter, this volume is cited as *Papers*.

2. The article is included in Josiah Royce, *Fugitive Essays* (1920; reprint ed., Freeport, N.Y.: Books for Libraries Press, 1968), pp. 219–60.

3. Ibid., p. 229. In his introduction to this volume of Royce's papers and essays, Jacob Loewenberg records Royce treating succession as unreal, as a kind of illusion. See p. 31 for the relevant entries from Royce's diary for 1879–80.

4. Ibid., p. 249. Loewenberg says that Royce derives past and future from the time-axiom (p. 19).

5. Ibid., p. 249.

6. Ibid., p. 250. In G. H. Howison, "Josiah Royce: The Significance of His Work in Philosophy," in Creighton, *Papers*, pp. 3–16, Howison relates Royce's "perfect confidence" here to another basic aspect of the philosophy, to the monistic nature and existence of God. "The defense of our capacity for absolute certainty must rest upon an idealistic metaphysics" (p. 8).

7. Royce, *Fugitive Essays*, p. 251. There is circularity in expression here if not circularity in idea. Loewenberg holds that the circularity of definition at this level in Royce's thought, or anyone else's, cannot really be avoided. Circular definitions are "inevitable in dealing with all philosophical ideas of a fundamental nature." See Loewenberg, "Royce's Synthetic Method," in the memorial issue for Royce's centenary in *Journal of Philosophy* 53 (Feb. 1956): 68.

8. Royce, *Fugitive Essays*, p. 252.

9. Ibid., p. 253. In a diary entry for April 3, 1879, Royce avers that "the future and the past are shadows both, the present is the only real" (p. 31).

10. Ibid., pp. 251, 254.

11. Ibid., p. 255, for this and the following quotation.

12. Ibid., p. 259. The goal of constructing a unified picture of the world of experience is caught up neatly in one of the names Royce gave to his early philosophy: synthetic idealism. He used this name to distinguish his version of idealism from that of Berkeley, Kant, and the major post-Kantian idealists. See Josiah Royce, *The Spirit of Modern Philosophy* (1892; reprint ed., New York: W. W. Norton & Co., 1967), p. 372.

13. Loewenberg observes that Royce opposes the present on the one hand, to the past and future on the other. See his introduction to Royce, *Fugitive Essays*, p. 19. From this point of view, the present is immediately actual, and past and future are derivative; there is ontological diversity among the modes of time.

14. This discussion of *datum, positum*, and *postulatum* is in "Tests of Right and Wrong," pp. 199–203, in ibid. See also note 16 below.

15. See Loewenberg's judgment that what is new in Royce's position is his theory of the present moment. See his introduction to ibid., p. 32. Cotton stresses the importance of Royce's theory of the present moment. "It was in terms of the present moment that Royce formulated the problem of knowledge. . . . The only self is the thinker of the present moment. All else is not-self, including the self of the past or of the future." See James Harry Cotton, *Royce on the Human Self* (Cambridge: Harvard University Press, 1954), p. 24.

16. The term 'postulatum' is not used by Royce. I introduced it here to round out a nomenclature that Royce mostly did develop, and chose a version of 'postulate', a term Royce does use.

17. Royce, *Fugitive Essays*, p. 205.

18. Ibid., p. 209. Such a view of Royce illustrates Loewenberg's judgment that the ethical significance of time as it is disclosed in Royce's later works is already prefigured in these early papers. Loewenberg speaks in this context of Royce's "chrono-synoptic and superpersonal standard." See his introduction, ibid., p. 21.

19. Ibid., p. 213, for this and the following quotation.

20. Josiah Royce, "The Decay of Earnestness," p. 302, in ibid. This early paper appeared in 1881, and reveals Royce working his way free of the more traditional understanding of time. In all of these early papers, Royce shows that time is not a preexistent forum in which man works out his destiny in fear and trembling, but is a dimension to life that arises out of human acts. He makes the temporal depend upon the ethical and religious dimensions of human experience.

21. Ibid., p. 303. Still, Royce finds in the concept of attention a mediating idea that catches up a naturalistic aspect of human consciousness that allows him to pass easily from the more empirical sides of experience to the anticipatory, postulational features of a more fully rationalized experience. See his 1882 article, "How

Beliefs Are Made," pp. 351, 360, in ibid., for the idea that will develops out of attention, and that the tendency to err that is present in the will arises out of this naturalistic feature of attention. It is instructive to compare this 1882 article with Peirce's well-known 1877 article, "The Fixation of Belief."

22. Josiah Royce, *The Religious Aspect of Philosophy* (1885; reprint ed., Gloucester, Mass.: Peter Smith, 1965), pp. 237, 242, 354–55, 423. Royce's "journey" toward the idea of an absolute reason that apportions to each existent its proper place and its extent of influence is his way of grasping a logos in philosophy which functions about the way the law of the conservation of energy functions in physics. There must be some sufficient reason for things and events being about the way they are. See Charles L. Bakewell, "Novum Itinerarium Mentis In Deus," in Creighton, *Papers*, pp. 27–36.

23. Royce, *Religious Aspect*, pp. 388, 356, 419.

24. Royce, *Fugitive Essays*, p. 356.

25. Royce, *Religious Aspect*, p. 357.

26. Ibid., p. 461.

27. Josiah Royce, *The Spirit of Modern Philosophy* (1892; reprint ed., New York: W. W. Norton & Co., 1967), pp. 61–62.

28. Ibid., pp. 122, 138.

29. According to Bakewell, Royce avoided the overemphasis upon the intellect which was typical of German idealism. See Charles Bakewell, "The Significance of Royce in American Philosophy," in *Proceedings of the Seventh International Congress of Philosophy*, ed. Gilbert Ryle (London: Oxford University Press, 1931), p. 471.

Muirhead speaks of the "reconstructed idealism of which Royce was the chief representative," in J. H. Muirhead, *The Platonic Tradition in Anglo-Saxon Philosophy* (London: George Allen & Unwin, 1931), p. 326. It was a reconstructed idealism because Royce was "working out a view that sought to do more justice to the will" (p. 275).

30. Royce, *Spirit*, p. 422.

31. Ibid., p. 430.

32. Ibid., p. 431. Gabriel Marcel agrees with Royce that our regular experience allows us on occasion to have such encompassing insights. "It would be playing with words to say that eternal knowledge differs wholly and inexplicably from our own. For everyday experience, in the apperception of succession, gives us the image, almost the pattern, of what eternity may be." See Gabriel Marcel, *Royce's Metaphysics*, trans. Virginia and Gordon Ringer (Chicago: Henry Regnery Co., 1956), p. 79. For an opposing judgment regarding the propriety of the example of music, see William Ernest Hocking, "On Royce's Empiricism," in *Journal of Philosophy* 53 (Feb. 1956): 61. Hocking speaks of "Royce's favorite example, the musical idea, which I held to be an atypical special case." John Dewey also criticizes Royce's musical metaphor. See his review of the second series of Royce's Gifford lectures in *Philosophical Review* 11 (1902): 405.

33. Royce, *Spirit*, pp. 456, 457.

34. Ibid., pp. 326–27.

35. Bakewell, "Significance of Royce," p. 471, shows Royce struggling with the reality of time, and judges that Royce came to the view that time is unreal.

36. Royce, *Spirit*, pp. 432, 433.

37. The mirroring of the structures of wholes to parts is suggestive of organic

wholes. Thomas F. Powell, *Josiah Royce* (New York: Washington Square Press, 1967), p. 44, says of Royce that "in all of his work, there is one dominant theme, that of organic unity. His was a lifelong quest for the commonly experienced, the general, the universal."

38. Josiah Royce, *The World and the Individual*, 2 vols. (1899; reprint ed., New York: Dover Publications, 1959), 1:410.

39. John M. E. McTaggart, "The Unreality of Time," *Mind* 68 (Oct. 1908): 457–74.

40. Royce, *World and Individual*, 1:418.

41. Ibid., 1:420, 421.

42. Ibid., 1:425.

43. Buranelli suggests another source for Royce's idea that all phases of the temporal are drawn up into the eternal: Goethe. See Vincent Buranelli, *Josiah Royce* (New York: Twayne Publishers, 1964), p. 29. "Among the persistent problems of Royce's philosophy is the problem of time. Royce thought that if the relations of past, present, and future, and the relations of all three to eternity, could be given a definitive analysis, most of metaphysics would be established, by implication if not directly. Goethe may have put the germ of this idea in his mind."

For an opposing view of the source of Royce's key metaphysical notions, McTaggart's review of the first volume of *The World and the Individual*, in *Mind* 25 (1900): 258, suggests of Royce that "his system may be considered as based on Hegel, and as profoundly influenced by Mr. Bradley, but there is much in it that is distinctively his own."

44. For a sympathetic treatment of Royce's analysis of the relations between the temporal and the eternal, see chap. 6, "Time and Eternity," in Marcel, *Royce's Metaphysics*.

45. Royce, *World and Individual*, 2:x.

46. Ibid., vol. 2, sec. 1, of lecture 3, "The Temporal and the Eternal," pp. 113–26, for a discussion of these five leading characteristics of time.

47. Ibid., 2:117.

48. Ibid., 2:124. Such statements by Royce give special weight to the judgment of expositors like Richard Hocking that Royce had a fundamental interest in the problem of time. See Hocking's contribution to the memorial issue of *Journal of Philosophy* 53 (Feb. 1956), entitled "The Influence of Mathematics on Royce's Metaphysics," pp. 78–79, where he holds that "in one light Royce is a thinker beset by the problem of time. The preoccupation with the relations between temporal succession and the reflective life of the will is a ground theme running through his writings from the earliest to the latest. . . . The basis of temporal succession is, in the last analysis, the will manifested through rational construction. Such a view bears comparison with Augustine's doctrine of time."

49. Royce, *World and Individual*, 2:133. John Dewey was puzzled by the way Royce's concepts of the temporal and the eternal were given as convertible with each other, and concomitantly, by the way the finite and Absolute consciousness were convertible with each other. "Royce's entire metaphysics seems to me permeated with this illusion of double vision, of reduplication. . . . Professor Royce seems to have two minds about time and two about eternity. On one side, the temporal process in each and every phase is equally fragmentary and finite. The eternal is simply the temporal process taken as an object of knowledge all at once. The other view is that the meaning of the whole time process somehow manifests

itself in every member of the process. Each part of experience has an eternal meaning, because it embodies in its own significance the meaning of all others being linked to them in the Absolute." See Dewey's review of the second series of Gifford lectures in *Philosophical Review* 11 (1902): 405.

50. Royce, *World and Individual*, 2:134.

51. Etymologically, the word 'time' arises out of the word 'tide'. Only when processes of change steady into repetitive, ordered, and directed kinds of change do we speak of tides and, *mutatis mutandis*, times.

52. See Dewey's article, "Voluntarism in the Roycean Philosophy," in Creighton, *Papers*, and see note 49, above.

53. Royce, *World and Individual*, 2:140–41.

54. Ibid., 2:127.

55. Ibid., 2:128.

56. Ibid., 2:131.

57. The title of Charles Bakewell's contribution to *Papers*, "Novum Itinerarium Mentis In Deum," precisely catches up this sense of the fulfillment of the temporal within the eternal, a strong Bonaventuran motif. Bakewell says of Royce that "he has read his Socrates through the eyes of Kant and in the spirit of Bonaventura" (p. 31).

58. Bruce Kuklick, *Josiah Royce: An Intellectual Biography* (Indianapolis: Bobbs-Merrill Co.), p. 149, where he judges that "Royce has restated Bradley's riddle in a mathematically more sophisticated form: how are we to reconcile the finite world, marked by a dense series, with an Absolute, marked by a well-ordered series?"

59. Royce, *World and Individual*, 2:68, 76–86.

60. Ibid., 2:91. See Cotton, *Royce on the Human Self*, pp. 159–64, for a discussion of the concept of series and its importance in Royce's thought. Cotton shows that System Sigma is a series of series or a system of relations whose relata are relations.

61. Royce, *World and Individual*, 2:227.

62. Josiah Royce, "The Eternal and the Practical," *Philosophical Review* 13 (March 1904): 113–42.

63. Ibid., pp. 117, 140–41.

64. Josiah Royce, "The Reality of the Temporal," *International Journal of Ethics* 20 (1910): 257–71.

65. Ibid., p. 260. See also notes 58 and 60, above.

66. Ibid., p. 261.

67. Ibid., p. 267.

68. Ibid., p. 269.

69. Such views provide justification for the importance of the historical dimension to human experience. In his presidential address to the Pacific Coast branch of the American Historical Association, Earl Pomeroy said of Royce that "he was the only major American philosopher who before the second quarter of the twentieth century took much interest in history. See Earl Pomeroy, "Josiah Royce, Historian in Quest of Community," *Pacific Historical Review* 40 (1971): 1. Pomeroy judged regarding Royce that "his overarching theme was the tension of individualism and social responsibility" (p. 7).

70. Oppenheim concludes that "Royce's mature epistemology, borrowed largely from Peirce, was basically triadic, requiring three selves or signs of selves: the self or sign interpreted, the interpreter, and the one who receives the interpretation."

See Frank M. Oppenheim, "A Roycean Road to Community," *I.P.Q.* 10 (1970): 345.

71. Royce, "Reality of the Temporal," p. 271.

72. Royce, "Mind," *Encyclopedia of Religion and Ethics*, 1913, reprinted in *Royce's Logical Essays*, ed. Daniel S. Robinson (Dubuque, Iowa: Wm C. Brown Co., 1951), p. 151.

73. Such a method would include practical aspects of experience within logical universals. See Bakewell, in Creighton, *Papers*, p. 32.

74. Royce, "Mind," p. 156, for both quotations in this paragraph. See also note 70, above. In *Josiah Royce*, Vincent Buranelli says of Royce's view that "interpretation is a system that uniquely relates to time and the self. The sign pertains to the past; the interpreter, to the present; the interpretee, to the future" (p. 95). Buranelli also relates Royce's theory to Peirce's views.

75. Royce, *Royce's Logical Essays*, p. 160.

76. John E. Smith argues that Royce introduced a fundamental confusion into his philosophy through virtually identifying interpretation and comparison. Unlike comparison, interpretation is fundamentally related to time. See Smith's introduction to Royce, *The Problem of Christianity* (1913; reprint ed., Chicago: University of Chicago Press, 1968), p. 29. Smith judges that "the later Royce took time seriously" (p. 3).

77. The title of chapter 5 is "Time and Guilt," and the title of chapter 9 is "The Community and the Time Process."

78. Royce, *Problem of Christianity*, p. 38.

79. Ibid., p. 162. Such views of Royce, and indeed the whole of the chapter on "Time and Guilt," would be consistent with George Santayana's judgment that Royce "was heir to the Calvinistic tradition." See George Santayana, *Character and Opinion in the United States* (New York: W. W. Norton & Co., 1967), p. 100.

80. Royce, *Problem of Christianity*, p. 243. John Smith points out that there can be no community at an instant, and believes that this is analogous to Whitehead's "no nature at an instant." See p. 23 of his introduction.

81. See note 46, above.

82. Royce, *Problem of Christianity*, pp. 268, 288–89.

83. Ibid., p. 346.

84. Ibid.

85. Royce, *World and Individual*, vol. 2, chap. 3, sec. 4.

86. Ibid., 2:143.

CHAPTER IV. SANTAYANA AND
THE TEMPORAL COMPULSION

1. George Santayana, *Persons and Places* (New York: Scribner's, 1944–53), 3:136. Matter and time are quite closely linked as principles of reality in this philosophy. According to VanWesep, "the deepest thing to Santayana is his commitment to the reality not of matter but of time." See H. B. VanWesep, *Seven Sages* (New York: David McKay Co., 1960), p. 296.

2. Corliss Lamont, ed., *Dialogue on George Santayana* (New York: Horizon Press, 1959), pp. 38–39.

3. George Santayana, *The Idler and His Works*, ed. Daniel Cory (Freeport, N. Y.: Books for Libraries Press, 1969), p. 7.

4. Santayana, *Persons and Places*, 3:136, and 1:239. In a conversation with Corliss Lamont, Santayana said that when he was an undergraduate at Harvard, he carried around a pocket copy of Lucretius and read it on the horse car. Corliss Lamont, *Voice in the Wilderness* (Buffalo: Prometheus Books, 1974), p. 45.

5. George Santayana, "A General Confession," in *The Philosophy of George Santayana*, ed Paul Schilpp (Evanston: Northwestern University Press, 1940), p. 24.

6. George Santayana, *The Birth of Reason and Other Essays*, ed. Daniel Cory (New York: Columbia University Press, 1968), p. 151. Some commentators trace Santayana's notion of flux to William James or to Henri Bergson, but Heraclitus is a much more likely influence because of Heraclitus's emphasis upon *logos* or form amidst the swirl of change.

For the view that William James was a main influence in this regard, see Herbert Schneider, *A History of American Philosophy*, 2d ed. (New York: Columbia University Press, 1963), p. 504. For the view that Henri Bergson provides Santayana's point of departure regarding the flux, see Harold A. Larrabee, "George Santayana, II: Philosopher for America?" *Sewanee Review* 39 (1931): 327. But for the more obvious Heraclitean emphasis upon form in the midst of the flow of matter from one state to the next, see Santayana's letter to Sidney Hook on June 8, 1934, where Santayana said "matter cannot exist without form, and its form gives definition to its powers; but matter flows through these forms which are not magic bodiless forces magnetizing it from outside; they are the forms it has assumed in flowing. That, to my mind, is the essence of materialism." In Sidney Hook, "Letters from George Santayana," *American Scholar* 46 (1977): 80.

7. George Santayana, *The Letters of George Santayana*, ed. Daniel Cory (New York: Scribner's, 1955), p. 170.

8. George Santayana, *The Realm of Matter* (New York: Scribner's, 1930), p. 39. Santayana did not accept the flux composed of atoms as it was set out in Lucretius and, behind Lucretius, Democritus. He corrected the atomists by attending to Heraclitus and, it seems at least sometimes, Anaximander. For nuances of the main theme from Anaximander, see Michael C. J. Putnam, "Three Philosophical Poets," *Daedalus* 103 (1973): 132: "In Lucretius' philosophy, though the substance of our world may seem permanent, life is always in a state of flux, happy or sad. Only mutation is universal: nothing is born without the death of something else. . . . Santayana searches for the same flux in the mind of Lucretius as Lucretius envisions in nature." The retributive notion that the birth of some new thing will have its recompense in the death of something else is from Anaximander, and also finds its register in several of the fragments of Heraclitus.

9. Santayana, *Birth of Reason*, p. 151.

10. Ibid., p. 152. Among the pre-Socratic philosophers, in Howgate's judgment, neither of the two great proponents of changeless being or beings, Parmenides and Democritus, touched Santayana as deeply as did Heraclitus. See George W. Howgate, *George Santayana* (New York: Russell & Russell, 1971), pp. 198, 240.

For an opposing view which stresses Santayana's fundamental acceptance of Lucretius and Democritus at face value without any modification of their views in the light of Heraclitean motifs, see Stuart Gerry Brown, "Lucretius and Santayana: A Study in Classical Materialism," *New Mexico Quarterly* 15 (1945–46): 12, to the effect that Santayana "identifies himself clearly with the writers we have considered here, with Mo Ti, Epicurus, and Lucretius, as well as others whom we have not touched, especially Democritus, the atomist, and Spinoza." See also pp. 15–16 of

this same article where Santayana is grouped with Democritus and Lucretius as proponents of classical, atomistic materialism. But to ignore the Heraclitean features of Santayana's thought to this degree is simply to misread the record.

11. Santayana, *Realm of Matter*. Compare chapters 1 and 3.

12. Santayana, *Realm of Matter*, p. 67. According to Williams, Santayana "often means by 'matter' no more than whatever flux of existence engenders our lives and experience." In Donald C. Williams, "Of Essence and Existence and Santayana," *Journal of Philosophy* 51 (1954): 35.

13. Santayana, *Letters of George Santayana*, p. 174. Although Santayana sometimes uses 'matter' and 'substance' interchangeably, according to Lachs, the two concepts are clearly not to be identified in his work. See John Lachs, "Matter and Substance in the Philosophy of Santayana," *Modern Schoolman* 44 (Nov. 1966): 2–3. My use of 'substance' and also 'material substance' in this section is meant, accordingly, to show that Lachs has raised an important issue about Santayana's metaphysics.

14. George Santayana, *Scepticism and Animal Faith* (New York: Dover, 1955), p. 42. Santayana's emphasis on external relations holding between existing things, relations which issue often enough in groundless reactions between coexisting entities, is reflected in Williams's judgment that "matter as existence is the plain fact or status of occurring; and occurrence is the irreducible circumstance that essences enter into external relations. . . . As no external relation has any ground in the essences it connects, so existence has no ground in any essence." See Donald Williams, "Of Essence and Existence and Santayana," p. 39.

15. George Santayana, *The Life of Reason*, rev. ed. in 1 vol. (New York: Scribner's, 1953), p. 19. In commenting on a discussion of care or uneasiness (Sorge) by Heidegger, Santayana says that "the transitoriness of life is its radical essence. It is engulfed in the flux of existence." See Martin Heidegger and George Santayana, *Sein und Zeit*, Dritte Auflage, Erste Hälfte with marginalia by George Santayana (Halle: Max Niemeyer, 1931; from the papers of George Santayana, Columbia University Libraries), p. 250.

16. Santayana, *Realm of Matter*, p. 65. Alfred North Whitehead thought that time in the sense of passage could not really be known but must simply be endured. See our discussion of Whitehead's view below, in chapter 6, sect. 4, pt. B.

17. Santayana, *Persons and Places*, 1:248. The same kind of will, Santayana thought, was exhibited in the drive to accomplish and to produce that was found in the American working man, and not in the "genteel tradition" of the puritan intellectual. See Richard Colton Lyon, *Santayana on America* (New York: Harcourt, Brace & World, 1968), p. xxvii, where Lyon judges of Santayana that "his fundamental distinction between the theorizing Intellect of the country and its working Will clearly declares a preference for the Will."

18. Santayana, *Realm of Matter*, p. 15. The background argument here would contrast the realm of essence and the realm of matter with respect to the distinctive principle of each. For Santayana, the principle of essence is identity, whereas the principle of matter is change and otherness. Matter or substance is the principle of creative change, where things issue forth that are ontologically distinct from the creative ground. Matter or substance is precisely such a creative ground for Santayana, a creative ground of endless potentiality.

Richard Butler judges that a naturalized version of the Christian Trinitarian doctrine is being set out in Santayana's thought at this point. "Santayana . . . dissolves

the Trinity into his own terms. Father, Son, and Holy Spirit are transposed into matter, essence and spirit. Shocking as this divinization of nature is, Santayana has done a service to philosophy by extending the principles of naturalism to their logical termination." See Richard Butler, *The Life and World of George Santayana* (Chicago: Henry Regnery Co., 1960), p. 144. In a peevish and rather graceless aside, Butler also opines that Santayana's "claim to recognition, to a deserved reputation, is not as a philosopher, but as a poet. His philosophy belonged to him and should die with him." See Richard Butler, *The Mind of Santayana* (New York: Green Press, Pub., 1968), p. 194.

19. George Santayana, *Physical Order and Moral Liberty*, ed. John Lachs and Shirley Lachs (Nashville: Vanderbilt University Press, 1969), p. 37. In a letter to Daniel Cory on February 1, 1940, Santayana held that identity of stuff was important in proving matter and aiding in our conception of nature. But beyond those functions of the concept of the fluxing matter, it also contributed to continuity and derivation, helping us to distinguish genesis proper from a mere succession of phenomena. See Daniel Cory, *Santayana: The Later Years* (New York: George Braziller, 1963), p. 227.

21. Santayana, *Physical Order*, p. 75.

22. Ibid., pp. 30, 63, 52. Taken together, the ideas that the flux is generative and that the minimum units of the flux are tropes allow us to conclude that Santayana's flux is *not* absurd, irrational happening, a mere chaos. Perhaps seeing too much of Lucretius and Democritus in Santayana, and not enough of Heraclitus (cf. note 10, above), some very able commentators on Santayana take his flux as nonformed, nongenerative.

For the view that the flux of Santayana is irrational, see Milton K. Munitz, *The Moral Philosophy of Santayana* (Westport, Conn.: Greenwood Press, 1972), p. 39: "The realm of matter . . . is nevertheless in its very existence and arbitrary determinations an irrational and absurd flux of events." For a view that denies that Santayana's notion of change has any specifiable characters or determinations, such as tropes or a generative order, see Charles Hartshorne, "Santayana's Doctrine of Essence," in Schilpp, *Philosophy of George Santayana*, p. 174, where Hartshorne judges that "Santayana's account makes the character of change identifiable with the mystery of a 'matter' which is a mere surd to character, rather than a system of more or less general or determinable characters."

For a more adequate view, which sees the flux as chaos but also ascribes a course of events to it, see Schneider, *History of American Philosophy*, p. 507. For the view that Santayana's flux is not a chaos, but has a logos, see Beth Singer, "Matter and Time," *Southern Journal of Philosophy* 10 (Summer 1972): 198–99.

23. Santayana, "General Confession," p. 11.

24. George Santayana, *Three Philosophical Poets* (Garden City, N. Y.: Doubleday & Co., 1938), p. 47. Singer, "Matter and Time," p. 198, notes that for Santayana time is a function of the order of events. Hartshorne, "Santayana's Doctrine of Essence," p. 145, observes that "existence is temporal or nothing, as Santayaya himself insists." But for Santayana, once there existed nothing except matter or material conditions, and time arose from them. As opposed to Hartshorne's "existence is temporal or nothing," Santayana would say that existence is temporal or nontemporal.

25. Santayana, *Realm of Matter*, p. 46.

26. Santayana, *Physical Order*, p. 62.

27. Santayana, *Realm of Matter*, p. 58. Taken together, the two definitions of physical time suggest that physical time exhibits different aspects of the earlier/later relation. For some discussion of the degree to which Santayana may conflate the earlier/later relation with the past/future relation, see chap. 9, "Truth and Time," in Timothy L. S. Sprigge, *Santayana: An Examination of His Philosophy* (London: Routledge & Kegan Paul, 1974), pp. 180–81.

28. Santayana, *Realm of Matter*, p. 83.

29. Santayana, *Physical Order*, p. 75; idem, *The Last Puritan* (New York: Scribner's, 1936), p. 530. As did Peirce, Santayana raises the issue of cyclical time in order to dismiss it.

30. Santayana, *Physical Order*, p. 63. It seems that it is the procreative power of nature, the sheer fecundity, that keeps time from being reversible. The power of time and the procreative power of nature are closely related conceptions for him when he speaks of ". . . the strength of time, the fertility of matter, the variety, the unspeakable variety, of possible life." See Santayana, *The Genteel Tradition*, ed. Douglas L. Wilson (Cambridge, Mass.: Harvard University Press, 1967), p. 63.

31. Santayana, *Physical Order*, p. 52; idem, *Realm of Matter*, p. 88. It is difficult to know how much weight we are to attach to Santayana's view here that these natural moments are the ultimate elements of existence. Is this a temporalist form of atomism, where "natural moments" are vestigial "atoms" from Democritus and Lucretius? Taken at face value, natural moments as ultimate elements would constitute just that sort of central datum Santayana explicitly discounted. In addition to our own discussion of Lucretius earlier, see Santayana's judgment that "in nature, there is no foreground or background, no here, no now, no moral cathedra, no center so really central as to reduce all other things to mere margins and perspectives." In George Santayana, "Dewey's Naturalistic Metaphysics," *Journal of Philosophy* 22 (1925): 680. It was in this famous article that Santayana criticized "Dewey's half-hearted naturalism" (p. 678). But taking natural moments as ultimate existents might open Santayana to his own charge of half-hearted naturalism.

For a discussion that makes a strong case for natural moments as the key to Santayana's materialism, see Singer, "Matter and Time," p. 198, where she says that "Santayana has an elaborate theory of material substance. Its central doctrine is, in my judgment, the doctrine of natural moments." His naturalism, Singer holds, "culminates in a doctrine of process."

Timothy Sprigge calls special attention to difficulties that arise if we make natural moments the pivotal elements in Santayana's material substance. Sprigge judges that "the aspect of Santayana's treatment of space and time which may seem most contentious lies in his conviction that physical things and successions have ultimate components such as he calls 'natural moments'," in Sprigge, *Santayana*, p. 156. It seems contentious because it is not supported by our own experience of space and time. But Sprigge holds that this objection can be removed by (1) allowing any number of actual entities to comprise a given region, and (2) questioning whether our experience might not need to be rethought instead of rethinking natural moments (p. 157). Sprigge compares Santayana's natural moments with Whitehead's actual entities in arguing the first of these two points. Both Sprigge and Singer seem to be looking at Santayana's view of time as would investigators schooled in a Whiteheadean kind of process philosophy. Our own text mostly conflates natural moments and tropes.

32. Santayana, *Physical Order*, p. 52; idem, *Realm of Matter*, p. 95.

33. Santayana, *Physical Order*, p. 52; idem, *Realm of Matter*, p. 95.

34. Santayana, *Realm of Matter*, pp. 100–101.

35. Ibid., pp. 41, 42.

36. Santayana, *The Idler and His Works*, p. 235.

37. Santayana, *Realm of Matter*, pp. 100, 133.

38. Ibid., p. 62.

39. Santayana, *Physical Order*, p. xii.

40. Ibid., pp. 72, 62.

41. George Santayana, *The Idea of Christ in the Gospels* (New York: Scribner's, 1946), p. 254.

42. Santayana, *The Idler and His Works*, p. 151. This notion, that nature has the hierarchical habit which it exhibits differentially in cumulative levels or realms of being, is paralleled in an excellent recent treatment of time by J. T. Fraser, *The Genesis and Evolution of Time* (Amherst: University of Massachusetts Press, 1982), p. 1, where he notes that "the interpretative proposition made and examined in this book is called the principle of temporal levels. It maintains that each stable integrative level of the universe manifests a distinct temporality and that these temporalities coexist in a hierarchically nested, dynamic unity."

43. Santayana, *Realm of Matter*, p. 28.

44. Santayana, *Physical Order*, p. 21, for the account of these different levels of the morphological flux.

45. Ibid., p. 26.

46. Santayana, *The Letters*, p. 175. Other philosophers have noted this duality in Santayana's thought, differing though in their judgments as to which motif predominates, the naturalistic or the idealistic. Dewey called Santayana's approach a naturalistic idealism, as noted by Gary R. Stolz, "The Reception of Santayana's Life of Reason among American Philosophers," *Journal of the History of Philosophy* 14 (1976): 324. Buchler concludes that "there are two strains in his philosophy. But they are not sequential. They cohabit in *each* of his major works." See Justus Buchler, "One Santayana or Two?" *Journal of Philosophy* 51 (1954): 53. For John Herman Randall, Jr., the idealistic, imaginative, transcendental theme is quite overpowered by the naturalistic theme. Randall judges that "Santayana has thoroughly taught men that the imagination is a natural inhabitant of the realm of being." In John Herman Randall, Jr., "George Santayana—Naturalizing the Imagination," *Journal of Philosophy* 52 (Jan. 1954): 50–52. Richard Butler also believed, and was dismayed, that Santayana's naturalism had quite overtaken the idealistic and religious aspects of the system of thought. See note 18, above.

47. Santayana, *Life of Reason*, p. 429.

48. Ibid., p. 430. Heidegger had held that uneasiness of anxiety (Sorge) is the defining mark of human existence. Santayana disagrees, holding that "care is not the *first* characteristic of incarnate spirit: time of flux or expectancy precedes." See Heidegger and Santayana, *Sein und Zeit* (with marginalia by Santayana), p. 230.

49. Santayana, *Physical Order*, p. 66.

50. Ibid., p. 67.

51. Santayana, *Scepticism and Animal Faith*, p. 34.

52. George Santayana, *Character and Opinion in the United States* (1920; reprint ed., New York: Norton, 1967), p. 17.

53. Santayana, *Physical Order*, pp. 63, 75.

54. Santayana, *Realm of Matter*, pp. 77, 74, 64. See also Sprigge, *Santayana: An*

Examination of His Philosophy, p. 149, for the view that temporal succession at the level of material substance, where one stage of existence inherits from previous stages, makes possible the common space and time world that we find amidst specious space and time.

55. Santayana, *Physical Order*, p. 65; and idem, *Realm of Matter*, p. 65.

56. Ibid., pp. 66–68.

57. Santayana, *Physical Order*, p. 39.

58. George Santayana, *Some Turns of Thought in Modern Philosophy* (1933; reprint ed., Freeport, N.Y.: Books for Libraries Press, 1967), p. 76.

59. Santayana, *Realm of Matter*, p. 92.

60. Ibid., p. 58.

61. Santayana, *Physical Order*, p. 65.

62. Santayana, *Life of Reason*, p. 394.

63. Santayana, *Realm of Matter*, p. 70.

64. See also the thesis of J. T. Fraser mentioned in note 42, above.

65. What these temporal levels in social consciousness would look like if Santayana had treated them could perhaps be reconstructed from what he does say about the material conditions exhibited at the different levels of society. Initial steps to such a reconstruction seem implicit in Beth J. Singer, *The Rational Society* (Cleveland: The Press of Case Western Reserve University, 1970), chap. 3, "The Ambiguities of Santayana's Materialism," esp. pp. 25–29.

CHAPTER V. DEWEY AND THE TEMPORALIZING OF TIME

1. John Dewey, "From Absolutism to Experimentalism," in George P. Adams and William P. Montague, eds., *Contemporary American Philosophy* (New York: Russell & Russell, 1962), 2:22.

2. John Dewey, "The Metaphysical Assumptions of Materialism," *Journal of Speculative Philosophy* 16 (1882): 208–9. The paper was written in 1881 but its publication was delayed for a year.

3. Dewey, "Metaphysical Assumptions," p. 211. This would be a very early example of what Geiger sees as Dewey's emphasis upon a kind of continuity that goes beyond mere change and flux. See George Geiger, *John Dewey in Perspective* (New York: Oxford University Press, 1958), pp. 26–27.

4. John Dewey, "The Pantheism of Spinoza," *Journal of Speculative Philosophy* 16 (1882): 250.

5. Ibid., p. 254. From first to last, Dewey discounts the significance of the eternal. Over forty years later, he repeats the thought that the eternal cannot be meaningfully associated with change. See John Dewey, "Events and the Future," *Journal of Philosophy* 23 (1926): 254. According to Stephen Cahn, ed., *New Studies in the Philosophy of John Dewey* (Hanover, N.H.: University Press of New England, 1977), p. 59, Dewey was to emphasize "the temporality and contingency which Augustine and Spinoza used the notion of 'eternity' to exclude."

According to Boas, Dewey was "willing to accept the consequences of temporalized thinking. He has never, except in his youth, believed in Eternity and as a consequence he has never believed that one should turn to the past for a solution of present problems." See George Boas, "Instrumentalism and the History of Philosophy," in *John Dewey: Philosopher of Science and Freedom*, ed. Sidney Hook (New York: Barnes & Noble, 1967), p. 66.

6. John Dewey, "The New Psychology," *Andover Review* 2 (1884); reprinted in Jo Ann Boydston, ed., *The Early Works of John Dewey, 1882–1898* (Carbondale: Southern Illinois University Press), 1:48.

7. Dewey, "New Psychology," pp. 53–54. G. Stanley Hall had a very cautious if not negative view of the significance of Dewey's work in psychology. He judged that Dewey was a mediator between child study and the old philosophical orthodoxy of men like Herbart and Hegel, and that even though his influence was beneficial, "it is transient because he lacks originality." See G. Stanley Hall, *Life and Confessions of a Psychologist* (New York: D. Appleton and Company, 1923), p. 500.

8. Dewey, "New Psychology," pp. 53–54. It is consistent with Dewey's rejection of the eternal that he reject the significance of the *now* as immediately given. We have seen Royce argue that the eternal is presaged in the *now* as given. In rejecting the *now*, Dewey implicitly denies that it has any special significance in our understanding of time. His mature doctrine accordingly has it that present, past, and future all have the same status and are mutually implicated in each other. See, for example, Dewey, "Events and the Future," *Journal of Philosophy* 23 (1926): 257–58.

9. John Dewey, "Soul and Body," in Boydston, *Early Works of John Dewey*, 1:129.

10. John Dewey, "Psychology As Philosophical Method," in ibid., p. 160. Having rejected the eternal and the *now*, Dewey is consistent in rejecting the idea of a self or consciousness that might stand outside of temporal processes.

11. Dewey, "Psychology As Philosophical Method," p. 161.

12. John Dewey, "Illusory Psychology," in Boydston, *Early Works of John Dewey*, 1:172.

13. Ibid., p. 186.

14. John Dewey, "Ethics and Physical Science," in Boydston, *Early Works of John Dewey*, 1:209. Sixty years later, when in his judgment relativity theory had temporalized the physical world, allowing that it be a telic realm, Dewey had clearly reversed his judgment on the physical sciences. See John Dewey and Arthur Bentley, *Knowing and the Known* (Boston: Beacon Press, 1949), p. 113, where the coauthors refer to physics as "the most potent of all existing sciences." The old, Newtonian physics was merely interactional, whereas the new physics was transactional, fully temporalized.

15. Dewey, "Ethics and Physical Science," pp. 223, 225. For a contemporary argument which uses reasons that parallel Dewey's reasons, see Nathaniel Lawrence, "Time Represented As Space," *Monist* 53 (1969), esp. p. 456, where Lawrence concludes that "a more concrete approach to time does not confine itself to the factual, the physical, and the mathematical . . . but rather extends to the realm of value, intent, and purpose as well."

16. George Dykhuizen, *The Life and Mind of John Dewey* (Carbondale: Southern Illinois University Press, 1973), p. 64.

17. John Dewey, *Leibniz's New Essays concerning the Human Understanding* (Chicago: S. C. Griggs and Co., 1888), reprinted in Boydston, *The Early Works of John Dewey*, 1:317, where Dewey judges that "the treatment of sensation always reflects the fundamental philosophical category of the philosopher."

18. Dewey, *Leibniz's New Essays*, p. 267.

19. Ibid., p. 415. The Leibniz book is typical of this stage of Dewey's work, according to Morton White, *The Origins of Dewey's Instrumentalism* (New York: Octagon Books, 1964), p. 60.

20. Dewey, *Leibniz's New Essays*, p. 281.

21. Ibid., pp. 283, 285. Dewey took a version of just this problem and dealt with it as *the* philosophical problem in his late essay, "Time and Individuality," 1940. See note 70, below.

22. Ibid., p. 347.

23. Ibid., p. 355. Sherover observes that Dewey's study of Leibniz helped frame the context in which his thought developed. He judges that "significantly, two of [Dewey's] first books were on Leibniz and Darwin; they set much of the mood that was to pervade the development of his thinking. The first suggests his abiding interests in the fundamental import of individuality, context, dynamicity and temporal quality; the second, his continuing concern for the significance of the scientific experience and his conviction that rationality and understanding of natural processes are to be found in development, evolution, and growth." See Charles M. Sherover, *The Human Experience of Time* (New York: New York University Press, 1975), p. 364.

24. Dewey, *Leibniz's New Essays*, p. 364.

25. Ibid.

26. Ibid., p. 365. Dewey never forgot this distinction that he found in the work of Leibniz. The distinction is the direct antecedent of Dewey's own distinction between temporal quality and temporal order.

27. Ibid., p. 366. Part of Dewey's temporalizing of time is due to the fact that temporal order is a matter of relations and mere possibilities, and thus is timeless (or related to the eternal), whereas temporal quality is much closer to the appetitive, striving aspects of actual experience. The idea of time, for Dewey and Leibniz, is close to being infected with eternality. Royce embraced that fact while Dewey eschews it.

28. John Dewey, *Psychology* in Boydston, *Early Works of John Dewey*, 2:75, 89.

29. Ibid., pp. 139, 140, 158.

30. Ibid., p. 161. The concept of rhythm, once it had been introduced in this book, for the most part lay dormant in Dewey's philosophy of time for three decades and more. It was activated to play an expanded role in his account of time in the natural world. See section 5 of this chapter.

31. Ibid., p. 163. Some of what Dewey says about the concept of rhythm makes clear that it is a surrogate concept for certain notions about the transcendent and the eternal. Royce saw evidence of the presence of the eternal in just these features of what are for Dewey simply rhythmic gestalts. Put otherwise, Dewey would say that Royce has, in his concept of the eternal, simply hypostatized some sophisticated natural functions of the psyche as it actively organizes and responds to experience.

32. Ibid., p. 166.

33. Dykhuizen, *Life and Mind of John Dewey*, p. 38.

34. John Dewey, "Some Stages in Logical Thought," *John Dewey: The Middle Works, 1899–1924*, ed. Jo Ann Boydston (Carbondale: Southern Illinois University Press, 1976), 1:170, 211.

35. Ibid., p. 193.

36. See Thomas P. Neill, "Dewey's Ambivalent Attitude toward History," in John Blewett, ed., *John Dewey: His Thought and Influence* (Westport, Conn.: Greenwood Press, 1973), p. 149, for the judgment that "despite his concession that a knowledge of history is useful, Dewey is basically hostile toward the past and apparently afraid that history will be studied so as to become a hindrance to progress."

In his conclusion, Neill adds that "Dewey considered the past only as a lever to use in the present" (pp. 157–58). Dewey's logical theory provided backing to validate his indifference to the past *qua* past.

37. White, *Origins of Dewey's Instrumentalism*, pp. 134, 146. Richard Bernstein, *John Dewey* (New York: Washington Square Press, 1966), p. 78, holds that a key to Dewey's logical essays is the notion of the temporal development of experience.

38. Dykhuizen, *Life and Mind of John Dewey*, p. 125. Some who were sympathetic with Dewey's basic approach to philosophy nevertheless could see the influence of idealistic categories upon it. John Randall, 1859–1952," *Journal of Philosophy* 50 (1953): p. 5, said of Dewey's language that it "owed its difficulty primarily to being the language of the idealistic philosophy of social experience in which he grew up." More recently, Maritain, a less sympathetic commentator, judged that "it is by reason of the incomplete rupture with Hegelianism that Dewey gives in his philosophy a pseudo-Hegelian interpretation and flavor to the typically American conviction of the inherent necessity for things to change, to progress; whereas in fact this feeling has absolutely nothing to do with a metaphysics of pure Becoming and derives solely from a moral disposition combining creative energy and detachment." See Jacques Maritain, *Moral Philosophy* (New York: Charles Scribner's Sons, 1964), p. 401. Dewey was not, of course, interested in a metaphysics of pure Becoming. From his first publication on, he was concerned with value, order, and stability in the midst of change.

39. Dewey, "From Absolutism to Experimentalism," p. 13.

40. John Dewey, *The Influence of Darwin on Philosophy* (Bloomington: Indiana University Press, 1965), pp. 1, 47, 70. The concepts of evolution and experience are singled out by John Smith to show how the idea of evolution shaped Dewey's general outlook. See John Smith, "John Dewey: Philosopher of Experience," in *John Dewey and the Experimental Spirit in Philosophy*, ed. Charles W. Hendel (New York: Liberal Arts Press, 1959), p. 94. See also note 23, above.

41. Dewey, *Influence of Darwin*, p. 179. In the 1920s Dewey and Lovejoy made the telling point that if the meaning of the past lies in the future, then we will be unable to make judgments about the past that can be either confirmed or disconfirmed in the future because we will never have a stable belief or judgment to test. See Arthur Lovejoy, "Time, Meaning and Transcendence," *Journal of Philosophy* 19 (1922): 505–15. Thus, Lovejoy concluded, the "alleged futurity of yesterday" is a confused conception.

42. Dewey, *Influence of Darwin*, p. 200. Smith, "Dewey: Philosopher of Experience," p. 101, judges that "the secret of Dewey's instrumentalism lies in his view that the present (and the past also as retained) is not chiefly for observation, but is to be used by us in a strategic way; from it we have our only chance to obtain a foothold on the future, which alone counts."

The future as infinite *progressus* would not count for much to Dewey. It is the future as the arena for the fulfillment of intelligent experience that counts. "The future just as future lacks urgency and body," says Dewey in "Democracy and Education," in *Dewey: The Middle Works*, 9:59.

43. John Dewey, "The Subject Matter of Metaphysical Inquiry," *Journal of Philosophy* 12 (1915), reprinted in *Dewey and His Critics*, ed. Sidney Morgenbesser (New York: Journal of Philosophy, 1977), p. 312.

44. Dewey, "Subject Matter of Metaphysical Inquiry," p. 317.

45. John Dewey, "Reconstruction in Philosophy," in *Dewey: The Middle Works,* 12:129, 133.

46. Dewey, *Reconstruction in Philosophy,* p. 33. W. T. Feldman, *The Philosophy of John Dewey* (1934; reprint ed., New York: Greenwood Press, 1968), chap. 6, "Futurism." Feldman speaks of "Dewey's unmistakable bias towards all things future" (p. 59).

47. Dewey, *Reconstruction in Philosophy,* pp. 60–61. In recounting certain leading ideas in Dewey's philosophy, A. H. Johnson observes that "he contends that every existent is an 'event.' That is to say, 'change' is an essential characteristic of the universe. Events (persons and things) are in constant 'interaction.' " A. H. Johnson, ed., *The Wit and Wisdom of John Dewey* (1949; reprint ed., New York: Greenwood Press, 1969), p. 15.

48. Dewey, *Reconstruction in Philosophy,* p. xiii. In the judgment of George Boas, "Instrumentalism and the History of Philosophy," p. 66, "[Dewey's] entire orientation is in a sense historical, for like Croce and Bergson, from both of whom he differs on most points, he has integrated thought into historical processes and, unlike them and many others, he has been willing to accept the consequences of temporalized thinking."

49. John Dewey, "Events and Meanings," *New Republic* 32 (August 1922): 9–10. Bernstein, *John Dewey,* p. 88, holds that a key to Dewey's philosophy is his idea of quality. Bernstein also judges that immediacy is an emphasis in American philosophy (p. 92).

50. John Dewey, *Experience and Nature* (1925; reprint ed., La Salle, Ill.: Open Court Publishing Co., 1958), pp. 41, 124, 214, 110.

51. Ibid., p. 54. David W. Mancell, *Progress and Pragmatism* (Westport, Conn.: Greenwood Press, 1974), p. 231, where he concludes that "Dewey, like James, saw pragmatism as a middle way between the extremes of flux and stability."

52. Dewey, *Experience and Nature,* p. 57.

53. Ibid., pp. 62, 64. Irwin Edman, ed., *John Dewey: His Contribution to the American Tradition* (New York: Greenwood Press, 1968), p. 30, concluded in his introduction to a selection of Dewey's writings that "most classical philosophies regard the universe as something fixed and eternal, as a stable order. . . . But Dewey's conception of the nature of things implies in its very terms the notion of a universe which is always in process, always changing, in which time is real and in which time makes a constant difference, the difference being specific variation and change. . . . To Dewey the reality *is* change, the universe is process."

54. Dewey, *Experience and Nature,* p. 62. Thomas R. Martland, Jr., *The Metaphysics of William James and John Dewey* (New York: Greenwood Press, 1969), p. 54, judges that pragmatism sacrifices structure to process.

55. Dewey, *Experience and Nature,* p. 97.

56. Ibid., p. 93. J. Oliver Buswell, Jr. (*The Philosophies of F. R. Tennant and John Dewey* [New York: Philosophical Library, 1950], p. 427) believes that "Dewey is confused in his own definitions of time and space. . . . It does not seem to concern him in the least whether he is consistent in his definitions and usages of such terms as time and space." Given his essential distinction between temporal quality and temporal order, and that time is derived from temporal order, Dewey is dependably consistent in his usage of these key terms. An exception, one which might lend some support to Buswell's judgment, does occur quite late in Dewey's work, where he coauthored (with Arthur Bentley) his preferred definitions. See notes 85 and 86, below.

57. Dewey, *Experience and Nature*, pp. 124, 352.

58. George Santayana observed that Dewey had chosen events to be his metaphysical elements. See Santayana, "Dewey's Naturalistic Metaphysics," in *The Philosophy of John Dewey*, ed. Paul A. Schilpp (Evanston and Chicago: Northwestern University, 1939), p. 250.

59. Dewey, *Experience and Nature*, p. 92.

60. Ibid., pp. 82, 83. John Smith recounts that "[Dewey] was fond of saying that the proper contrast to appearance is not reality but disappearance," in "John Dewey: Philosopher of Experience," p. 115.

61. Dewey, *Experience and Nature*, p. 64.

62. Ibid., p. 158.

63. John Dewey, *The Quest for Certainty: A Study of the Relation of Knowledge and Action* (New York: Minton, Balch & Co., 1929), p. 126.

64. Ibid., p. 145.

65. Ibid., p. 290–91. In the context of his argument in chapter 11, "The Copernican Revolution," Dewey points out that philosophy is now moving beyond the Copernican revolution of Kant, and the mind is seen as an operating center within the on-going processes of the world. Operationalism and Instrumentalism, Dewey thought, were ways to secure the advances of this new understanding.

66. The concept of rhythm mostly remained unused by Dewey after his initial introduction of it to secure certain views within his psychology; see note 30, above. Dewey later refurbishes 'rhythm' for special use in his metaphysics.

67. John Dewey, *Art As Experience* (1934; reprint ed., New York: G. P. Putnam's Sons, 1958), pp. 209–10, 14. Paul Welsh notes the interplay between the notions of change and endurance in Dewey's metaphysics. He characterizes the uniqueness of events and the recurrence of relations as quite central: "Here in brief are two assumptions of Dewey's philosophy." See Paul Welsh, "Some Metaphysical Assumptions in Dewey's Philosophy," *Journal of Philosophy* 51 (1954): 861. Welsh adds the telling observation that Dewey's claim about the uniqueness of events and the qualities that comprise them is not empirically verifiable, pp. 866–67.

68. Dewey, *Art As Experience*, p. 23.

69. Dewey, *Art As Experience*, pp. 218, 17. In "Events and Meanings" (1922), Dewey had held that "thinking about events and celebrating them in tone and color and form might become more important than being an event. It is even possible that temporary abstinence from the course of events for the sake of conversing about them might moderate their violence, and by tempering power, render it more stable." Times of intelligent, consummatory experiences could have a catalytic effect in redirecting and modulating power.

70. John Dewey, "Time and Individuality," *Time and Its Mysteries*, series 2 (New York: New York University Press, 1940; reprinted in Sherover, *Human Experience of Time*), p. 430.

71. Dewey, "Time and Individuality," p. 434. In his review of *Time and Its Mysteries*, Ernest Nagel gave almost all of his attention to Dewey's contribution, "Time and Individuality." He thought the essay was provocative but its arguments puzzling. He believed Dewey was working at cross-purposes in some of what he said, and concluded that Dewey's effort to supply a "metaphysical underpinning" for his faith in democracy was neither effective nor desirable. Nagel's review appeared in *Journal of Philosophy* 39 (1942), and is reprinted in Morgenbesser, *Dewey and His Critics*, pp. 401–3.

72. Dewey, "Time and Individuality," p. 423.

73. Ibid., pp. 427–28.

74. Ibid., p. 429.

75. Ibid., p. 431. On p. 428, Dewey makes a very extended application of the principle of indeterminacy of Heisenberg, saying that the principle is "a way of acknowledging the pertinency of time to physical beings." Arthur Lovejoy questioned Dewey's use of the principle in some of Dewey's arguments in *The Quest for Certainty*, holding that "no metaphysical consequences . . . can be deduced from the physical principle of indeterminacy except with the aid of a purely metaphysical assumption." See Lovejoy, *The Revolt against Dualism* (1929; reprint ed., La Salle, Ill.: Open Court Publishing Co., 1955), p. 356. In Ernest Nagel's review of *Time and Its Mysteries* (see note 71, above), he held that "it is not clear . . . what relevance the Heisenberg principle has for Professor Dewey's argument," p. 402.

76. Dewey, "Time and Individuality," p. 433.

77. John Dewey and Arthur Bentley, *Knowing and the Known* (Boston: Beacon Press, 1949), p. 108.

78. Ibid., pp. vi, 303.

79. Ibid., pp. 290, 60.

80. Ibid., p. 63.

81. Ibid. The coauthors in all likelihood adopt circularity in the spirit of recognizing what Ralph B. Perry had called "the egocentric predicament." That is, reason is experiential and never ontological, never able to pierce beyond experience to grasp essences or forms as they are in reality. Somewhere, the English philosopher Robin G. Collingwood remarks that all thinking is circular, and the only important matter is whether the circle is so narrow that it is barren, or extended enough to be fruitful.

82. Ibid., pp. 63–64. There is an effective summary of Dewey's classification of events in Robert E. Dewey, *The Philosophy of John Dewey* (The Hague and Boston: Martinus Nijhoff, 1977), in chapter 5, "Change," especially p. 102. After showing that Dewey has assigned a dual role to events—experiential and metaphysical— Robert Dewey judges that the duality "reflects opposing tendencies in Dewey's thought," and that the opposition was "never fully reconciled by him" (pp. 110, 166). See also note 56, above.

83. Dewey and Bentley, *Knowing and the Known*, pp. 69, 70.

84. Ibid., p. 113. The references to Newton, Maxwell, and Einstein in the remainder of the paragraph are to ideas proposed by the coauthors on pp. 111, 106, and 112, respectively. Bentley had held independently that "Einstein's work opened new vistas of freedom to psychologies of the future." See Arthur Bentley, "The Factual Space and Time of Behavior," *Journal of Philosophy* 38 (1941): 478. Bentley meant this judgment to be taken in a methodological sense, concerning the freedom of inquiry, and not in a physicalistic sense, p. 478.

85. Dewey and Bentley, *Knowing and the Known*, pp. 289–93.

86. Sidney Ratner and Jules Altman, eds., *John Dewey and Arthur F. Bentley: A Philosophical Correspondence, 1932–1951* (New Brunswick: Rutgers University Press, 1964), p. 202. See also John Dewey, "Events and the Future," *Journal of Philosophy* 23 (1926): 253, 256, 257, for some of Dewey's analysis of 'event' that makes that term central for him.

Another difficulty with 'existence' as the key term is that, as noted by Dewey in the first of his published papers, it had been closely associated with the idea of eternity by Spinoza. See Spinoza's Definition 8 in Dewey, "Pantheism of Spinoza," p. 579.

87. Ratner and Altman, *Dewey and Bentley*, p. 579.

88. John Dewey, "Events and Meanings," *New Republic* 32 (1922): 9.

89. Ibid., p. 10.

CHAPTER VI. WHITEHEAD AND TEMPORAL EXTENSION

1. Lucien Price, *Dialogues of Alfred North Whitehead* (London: Max Reinhardt, 1954), p. 146. Whitehead thought that a "feebleness of language" lay behind the difficulties of philosophical discussion. See Alfred N. Whitehead, *Modes of Thought* (New York: Free Press, 1968), p. 101.

2. Alfred N. Whitehead, "On Mathematical Concepts of the Material World," *Philosophical Transactions of the Royal Society of London*, Series A 205 (May 1906): 465–66. The paper was received by the society on September 22, 1905, and read on December 7, 1905.

3. In commenting on Nathaniel Lawrence, *Whitehead's Philosophical Development* (1956; reprint ed., New York: Greenwood Press, 1968), Leclerc contends, against Lawrence, that Whitehead's problems were cosmological in this early period. See Ivor Leclerc, "Whitehead's Philosophy," *Review of Metaphysics* 11 (1957): 85.

4. The linear concepts afford a more secure purchase on physics. See Janet A. Fitzgerald, *Alfred North Whitehead's Early Philosophy of Space and Time* (Washington, D.C.: University Press of America, 1979), p. 39.

5. Whitehead, "On Mathematical Concepts," p. 484.

6. Ibid., p. 469.

7. But these main features of Concept V are *not* the channels of that thought. Whitehead was suspicious of modeling philosophical method upon mathematical method. Perhaps it is John Dewey who did most to popularize the idea that a mathematical pretension controls Whitehead's philosophy. See Dewey, "The Philosophy of Whitehead," in Paul A. Schilpp, ed., *The Philosophy of Alfred North Whitehead*, 2d ed. (New York: Tudor Publishing Co., 1951), p. 646, where Dewey judges that a "mathematical strain" dominates Whitehead's cosmology. David Harrah pursues this viewpoint at some length in "The Influence of Logic and Mathematics on Whitehead," *Journal of the History of Ideas* 20 (1959): 420–30, saying that "the central thesis of this paper, briefly, is this: Whitehead was a creative mathematician; his cast of mind was shaped in and through his procedures as a creative mathematician; these procedures were later sublimated into the basic principles of his cosmology" (p. 422). See also Fitzgerald, *Whitehead's Early Philosophy*: "Whitehead's method of extensive abstraction from its origins in 1905 through its final, metaphysical appearance in *Process and Reality*, is a mathematical model" (p. ix).

8. Alfred N. Whitehead, *The Axioms of Projective Geometry* (New York: Hafner Publishing Co., 1971), p. 2.

9. Immanuel Kant, "On the First Ground of the Distinction of Regions in Space," in *Kant's Inaugural Dissertation and Early Writings on Space*, trans. John Handyside (Chicago: Open Court Publishing Co., 1929), pp. 19–29.

10. Alfred N. Whitehead, *An Introduction to Mathematics* (1911; reprint ed., New York: Oxford University Press, 1958), p. 91.

11. Chapter 12 of Whitehead's *Introduction to Mathematics* is entitled "Periodicity in Nature," and develops out of an analogy between periodicities in nature and periodicities in bodily events.

12. Whitehead, *Introduction to Mathematics*, pp. 122, 125.

13. Ibid., p. 179.

14. Ibid., pp. 181–82. According to Paci, Whitehead was particularly interested in the problem of space or spatial existence. See Enzo Paci, *La Filosofia Di Whitehead* (Milano: La Goliardica, 1965), pp. 41–42. I appreciate the help of Frank Mazzella in translating a section of Paci's book for me.

The considerable weight of the expositions of Whitehead's work that are found in Robert M. Palter, *Whitehead's Philosophy of Science* (Chicago: University of Chicago Press, 1960), is due to Palter's remaining bound by the experiential lines of evidence Whitehead used (see pp. 3–4).

15. Whitehead, *Introduction to Mathematics*, pp. 184, 185–86. But already a problem about time shows up here as we deal with measurement by means of the repetition of the same kind of event, for we are *less* sure that these canonical events are of the same duration than we are that our footrule is of the same length.

16. Alfred N. Whitehead, "The Mathematical Curriculum," in *The Aims of Education and Other Essays* (New York: The Free Press, 1967), pp. 78–79.

17. Whitehead, "Mathematical Curriculum," pp. 84–85.

18. Alfred N. Whitehead, "La Théorie Relationniste de l'Espace," translated as "The Relational Theory of Space" by Janet Fitzgerald in her appendix to *Whitehead's Early Philosophy*, p. 169.

19. Ibid., p. 21, for this and the next quotation.

20. Ibid., p. 170. See also idem, *Introduction to Mathematics*, p. 122.

21. Filmer S. C. Northrop, "Whitehead's Philosophy of Science," in Schilpp, *Philosophy of Whitehead*, p. 200.

22. Alfred N. Whitehead, "Space, Time, and Relativity," in *The Interpretation of Science*, ed. A. H. Johnson (Indianapolis: Bobbs-Merrill Co., 1961), p. 91.

23. Alfred N. Whitehead, "Autobiographical Notes," in Schilpp, *Philosophy of Whitehead*, p. 7, where Whitehead says that "I nearly knew by heart parts of Kant's *Critique of Pure Reason*. Now I have forgotten it, because I was early disenchanted."

24. Whitehead, "Space, Time, and Relativity," pp. 92–93.

25. Ibid., p. 94, where the analogy is developed. While he apparently believed it was fruitful to pursue the analogy, he was aware of an important, obvious dis-analogy. Spatial relations are reversible, whereas temporal relations mostly are not. Nathaniel Lawrence judges that "the opinions expressed in this article are very heterodox in comparison with those expressed in the works of 1919–1920. . . . These views are inconsistent with some of the most stable underlying features of the subsequent philosophy." See Lawrence, *Whitehead's Philosophical Development*, p. 143.

If there is heterodoxy or inconsistency between the two sets of writings, it may be traced to the circumstance (which is argued for later on) that Whitehead had been modeling time upon space. But time is on the point of having its fortunes reversed in Whitehead's thought, and is to be dominant over space.

26. Rudolf Metz held of Whitehead that "his awakening from dogmatic slumber resulted, as he himself confessed, from the great changes in the field of mathematical physics that came especially from Einstein's theory of relativity and its criticism of the traditional doctrine of space and time." See Rudolf Metz, *A Hundred Years of British Philosophy*, trans. J. N. Harvey, T. E. Jessop, and Henry Sturt (New York: Macmillan Co., 1938), p. 591.

27. Whitehead, "Space, Time, and Relativity," p. 94.

28. Ibid., p. 101.

29. Ibid., p. 103.

30. Ibid.

31. Ibid., p. 107. Whitehead had probably *not* forgotten some parts of Kant's first *Critique* which he said he "knew by heart"; see note 23, above. Whitehead's thought here is thoroughly Kantian in form. See what Kant says regarding a Copernican-like change of emphasis in metaphysics in the *Critique*, B xvi–xvii. But where Kant wanted to pursue the hypothesis that objects must conform to our knowledge, Whitehead saves the form of Kant's insight, and varies its content by saying that "our problem is, in fact, to fit the world to our perceptions." As it develops, moreover, Whitehead will fit the world to our *bodily* perceptions. In part, "Space, Time, and Relativity" gives us a Lockean version of Kant's Copernican revolution.

32. In the Whitehead centennial issue of *The Journal of Philosophy* 58 (1961), edited by George Kline, Ivor Leclerc concluded in his paper, "Whitehead and the Problem of Extension," p. 559, that although Whitehead still believed that extension was basically spatial, "he realized that recent advances in scientific theory, culminating in the theory of relativity, had made time crucial. But it was only in his middle period, with his doctrine of 'events,' that he was able coherently to bring time into the notion of extension: events are essentially spatiotemporal—they have a temporal extensiveness as well as a spatial extensiveness."

33. Alfred N. Whitehead, "The Aims of Education," in *Aims of Education* (1929; reprint ed., New York: Free Press, 1967), p. 2. With a slight change, the same idea is repeated on p. 127, in "The Anatomy of Some Scientific Ideas," published in this same collection of essays.

34. Whitehead, "Aims of Education," p. 3. This is the first statement in Whitehead's works of the way all of the modes of time are interwoven in the present. We examine this issue at some length farther on, both in this chapter and the next.

35. Ibid., p. 14.

36. Price, *Dialogues of Alfred North Whitehead*, p. 128, where Whitehead says, "I have lived three distinct lives in this single span; one from childhood to the first world war, one from 1914 to my residence in America in 1924; and a third since 1924. The first seems the most fantastic; in those years from the 1880's to the first war, who ever *dreamed* that the ideas and institutions which then looked so stable would be impermanent?"

37. Alfred N. Whitehead, "The Organisation of Thought," in *Aims of Education*, p. 104.

38. Ibid., p. 106. See also Justus Buchler, "On a Strain of Arbitrariness in Whitehead's System," *Journal of Philosophy* 66 (1969): 591, for the judgment that Whitehead is as addicted to the notion of concreteness as any other notion. Buchler finds two trends in Whitehead's philosophy which fit together uneasily: the attempt to define and justify a conceptual order having certain types of entities, and the attempt to judge how real the entities are.

39. Whitehead, "Organisation of Thought," p. 107.

40. Alfred N. Whitehead, "Technical Education and Its Relation to Science and Literature," in *Aims of Education*, p. 48.

41. Whitehead, "Technical Education," p. 58.

42. Whitehead, "Anatomy of Some Scientific Ideas," pp. 127, 128.

43. Ibid., p. 136. Point objects in space-time are not directly related to facts, but are in the first place intellectual constructs.

44. Ibid., p. 133. According to Duhem, Plato says that we know space by a hybrid sort of reasoning that is most like *imagination* or like our dream-life. See Pierre Duhem, "Plato's Theory of Space and the Geometrical Composition of Elements," in *The Concepts of Space and Time*, ed. Milič Čapek (Dordrecht, Holland: D. Reidel Publishing Co., 1976), pp. 21–22.

45. Whitehead, "Anatomy of Some Scientific Ideas," p. 134. From this point on, it would be correct to say that time is primary and space is derivative for Whitehead. See also Robert Brumbaugh, *Whitehead, Process Philosophy, and Education* (Albany: State University of New York Press, 1982), for the view that "Whitehead himself, particularly concerned to protect the primary role of time in his physical theories, made space abstract and derivative" (p. 22).

46. Whitehead, "Anatomy of Some Scientific Ideas," p. 147. See also Wilbur M. Urban, "Whitehead's Philosophy of Language and Its Relation to His Metaphysics," in Schilpp, *Philosophy of Whitehead*, for the judgment that although Whitehead does balance permanence and flux, "it would not seem unfair to say that at all critical points throughout Whitehead's entire philosophy time and flux are given the last word" p. 320. We have seen that this does not hold for Whitehead's "entire philosophy" but does reflect a position Whitehead developed from about 1915 to 1917 on, and then time and flux, or events upon which they are based, are "given the last word."

47. Whitehead, "Anatomy of Some Scientific Ideas," pp. 136–37.

48. Ibid., p. 137.

49. Ibid., pp. 138–39, 140.

50. Pierre Duhem, "Place and Void according to John Philopon"; and idem, "Absolute Frame of Reference according to St. Thomas," pp. 39–42 in Čapek, *Concepts of Space and Time*.

51. Whitehead, "Anatomy of Some Scientific Ideas," p. 149. As part of his conclusion to this significant paper, Whitehead says that "we commenced by excluding judgments of worth and ontological judgments. We conclude by recalling them. Judgments of worth are no part of the texture of physical science, but they are part of the motive of its production" (p. 151). This bears on what we are to make of the statement in the *Concept of Nature* that "nature is closed to mind," and supports the *methodological* context in which that famous statement is embedded.

52. Alfred N. Whitehead, *The Concept of Nature* (1920; reprint ed., Cambridge: University Press, 1964), pp. vii, 55. This book is comprised of Whitehead's Tarner lectures from November 1919.

53. Alfred N. Whitehead, *The Principle of Relativity* (Cambridge: University Press, 1922), p. 4.

54. Victor Lowe comments that Whitehead's 1919 paper, "Time, Space, and Material," is a summary of Whitehead's *An Enquiry concerning the Principles of Natural Knowledge*, written for an Aristotelian Society meeting. See Lowe, "Whitehead's Philosophical Development," in Schilpp, *Philosophy of Whitehead*, p. 70.

55. Whitehead, "Time, Space, and Material: Are They, and If So in What Sense, the Ultimate Data of Science?" in idem, *Interpretation of Science*, p. 56.

56. Alfred N. Whitehead, *An Enquiry concerning the Principles of Natural Knowledge*, 2d ed. (1921; reprint ed., Cambridge: University Press, 1925), p. vi. Bertrand Russell judged that although there were still certain problems of a psychological and physiological nature, Whitehead's work is "far above anything else" in re-

lating abstract physics to the world given in sense experience. See Bertrand Russell, *The Analysis of Matter* (1927; reprint ed., New York: Dover Publications, 1954), p. 138.

57. See notes 23 and 29, above. Still, Kant like Whitehead gave time priority over space. For Kant, space is the form of external intuitions, whereas time is the form of *all* intuitions, both external and internal; Kant, *Critique of Pure Reason*, A 31–34.

58. Alfred N. Whitehead, *The Principle of Relativity with Applications to Physical Science* (Cambridge: University Press, 1922), p. 64.

59. Whitehead, *Enquiry*, 1.1.

60. Whitehead, "Time, Space, and Material," p. 56.

61. Whitehead, *Concept of Nature*, p. 33.

62. Whitehead, *Enquiry*, 1.1.

63. Whitehead, *Concept of Nature*, pp. 22–23.

64. Ibid., p. 19.

65. Whitehead, *Enquiry*, 1.2.

66. Whitehead, "Time, Space, and Material," pp. 57, 56; and *Enquiry*, 1.2. As early as the 1905 memoir, Whitehead had spoken of the need to account for velocity and acceleration. See the quotation on p. 223.

67. The metaphor that nature is impaled on the present, immobile instant is used by William W. Hammerschmidt, *Whitehead's Philosophy of Time* (New York: Russell & Russell, 1975), p. 18. By way of contrast, "the analysis of continuous change may be regarded as the basis of Whitehead's physical philosophy" (p. 18). Hammerschmidt divides Whitehead's work into three periods, and "the first period extends from his earliest publication through 1924" (p. 7). But we have shown that in the period from roughly 1915 to 1917, Whitehead made time and passage equal or dominant, whereas from 1905 to about 1914, Whitehead's dominant concept was space. That change is as striking or more so than the change from Hammerschmidt's second period, beginning with *Science and the Modern World*, to the third period, commencing with *Process and Reality*.

68. Whitehead, *Enquiry*, 5.4.

69. Whitehead, *Concept of Nature*, p. 40, and *Enquiry*, 2.2, 2.5. See also Whitehead, "Einstein's Theory: An Alternative Suggestion," in idem, *Interpretation of Science*, p. 126, where he says that "if absolute motion is imperceptible, absolute position is a fairy tale, and absolute space cannot survive the surrender of the absolute position."

70. Whitehead, *Concept of Nature*, pp. 33–34; idem, "Time, Space and Material," p. 58. Instants as ultimate existents had been included under every concept, both punctual and linear, in the 1905 memoir. See "On Mathematical Concepts of the Material World," p. 467. The assumptions Whitehead made in the memoir are now being discharged in his mature physical theory.

71. Whitehead, *Enquiry*, 2.4; idem, *Concept of Nature*, p. 68. Except as an ideal of observation, the knife-edge present does not exist; experience gives us nothing but durations with temporal thickness (p. 69). Whitehead's language here seems almost Jamesian in its images.

72. Ibid., pp. 32–33, 34.

73. H. Wildon Carr, "Discussion: The Idealistic Interpretation of Einstein's Theory," *Proceedings of the Aristotelian Society* 22 (1921–22): 127.

74. Alfred N. Whitehead, "Discussion: The Idealistic Interpretation of Einstein's Theory," *Proceedings of the Aristotelian Society* 22 (1921–22): 131.

75. Whitehead, *Enquiry*, 1.5; see also 2.4 and 3.5.

76. Arthur E. Murphy, "What Is an Event?" *Philosophical Review* 37 (1928): 574, observed that "the disciples of the event are many, but for the most part their altars are raised to an unknown god." For when something happens, we seem to be left with mere occurrence if we do not specify a substrate for the change that has occurred. Murphy notes a confusion in the work of Samuel Alexander between event and space-time itself, and believed that Whitehead's work was infected by the confusion. "It is by no means absent from the philosophy of Professor Whitehead and is the source of the major confusions with which this great and ambiguous work is surrounded" (p. 579).

77. Whitehead, "Time, Space, and Material," p. 59.

78. Whitehead, *Concept of Nature*, p. 19. Arthur Murphy defined, in the context of objective relativism, the sense in which events are substantive. He held that objective relativism is a "theory grounded upon the ultimacy of the relative. . . . The relations of an event are internal, and it is precisely that fact which distinguishes it from an object. . . . The event is substantive and objects are characters of events. Thus, relatedness, in all its complexity and interconnections, is made basic for the objective world." See Arthur Murphy, *Reason and the Common End* (Englewood Cliffs, N.J.: Prentice-Hall, 1963), pp. 52–53. For Murphy, Dewey and Whitehead presented cases of objective relativism which proved inadequate due to their neglect in consistently applying their central contextualist principles.

Comparing Einstein's and Whitehead's views, Robert Palter, *Whitehead's Philosophy of Science*, suggests that the way event is handled is crucial: "In summary, one might say Einstein supposes that matter (or the gravitational field) is ontologically prior to space-time, while events are simply intersections of world-lines of particles; and Whitehead supposes that events are ontologically prior to space-time, while matter is simply a contingent characteristic of certain events" (p. 213). Given, of course, the monistic concepts of the 1905 memoir, matter is simply redundant. That is the Berkeleyian strain in Whitehead's thought.

79. Whitehead, *Concept of Nature*, p. 125.

80. Whitehead, *Principle of Relativity*, p. 26.

81. Whitehead, *Concept of Nature*, p. 52.

82. This may well be less a case of reading psychic states into nature than of noting that psychic states arise from nature. According to Wing-Tsit Chan, "The Chinese made no absolute distinction between physical things and human activities, both being represented by the word 'shih'. (Only the Whiteheadean term 'event' approximates this word.)" See Wing-Tsit Chan, "Chinese Theory and Practice with Special Reference to Humanism," in *Philosophy and Culture: East and West*, ed. Charles A. Moore (Honolulu: University of Hawaii Press, 1962, 1962), p. 83.

83. Whitehead, *Concept of Nature*, pp. 143, 75. As the event happens, it takes on being, but its finished phase is already entering into the becoming of other events. "Events are the unity of being and becoming," according to Paul F. Schmidt, *Perception and Cosmology in Whitehead's Philosophy* (New Brunswick, N.J.: Rutgers University Press, 1967), p. 45.

84. Alfred N. Whitehead, "The Philosophical Aspects of the Principle of Relativity," in idem, *Interpretation of Science*, p. 143.

85. Whitehead, *Concept of Nature*, p. 53; idem, *Enquiry*, p. 202; idem, "The Philosophical Aspects of the Principle of Relativity," p. 143; idem, "The First Physical Synthesis," in idem, *Interpretation of Science*, p. 17. See also Lawrence, *Whitehead's Philosophical Development*, pp. 141–45.

The transition is associated with greater priority being assigned to time, which

gradually caused different emphases to fall on other concepts as well, e.g., cogredience. See Victor Lowe, "The Influence of Bergson, James and Alexander on Whitehead," *Journal of the History of Ideas* 10 (1949): 276.

86. Whitehead, *Enquiry*, 3.4, 3.5.

87. Ibid., 3.5.

88. Alfred N. Whitehead, "A Revolution in Science," *Educational Review* 59 (1920): 152; idem, "Philosophical Aspects of Principle of Relativity," p. 136.

89. Schmidt, *Perception and Cosmology*, believes that "to understand the development of this doctrine [of significance] is in large part to understand the development of Whitehead's philosophy" (p. 64). See Palter, *Whitehead's Philosophy of Science*, p. 25, for the importance of the significance doctrine for Whitehead's view of sense perception.

90. Whitehead, "Time, Space, and Material," p. 57.

91. Whitehead, *Principle of Relativity*, p. 64.

92. Whitehead, *Concept of Nature*, pp. 51–52.

93. Whitehead, *Principle of Relativity*, p. 13.

94. Whitehead, "Philosophical Aspects of Principle of Relativity," p. 140; idem, *Principle of Relativity*, p. 25.

95. Alfred N. Whitehead, "Uniformity and Contingency," in *Interpretation of Science*, p. 118. Significance is the entire topic of this paper, according to Victor Lowe, *Understanding Whitehead*, (Baltimore: Johns Hopkins University Press, 1966), p. 207. See note 89 above.

96. According to Bertrand Russell, Arthur Eddington believed it necessary to adopt Einstein's "variable space," whereas Whitehead believed it necessary to reject it. But why agree with either view, Russell asks, holding that "the matter seems to be one of convenience in the interpretation of formulae" (Russell, *Analysis of Matter*, p. 78).

Evander B. McGilvary, "Space-Time, Simple Location and Prehension," in Schilpp, *Philosophy of Whitehead*, says that "Mr. Whitehead and Einstein started from the opposite sides of the field of co-operative enterprise; and, when they met in the same equations, Mr. Whitehead seems in effect to have greeted his fellow worker with the charge that there is only one side from which to start in order to secure a philosophy of nature" (p. 219).

97. Whitehead, "Uniformity and Contingency," p. 118.

98. Whitehead, *Enquiry*, 3.5; idem, *Concept of Nature*, p. 39.

99. Victor Lowe holds that "*the doctrine of significance underlies Whitehead's whole theory of nature.* Every application of the method of extensive abstraction is based on it. . . . *The doctrine of significance is not a doctrine of ordinary empiricism.*" See Lowe, *Understanding Whitehead*, p. 205. See also notes 89 and 95, above.

Lowe's judgment lends interesting weight to the assertion that Whitehead's philosophy is a "gigantic cryptogram" which would take a whole generation to decipher (Metz, *A Hundred Years*, p. 594). If Whitehead's philosophy seemed a cryptogram to Metz in 1938, it may be due to the fact that Whitehead's philosophy accurately portrays nature as an embodied, significant cryptogram which science progressively decodes, only to find that nature is changing the cipher.

100. Whitehead, *Concept of Nature*, p. 51.

101. Whitehead, "Time, Space, and Material," pp. 58–59.

102. Whitehead, *Concept of Nature*, pp. 14, 53.

103. Whitehead, "First Physical Synthesis," pp. 8–9.

104. Whitehead, "Time, Space, and Material," p. 59.

105. Whitehead, *Concept of Nature*, pp. 15, 14, 49–51.

106. Whitehead, *Principle of Relativity*, p. 15.

107. Ibid., p. 16. Bergson's degree of influence on Whitehead has been a contested issue. F. S. C. Northrop saw Bergson as influencing Whitehead strongly through the intermediary H. Wildon Carr: "From this source came the doctrine of primacy of process, which is as basic to Whitehead's philosophy as it is to his metaphysics" ("Whitehead's Philosophy of Science," p. 169). Alexander reinforced Whitehead's Bergsonianism, Northrop believed, and the Bergsonian factor "presented the basis and doctrine of Whitehead's entire scientific and philosophical outlook. . . . Whitehead conceived it to be one of his major tasks to follow Bergson in accepting duration and process as primary" (p. 169).

Wilbur Urban said that Whitehead admitted that it was from Bergson that "the organicist philosophy has got its main insights" ("Whitehead's Philosophy of Language and Its Relation to His Metaphysics," p. 304). Urban also conjectured that Whitehead's concept of pure experience was derived from Bergson and James (p. 307).

On the other side of the issue, Norman Kemp Smith thought that Bergson's influence was marginal and verbal. See Norman Kemp Smith, "Whitehead's Philosophy of Nature," in *The Credibility of Divine Existence*, Collected Papers of Norman Kemp Smith, ed. A. J. D. Porteous, R. D. Maclennan, and G. E. Davie (New York: St. Martin's Press, 1967), where he notes that Whitehead shares none of Bergson's antipathy to space (p. 245); and where Whitehead does not share Bergson's anti-intellectualism on the question of universals (p. 247).

According to Victor Lowe, Whitehead was interested in countering the idea that mathematics was a science of number and quantity, whereas Bergson needed to *maintain* that conception of mathematics; Lowe reminds us that Bergson had nothing to do with the 1905 memoir which had already given concepts of nature that improved upon Newton. Lowe concludes that on the question of Bergson's influence on Whitehead, "this influence was both less, and showed itself later, than Professor Northrop has supposed" ("Influence of Bergson, James and Alexander on Whitehead," pp. 271, 272, 278).

Nathaniel Lawrence, in *Whitehead's Philosophical Development*, does not deal with the issue of Bergson's influence upon Whitehead, so presumably he believes that Bergson was *not* important to Whitehead's philosophical development. On the same grounds, it is probable that Ivor Leclerc discounts any significant influence of Bergson on Whitehead in Leclerc, *Whitehead's Metaphysics* (New York: Macmillan, 1958).

In *Understanding Whitehead*, Victor Lowe finds that Bergson had less of an influence on Whitehead than the above cited article would allow. Lowe's summary of key points bearing on this issue can be used to support the conclusion that Whitehead's philosophy of time and process was developed quite independently of Bergson's ideas on time and process.

108. Whitehead, *Enquiry*, 13.2, 13.4.

109. Whitehead, *Principle of Relativity*, p. 39.

110. Whitehead, *Concept of Nature*, p. 150.

111. Whitehead, *Enquiry*, 13.2.

112. Whitehead, *Concept of Nature*, p. 149; and idem, "Time, Space, and Material," p. 63.

113. Whitehead, *Concept of Nature*, pp. 106–7.

114. Whitehead, "Philosophical Aspects of Principle of Relativity," pp. 142–43.

115. Whitehead, *Enquiry*, 14.1. But behind extension, process is basic. Whitehead came to this conclusion by the time the second edition appeared, p. 202.

116. Whitehead, *Concept of Nature*, p. 24.

117. Northrop observes that "just as the relation of simultaneity within the exetension [sic] of space-time separates out the purely spatial relatedness of events, so the relation of non-simultaneity gives the purely temporal order between them and the durations of which they are a part. Such a family of non-intersecting durations Whitehead calls a time-system. The non-intersection of the durations of such a time-system constitutes what Whitehead terms a 'parallelism' of durations" ("Whitehead's Philosophy of Science," p. 196).

118. Whitehead, *Concept of Nature*, pp. 52, 108.

119. Whitehead, *Enquiry*, 14.1, 18.1. In 35.1, the time-concept is said to spring from extension and cogredience. In *Concept of Nature*, pp. 52, 53, the structure of events is said to be the complex of events as related by extension and cogredience.

120. Whitehead, "Time, Space, and Material," p. 64.

121. Whitehead, *Principle of Relativity*, p. 21.

122. Whitehead, *Concept of Nature*, p. 65; and idem, *Enquiry*, 14.2.

123. Whitehead, *Concept of Nature*, p. 64.

124. Ibid., p. 68.

125. Ibid., p. 108.

126. Whitehead, *Enquiry*, 14.3.

127. Whitehead, *Concept of Nature*, p. 155.

128. Lawrence points out "that Whitehead was quite sure that the introduction of alternative time systems is his own invention, and not Einstein's" (*Whitehead's Philosophical Development*, p. 193).

129. Whitehead, *Enquiry*, 16.1.

130. Alfred N. Whitehead, "The Problem of Simultaneity: Is There a Paradox in the Principle of Relativity in Regard to the Relation of Time Measures to Time Lived?" in *Interpretation of Science*, p. 156. See also Palter, *Whitehead's Philosophy of Science*, pp. 30 ff, "Durations and Simultaneity."

131. Whitehead, *Principle of Relativity*, pp. 9, 76.

132. See Northrop, "Whitehead's Philosophy of Science," pp. 194–95, for a discussion of the case of Whitehead's rejection of Einstein's concept of simultaneity."

133. Whitehead, *Principle of Relativity*, pp. 60, 68.

134. Whitehead, *Concept of Nature*, pp. 95, 37 (to be compared with p. 52), and 142.

135. Whitehead, *Enquiry*, 17.2, 17.4.

136. Whitehead, *Concept of Nature*, pp. 16–17, 32.

137. Ibid., p. 185; and idem, *Principle of Relativity*, where Whitehead aligns himself with the authority of the two English physicists, Thomson and Poynting, in accepting as a rule of method that "our ultimate aim must be to describe the sensible in terms of the sensible" (pp. 4–5).

VII. WHITEHEAD AND THE EPOCHS OF TIME

1. Nathaniel Lawrence, *Whitehead's Philosophical Development* (1956; reprint ed., New York: Greenwood Press, 1968), p. 250, holds that "the transition is charac-

terized by Whitehead's thoroughgoing rejection of his earlier conviction that the problems of physical science are isolable from the general problems of cosmology." (The entire statement is italicized in the original text.)

2. See, for example, Victor Lowe, *Understanding Whitehead* (Baltimore: Johns Hopkins University Press, 1966), pp. 12–13; and Ivor Leclerc, *Whitehead's Metaphysics* (1958; New York: Humanities Press, 1965), pp. 4–5.

3. Alfred N. Whitehead, *The Principle of Relativity* (Cambridge: University Press, 1922), p. 5.

4. Roy Wood Sellars, "Philosophy of Organism and Physical Realism," in *The Philosophy of Alfred North Whitehead*, ed. Paul A. Schilpp, 2d ed. (New York: Tudor Publishing, 1951). Sellars judges that, as opposed to physical realism, the philosophy of organism "introspects and takes the path of a monadism with windows, a monadism of atomic ocasions expressive of an ultimate creativity operating under the control of God" (p. 423). Elsewhere, in *Reflections on American Philosophy from Within* (Notre Dame: University of Notre Dame Press, 1969), p. 111, Sellars speaks of Whitehead's approach as a concrescent monadism.

5. Alfred N. Whitehead, *Science and the Modern World* (New York: Free Press, 1967), pp. 57, 64. See also notes 2 and 52 of chapter 6. When Whitehead opens up a new line of inquiry, he commences with an investigation of time and space as indicator topics.

6. Ibid., p. 123. See Laurence Bright, *Whitehead's Philosophy of Physics* (New York: Sheed and Ward, 1958), chap. 4, "The Theory of Internal Relations," for a discussion of how Whitehead presents the internal/external relations contrast as parallel to the idea of physical laws as immanent/imposed laws. Bright says that "the danger in any doctrine of internal relations is that of neglecting the individual nature of events" (p. 57). Interestingly, however, Whitehead uses the internal relatedness concept in order to *secure* the individuality of events.

See F. Bradford Wallack, *The Epochal Nature of Process in Whitehead's Metaphysics* (Albany: State University Press, 1980), pp. 37–40, for an analysis of the significance of internal relatedness in elucidating key Whitehead concepts (in this case, nexus), and the role internal relatedness plays in making sense of individuality and creativity for epochal occasions.

7. Whitehead, *Science and the Modern World*, pp. 72, 152.

8. Ibid., pp. 25, 44; Whitehead had held earlier that the present is all there is, that it is holy ground; see note 34 of chapter 6 above. See also Whitehead, *An Introduction to Mathematics* (1911; reprint ed., New York: Oxford University Press, 1958), p. 91.

9. Whitehead, *Science and the Modern World*, p. 64.

10. Ibid. See also p. 70, where Whitehead has tended to replace Leibniz's monads with Spinoza's modes.

11. Ibid., p. 79.

12. Ibid., pp. 70, 65–66, 93.

13. Ibid., p. 71.

14. Ibid., p. 72. Paul Schmidt, *Perception and Cosmology in Whitehead's Philosophy* (New Brunswick, N.J.: Rutgers University Press, 1967), phrases it that "the being of an entity is resultant from its relations" (p. 9). Dorothy Emmet (*Whitehead's Philosophy of Organism*, 2d ed. [New York: St. Martin's Press, 1966]), says "it is clear that Whitehead's remarks about mutual immanence of things must be considered fundamental to his view" (p. xxiv).

Evander McGilvary, "Space-Time, Simple Location, and Prehension," says that

although Whitehead's mirroring idea is suggestive of Leibniz, "Leibniz's mirroring monads had, as we all know, no windows which they could *go out* and through which other monads could *enter.* Their mirroring took place by grace of 'pre-established harmony.' Not so with Mr. Whitehead's monads" (pp. 230–31). Each of those monads is a way of feeling the world.

15. Whitehead, *Science and the Modern World*, pp. 72–73, for this and the following two quotations. See also p. 175.

16. Ibid., p. 122. On p. 107, Whitehead holds that the theory of organic mechanism denotes this reflecting of a whole into its internal modifications. According to Charles Hartshorne (*Whitehead's Philosophy* [Lincoln: University of Nebraska Press, 1972]), some questions about internal relatedness can be answered by referring to the doctrine of prehension. "Are there *internal* relations of events to other events? Yes, for so far as events prehend others, they are constituted by their relations to these others" (p. 126).

17. Whitehead, *Science and the Modern World*, pp. 92, 104, 108.

18. Ibid., p. 119.

19. Whitehead, *Science and the Modern World*, pp. 118, 125. So far, thus, has he gone past the writings of 1919–23. Time and space are not in the first place externalizing media, but are aspects of the internal relatedness of events: "The theory of the relationship between events at which we have now arrived is based first upon the doctrine that the relatednesses of an event are all internal relations, so far as concerns that event, though not necessarily so far as concerns the other relata" (pp. 122–23).

20. Ibid., p. 126.

21. Ibid., p. 119.

22. As realized, the entity is both a novel appearance and is related to what has gone before. Charles Hartshorne, *Whitehead's Philosophy*, judges in this connection that "this is the first theory of time worthy of the name.... For it is the first that ascribes to time an intelligible logical structure, while allowing for a principle of flux or passage that transcends all fixed or already determinate structures, since it is an inexhaustible source of new relationships, extrinsic to reality as already actual" (p. 15).

23. Vere Chappell, "Whitehead's Theory of Becoming," in the Whitehead centennial issue of *Journal of Philosophy* 58 (1961): 516–17, argued that this view "that Whitehead defends in his later philosophical writings is untenable," namely, the view of "epochal theory of time." On p. 525, Chappell says that the epochal view is also unnecessary in Whitehead's theory. He notes that Whitehead uses 'time' in two ways, as a process and as a product of a process: "The epochal theory stands or falls with the notion of a becoming that is not extensive. For the act of becoming that constitutes an actual occasion is indivisible because it is not extensive, and the process of transition whereby each actual occasion gives way to its successor is discontinuous because its component concrescences are indivisible. But the notion of a becoming that is not extensive is an odd notion at best."

In the same centennial issue, William Christian, in "Whitehead's Explanation of the Past," says that Whitehead uses the relation of pastness to exhibit that aspect of experience which reveals that the world is rough in space and time, and not smooth, and that such a fact "makes possible a systematic explanation of the epochal character of time" (p. 540).

For a complete rebuttal of Chappell's criticism, see David A. Sipfle, "On the Intelligibility of the Epochal Theory of Time," *Monist* 53 (1969): 505–18. It should be

noted that, as stated on p. 525 of the above article, Chappell himself believes his criticism only slightly affects Whitehead's philosophical position.

In his "Causal Efficacy and Continuity in Whitehead's Philosophy," *Tulane Studies in Philosophy* 10 (1961): 64–70, Harold N. Lee contends that Whitehead's atomism is not necessary in the system, is an intrusion in it, and a source of paradox in it. Lee's paper was written about the same time as Chappell's paper.

24. Wilbur M. Urban, in Schilpp, *Philosophy of Whitehead*, says that Whitehead shares with Samuel Alexander the view that a form of nonhuman value is universal in the connectedness of things. Whitehead, Urban judges, "conceives it as his main task to overcome the isolation beween natural science and value experiences and, in order to bridge the gulf, he, like Alexander, reads value down into the elementary constituents of the universe" (p. 325).

25. Alfred N. Whitehead, *Religion in the Making* (New York: New American Library, 1974), pp. 98–99.

26. Ibid., p. 89.

27. Ibid., pp. 105, 101. "The moral order is merely certain aspects of the aesthetic order." By way of contrast, we have seen Royce hold the converse view, that all order is the result of the order of the will.

28. Ibid., p. 110.

29. Alfred N. Whitehead, "Time," in *The Interpretation of Science*, ed. A. H. Johnson (Indianapolis: Bobbs-Merrill Co., 1961), pp. 240–46.

30. Ibid., p. 241.

31. Ibid., p. 243.

32. Ibid., pp. 243, 244–45.

33. Ibid., pp. 242, 246. The interplay of possibility and actuality gives the basis of the two different trends in Whitehead's philosophy, according to Justus Buchler, "On a Strain of Arbitrariness in Whitehead's System, *Journal of Philosophy* 66 (1969), esp. pp. 590–92. Buchler concluded that if Whitehead had not sought to give equal play to the realm of the actual, the resulting philosophy would be at least as majestic, and rather more free of arbitrariness.

Leclerc thinks, however, that the greater emphasis upon actuality is helpful and clarifying. See Ivor Leclerc, "Whitehead and the Problem of Extension," in Schilpp, *Philosophy of Whitehead*, where Leclerc judges that "the recognition that continuity pertains to potentiality and not to actuality is central to the enormous advance in thought of Whitehead's later period. Herein lies a basic factor making the doctrine of *Process and Reality* importantly different from the doctrine of *The Concept of Nature*. For the doctrine of his middle period still involved that confusion" (p. 561).

34. I am referring to the passages in Whitehead, *The Concept of Nature* (1920; reprint ed., Cambridge: University Press, 1964), pp. 3–5, where he distinguishes between thinking of nature homogeneously and thinking of it heterogeneously. To think of nature homogeneously is to think about it *without* thinking about thought, as if mind were an outside observer. Thus, his methodological statement that "nature is closed to mind" (p. 5) means that we can treat each as external to the other. See also p. 34, where he says time extends beyond nature, and our thoughts are in time. So thinking in some important sense is outside nature and external to it.

35. On the topic of taking time seriously, see the opening lines of "Time," where Whitehead shows his agreement with Samuel Alexander's criteria for what is involved in "taking time seriously," namely, avoiding the thought that there is a

completed, existing totality, and avoiding the thought that there is a plurality of validly isolated actual entities. Put positively, the minimum condition for taking time seriously, according to Whitehead, is an openness in reality whose several actual states nevertheless interpenetrate.

36. William A. Christian, *An Interpretation of Whitehead's Metaphysics* (New Haven: Yale University Press, 1959), observes the "important fact that the term 'extension' is not used in the categoreal scheme set forth in *Process and Reality* (Pt. 1, ch. 2). . . . The extensive character of an actual occasion, its *region*, is derivative from its character as an act of experience" (p. 78). See also Whitehead's notes appended to the second edition of *An Enquiry concerning the Principles of Natural Knowledge* (Cambridge: University Press, 1925), where he said that it gradually became clear that the "unique preeminence" assigned to extension needed to be modified. "Extension is derivative from process, and is required by it" (p. 202).

37. Christian, *Interpretation of Whitehead's Metaphysics*, explains the significance of 'supersession' for Whitehead's concept of time as epochal. He concludes that "time is constituted by the becoming and perishing of actual occasions in the rhythmic process of creativity" in Whitehead's epochal theory (pp. 70–72).

38. Whitehead, "Time," p. 246.

39. Ibid., p. 245.

40. Whitehead, *The Concept of Nature* (1920; reprint ed., Cambridge: University Press, 1964), pp. 50–60.

41. Whitehead, "Time," p. 246, for this and the following quotation.

42. Alfred N. Whitehead, *Symbolism: Its Meaning and Effect* (1927; reprint ed., New York: Capricorn Books, 1959), p. 38.

43. Ibid., pp. 50–53, 38.

44. Ibid., p. 35.

45. Ibid., p. 36.

46. For Hume's view, see his *Treatise*, bk. 1, pt. 2, sect. 2.

47. Whitehead, *Symbolism*, pp. 45–46.

48. Ibid., pp. 42, 43.

49. The idea of conformation as a feature given in experience is close to what Whitehead means by sense reception as opposed to sense perception, a distinction he valued in Bergson's philosophy. See Whitehead, *Process and Reality*, corrected edition, ed. David Ray Griffin and Donald W. Sherburne (New York: Free Press, 1978), p. 114.

50. Whitehead, *Symbolism*, p. 47. See Martial's *Epigrams*, trans. Walter C. A. Ker (Cambridge: Harvard University Press, 1919), 5, 20, 13.

51. Whitehead, *Symbolism*, pp. 58–59, 47–49, 60.

52. Ibid., pp. 56–57. This is Whitehead's answer to the question he posed in his 1914–17 papers, namely, how do we achieve a social time sense, one which unifies the different subjective time centers?

53. Whitehead, *Process and Reality*, p. 50. William Ernest Hocking, "Whitehead on Mind and Nature," in Schilpp, *Philosophy of Whitehead*, p. 387, believes that Whitehead as rebel needed to have devilish doctrines with which to contend, and Aristotle's substance doctrine was one of these.

54. Alfred N. Whitehead, "Response," in *Interpretation of Science*, p. 218.

55. Whitehead, *Process and Reality*, p. 287.

56. William P. Alston, "Internal Relatedness and Pluralism in Whitehead," *Review of Metaphysics* 5 (1952): 547–58. In the context of showing that too much had

been made of internal relatedness in early statements of the philosophy (because internal relatedness is inconsistent with pluralism), Alston judged that Whitehead limited the principle of internal relatedness in giving ultimate significance to the temporal standpoint. So internal relatedness, Alston says, was restricted to the predecessors of actual occasions, thus allowing for pluralism in space-time. Alston concluded, however, that the restriction of internal relatedness is untenable in the system, with the result that Whitehead's system drives "relentlessly" into a monism.

William W. Hammerschmidt, *Whitehead's Philosophy of Time* (New York: Russell & Russell, 1947), p. 83, raised the question that goes to the heart of the matter: how do internal relations contribute to emergence? If in fact Whitehead's principle of individuation and limitation does include internal relatedness, as I have argued in the text, then Hammerschmidt's question may no longer arise.

57. Whitehead, *Process and Reality*, p. 287. Dorothy Emmet (*Whitehead's Philosophy of Organism*, p. 206) emphasizes "the extreme importance of the notion of extensive connection for the Philosophy of Organism." At this time, Bertrand Russell's widely influential book, *The Analysis of Matter* (1927) had just appeared. For Whitehead's method of defining points by means of enclosure series, Russell suggested another procedure, based on the idea of a relation of compresence, or partial overlapping, where classes partly include and partly exclude each other (p. 292). This also amounted to a revision of Whitehead's earlier emphasis upon a continuum of whole/part relations. Russell's relation of compresence allowed a treatment of entities as external to each other just as much as did De Laguna's "extensive connection." Whitehead does not allude to Russell's revision of enclosure series definitions, based on this "compresence" relation.

For those still interested in the question of Bergson's influence on Whitehead, it may be noted that in his review of *An Enquiry*, T. De Laguna judged that Whitehead appears to have felt "the force of Bergson's criticism of natural science as incapable of expressing the continuity of things." Thus, Whitehead sought to reform science so that it *could* account for continuity. See T. De Laguna, "Review," *Philosophical Review* 29 (1920): 269.

58. Whitehead, *Process and Reality*, pp. 288, 61. One reason that Charles Hartshorne regards Whitehead's philosophy as important is stated in the form of a rhetorical question: "Who before Whitehead presented a clear, fully articulated reason for temporal atomicity, a special quantitative illustration of which is given by quantum mechanics? Or for the wave structure pervasive in nature, which for Whitehead illustrates (though it would not, unless in extremely generalized form, be deducible from) the aesthetic laws of contrast and repetition to which all appetition is subject?" See Hartshorne, *Whitehead's Philosophy*, p. 16.

59. Whitehead, *Process and Reality*, p. 66.

60. William Hammerschmidt, *Whitehead's Philosophy of Time*, pp. 16, 29–30, says that actual occasion, creativity, and nexus are the important new concepts in *Process and Reality*.

61. Whitehead, *Process and Reality*, pp. 66, 107. Again, Whitehead refers to Bergson with regard to the word 'canalizing', and to the ways the origination of things provide a restraining inheritance for things yet to come. Both canalization and conformation are stronger than Whitehead's early term 'limitation' because they suggest inheritance and memory.

62. Ibid., pp. 66–67. There are parallels between Whitehead's views on the nature

of this background continuum and the conceptions of some Stoic philosophers. See S. Sambursky, "The Stoic Views of Time," in Milič Čapek, ed., *The Concepts of Space and Time* (Dordrecht; Boston: Reidel, 1976), who says that "in Greek antiquity it was again the Stoics who, by virtue of their dynamic notion of the continuum, succeeded more than anyone else during the whole period to develop a satisfactory theory of the structure of time and to present a lucid analysis of the nature of its ultimate elements" (p. 159).

Perhaps the use of "parallels" above is not strong enough. Certainly Whitehead himself thought that Stoicism—through its stress upon order, both moral and natural—helped create the mind-set in which modern science arose. See Whitehead, *Science and the Modern World*, p. 11. Robert Palter believes that such historical passages in Whitehead provide a bridge from Whitehead's work in mathematics and philosophy of science to his work in metaphysics. See Palter, "Science and Its History in the Philosophy of Whitehead," in the Hartshorne Festschrift, *Process and Divinity*, ed. William L. Reese and Eugene Freeman (La Salle, Ill.: Open Court Publishing Co., 1964), pp. 52–55. Palter's comments on Whitehead's references to the Stoics are on p. 54.

63. Whitehead, *Process and Reality*, p. 80.

64. Ibid., p. 283.

65. Ibid., p. 289.

66. Ibid., p. 289, for the view that nature "is always passing beyond itself. This is the creative advance of nature. Here we come to the problem of time."

Henry J. Folse, Jr., "The Copenhagen Interpretation of Quantum Theory and Whitehead's Philosophy of Organism," *Tulane Studies in Philosophy* 23 (1974): 38–39, judges that "activity, not endurance, is the basic ontological status of entities in the philosophy of organism," and that through the doctrine of prehensions, the influence of William James is shown in Whitehead's work. Victor Lowe doubts a Jamesean influence in "The Influence of Bergson, James and Alexander on Whitehead," *Journal of the History of Ideas* 10 (1949): 289, where Whitehead is said to have appreciated James's genius but "there was no question of James affecting the direction of his thinking."

67. Whitehead, *Process and Reality*, p. 208.

68. Ibid., p. 209.

69. Ibid., p. 338, where he says that "ideals fashion themselves around these two notions, permanence and flux. In the inescapable flux, there is something that abides; in the overwhelming permanence, there is an element that escapes into flux."

70. Whitehead, *Process and Reality*, p. 210. The two following quotations are also on this page.

71. Ibid., p. 340.

72. Ibid., p. 348.

73. Ibid., p. 350. See also p. 338, where timelessness is implanted in the passing world, and time becomes the moving image of eternity.

74. Robert Whittemore, "Time and Whitehead's God," *Tulane Studies in Philosophy* 4 (1955): 92, summarizes his consideration of the evidence bearing on whether Whitehead's God is temporal by saying, "Is Whitehead's theory of time compatible with his notion of God? In the light of the foregoing, I suggest that it is not. In no one of His natures, nor in His character as a Whole, can God be held clearly temporal in any sense of the word permitted by Whitehead's theory of time."

75. Alfred N. Whitehead, *Adventures of Ideas* (New York: Free Press, 1967), p. 188.

76. Ibid., pp. 187, 150, 210.

77. Ibid., pp. 187, 134, 150.

78. Ibid., p. 170.

79. Ibid., pp. 150, 153. As we saw in our discussion of the *logos* doctrine of Heraclitus in our chapter on Santayana, it is the function of the *logos* to provide continuous relatedness throughout the passage of events.

80. Ibid., p. 143. Ivor Leclerc, *Whitehead's Metaphysics*, pp. 68–69, says that "the doctrine Whitehead maintains is that the *existence* of an actual entity must involve 'process'. If that be so, then all other senses of 'existence' will accordingly also have reference to process, for, by the ontological principle, all other forms of existence are derivative from 'actual' existence. Whitehead's doctrine, in his own statement, is 'that "existence" (in any of its senses), cannot be abstracted from "process." The notions of "process" and "existence" presuppose each other' " (pp. 68–69).

George Boas, *Dominant Themes of Modern Philosophy* (New York: Ronald Press Co., 1957), uses just this point to distinguish in a fundamental way between the temporalisms of Bergson and Whitehead, saying that "to Bergson time as real duration was a characteristic of mental life, to Whitehead it was an essential feature of all reality" (p. 628). In other words, time is "in fact the one character of the real that is omnipresent" (p. 633).

See also note 57, above, and note 107 of chapter 6.

81. See chapter 1 on Peirce, above, pp. 30–32, for Peirce's notion that what we call the present is a mixture of the near past and the immediate future. Chapter 12 in Whitehead's *Adventures of Ideas* is entitled "Past, Present, and Future."

The idea that past and future comprise the present is a Stoic idea. See S. Samburatsky, "The Stoic Views of Time," Čapek, *Concepts of Space and Time*, pp. 162–63. Samburatsky notes the "remarkable similarity" of the Stoic and Whiteheadean conceptions of time. Both Peirce and Whitehead studied Kant intensively during their early work, and Kant may very well be one route by means of which there was direct influence of Stoic cosmology on both Peirce and Whitehead (as opposed to the background atmospherics Whitehead discussed in *Science and the Modern World*).

82. Whitehead, *Adventures of Ideas*, pp. 191–92.

83. Ibid., p. 192.

84. Stephen Pepper set out his thesis in a special Whitehead issue of *Tulane Studies in Philosophy* 10 (1961), in a paper entitled "Whitehead's 'Actual Occasion,' " where Pepper hoped to show "what modifications in Whitehead's treatment of the actual occasion might lead to a new world theory more adequate than his, if his is interpreted as an attempt to use the purposive act as a root metaphor" (p. 88). Pepper listed eight features of the actual occasion (p. 75), and then uses the list to sift Whitehead's metaphysics for evidences of its being the structure of the purposive act writ large.

For a discussion of the exchange Charles Hartshorne and Stephen Pepper had over this "world hypotheses" approach to explicating Whitehead's metaphysics, see Andrew J. Reck, *The New American Philosophers* (Baton Rouge: Louisiana State University Press, 1968), pp. 76–78.

85. Whitehead, *Adventures of Ideas*, p. 194.

86. Ibid., pp. 195, 196.

87. Alfred N. Whitehead, *Modes of Thought* (New York: Free Press, 1968), p. 102.

88. Whitehead, *Adventures of Ideas*, p. 196.

89. Whitehead, *Modes of Thought*, p. 164. According to William A. Christian, "Whitehead's Exploration of the Past," *Journal of Philosophy* 58 (1961), the categorial scheme in *Process and Reality* does not lay the hand of the past upon the present, and "we could put this by saying that the scheme leaves open the question whether contemporary actual entities influence one another. But it would be much better to say that this question is not even raised, much less decided, because the concepts of pastness and contemporaneousness are not introduced" (p. 536).

90. Whitehead, *Adventures of Ideas*, p. 194; and idem, *Modes of Thought*, p. 103.

91. Whitehead, *Adventures of Ideas*, p. 197. Whitehead used the notion of nexus to stand for a special or particular kind of togetherness in *Process and Reality*, and it importantly occurs there as one of his eight categories of existence (p. 22).

92. Whitehead, *Modes of Thought*, p. 102.

EPILOGUE

1. The initial volume in this group of posthumous publications of the work of George H. Mead was *The Philosophy of the Present* (1932; La Salle, Ill.: Open Court Publishing, 1959). There followed the series from the University of Chicago Press. These were: *Mind, Self and Society*, ed. Charles W. Morris (Chicago: University of Chicago Press, 1934); *Movements of Thought in the Nineteenth Century*, ed. Merritt H. Moore (Chicago: University of Chicago Press, 1936); and *The Philosophy of the Act*, ed. Charles W. Morris (Chicago: University of Chicago Press, 1938). Selections from the three Chicago volumes were published in *On Social Psychology*, ed. Anselm Strauss (1956; Chicago: University of Chicago Press, 1964). A fifth volume in this Chicago series is *The Individual and the Social Self*, ed. David L. Miller (Chicago: University of Chicago Press, 1982), and is comprised of previously unpublished Mead materials. Finally, *Selected Writings*, ed. Andrew J. Reck (Indianapolis: Bobbs-Merrill, 1964) makes readily available a representative selection of articles Mead himself had published.

2. It is doubtful that Mead's philosophical methodology could be analyzed without explicitly treating his views of time, but a more systematic approach to his philosophy can proceed along lines that leave his theory of time unstated and implicit. See, for example, the overview of the structure of Mead's philosophy that is presented by Israel Scheffler in *Four Pragmatists* (New York: Humanities Press, 1974), where there is no treatment at all of Mead's temporalist themes, and Scheffler is treating the *major* themes of his subjects.

3. George H. Mead, *The Philosophy of the Present*, ed. Arthur E. Murphy (La Salle, Ill.: Open Court Publishing Co., 1959), p. 24.

4. George H. Mead, *On Social Psychology*, selected papers ed. Anselm Strauss (Chicago: University of Chicago Press, 1964), p. xxv.

5. George H. Mead, *The Philosophy of the Act*, ed. Charles W. Morris (Chicago: University of Chicago Press, 1938), p. 65.

6. George H. Mead, *Philosophy of the Present*, pp. 37, 4–5, 9, 11. For an extended, admirably clear analysis of Mead's view of time and its relation to the philosophy of science, see Harold N. Lee, "Mead's Doctrine of the Past," *Tulane Studies in Philosophy* 12 (1963): 52–75.

7. George H. Mead, *Philosophy of the Present*, pp. 3, 9, 10, 12, 13; and esp. pp. 20–21, where he evaluates the approach Whitehead used in referring the "what" of events to the ingression of eternal objects.

8. Mead was a student of Royce's at Harvard. According to David L. Miller, "Mead's conception of the philosophical method of treating problems was taken from Royce," whereas the specific directions Mead's thought took arose later, perhaps in relation to his work in Germany. See David L. Miller's "George Herbert Mead: Biographical Notes," in *The Philosophy of George Herbert Mead*, ed. Walter Robert Corti (Winterthur, Switzerland: Amriswiler Bücherei, 1973), pp. 20–21. Still, there is a definite overlapping of the views of Royce and Mead on the nature of time. Certainly their views that both time and ideation are grounded in the will are all of a piece.

9. For Mead's influence on Wieman's theology, see the introduction by James Luther Adams, to Henry Nelson Wieman, *The Directive in History* (Glencoe, Ill.: Free Press, 1949), pp. x–xi.

DATE DUE

DEMCO 38-297